T0355182

Democracy's Child

Democracy's Child

*Young People and the Politics of
Control, Leverage, and Agency*

ALISON L. GASH AND
DANIEL J. TICHENOR

OXFORD
UNIVERSITY PRESS

OXFORD
UNIVERSITY PRESS

Oxford University Press is a department of the University of Oxford. It furthers
the University's objective of excellence in research, scholarship, and education
by publishing worldwide. Oxford is a registered trade mark of Oxford University
Press in the UK and certain other countries.

Published in the United States of America by Oxford University Press
198 Madison Avenue, New York, NY 10016, United States of America.

Library of Congress Cataloging-in-Publication Data
Names: Gash, Alison L., author. | Tichenor, Daniel J., 1966– author.
Title: Democracy's child : young people and the politics of control,
leverage, and agency / By Alison L. Gash and Daniel J. Tichenor.
Description: New York : Oxford University Press, [2022] |
Includes bibliographical references and index.
Identifiers: LCCN 2022018807 (print) | LCCN 2022018808 (ebook) |
ISBN 9780197581667 (hardback) | ISBN 9780197581674 (epub) |
ISBN 9780197581698
Subjects: LCSH: Children and politics—United States. | Youth—Political
activity—United States. | Youth—Social conditions—United States. |
Child welfare—United States. | United States—Politics and government.
Classification: LCC HQ784.P5 G37 2022 (print) | LCC HQ784.P5 (ebook) |
DDC 323.3/520973—dc23/eng/20220525
LC record available at https://lccn.loc.gov/2022018807
LC ebook record available at https://lccn.loc.gov/2022018808

DOI: 10.1093/oso/9780197581667.001.0001

1 3 5 7 9 8 6 4 2

Printed by Marquis, Canada

FOR ELIZA, ERIC, ISAIAH, MATIAS, and NATALIE

Contents

Contents

Acknowledgments

We drew our most significant inspiration for writing this book from the young people who inhabit and enrich our lives. This begins with our children—Natalie, Eric, and Isaiah (Dan) and Eliza and Matias (Alison)—to whom this book is dedicated. Their own democratic activism and political acuity showed us that we were on the right track when we began writing. Many of our students (we teach at a large public university) also motivated this project. They regularly defy familiar presumptions about youth apathy and narcissism by mobilizing for immigrant and refugee rights, climate reform, LGBTQIA+ rights, gun safety, racial justice, prison and police reform, gender equality, and other issues. Whether in large lecture halls or small seminars, they shared insights and passions that deeply inform this work.

Our partnership on this book springs not only from the fact that we are great friends and intellectual kindred spirits teaching in the same political science department, but also from lively conversations about separate research projects in which we drew similar conclusions about the centrality of children in politics. From distinct studies of the politics of gender and sexuality (Alison) and immigration and social movements (Dan), we were struck by the bravery and impact of young people "coming out" to demand democratic inclusion: undocumented Dreamers fighting for equal membership and LGBTQIA+ young people fighting for safety, dignity, and voice. The sociopolitical demonization and exploitation of some children and the vigilant protection of others were just as unmistakable in this previous research. We also noticed the inconsistent and arbitrary definitions of childhood as a consequential status in law and policy, as well as the ways in which being a child combines with class, race, gender, sexual orientation, and other categories of exclusion to shape tenacious systems of disadvantage or privilege. Over time, our marathon discussions evolved into more reading, research, and brainstorms on multiple white boards as we tested fresh concepts and theories (including once with a permanent marker, which we then frantically tried to wash off before being scolded by less forgiving colleagues). Along the way, we have become adept at finishing each other's sentences (and definitely at rewriting them). We know that our collaboration has produced a book far stronger than either of us could have produced alone, and we are eager to start the next one.

We could not have written *Democracy's Child* without the help of talented and supportive family members, friends, colleagues, students, and editors. As most authors know well, although writing is mostly a solitary process, producing a book often involves a strong team—and ours is incredible. Our first forays into children and politics led to conference papers and an initial journal article, efforts that included two impressive University of Oregon graduate students: Angelita Chavez and Malori Musselman. We also received excellent research assistance from, Dustin Ellis, Kahina Freeman, and Michael Magee. As we tested the waters with early work, we benefited from excellent feedback at conferences from two especially incisive colleagues and friends, David Gutterman and Melissa Buis Michaux. As our project picked up momentum, a number of brilliant scholars shared valuable advice and critical insights, including Saladin Ambar, Elizabeth Cohen, Cybelle Fox, Karthick Ramakrishnan, and Deborah Thompson. We are particularly indebted to Elizabeth Cohen who later provided sage recommendations and detailed comments on the entire manuscript. The development of this manuscript also benefited enormously from the anonymous reviewers at Oxford University Press. We owe special thanks to our gifted editor David McBride, whose steady enthusiasm for the project and thoughtful suggestions kept us energized and on course. We are grateful to our reviewers and the whole team at Oxford University Press, who made the final stages of producing this book smooth sailing.

Scholarly support is a critical component of many research projects—and we both have been very fortunate to have received institutional and financial investments from a range of academic resources. Dan is grateful for the incredible support he has received from the Philip H. Knight Chair at the University of Oregon (UO), which has facilitated his research and writing since arriving on campus twelve years ago. He is indebted to the Carnegie Corporation, whose Andrew Carnegie Fellowship provided crucial space to launch this book project, and the National Endowment for the Humanities, which supported research on immigration policy and politics. He is thankful that he works with wonderful colleagues across the UO campus, especially at the Wayne Morse Center of Law and Politics and the UO Senate. Dan also wants to give a big shout out to the 238 undergrad Wayne Morse Scholars he has worked with inside and outside the classroom over the last decade, sparking discussions and friendships that helped fuel his writing.

Alison credits her colleagues at UO for championing her continued commitment to policy-driven scholarship since joining the faculty as a newly minted PhD. She is especially grateful to the staff at University Communications—in particular Molly Blancett—for promoting her work as a public scholar on LGBTQIA+ issues. Molly and UO Communications made it feasible for Alison to reach a much wider audience, using a more journalistic lens. Alison is equally indebted to Lee Rumbarger and Jason Schreiner in UO's Teaching Effectiveness Program for modelling and nurturing research-informed programs that center and showcase youth resilience and resistance.

Most of all we thank our families. Writing this book inevitably led us to reflect more than a few times on our own childhoods and to appreciate just how lovingly our parents (and grandparents) nurtured, protected, and "governed" us. For giving us plenty of room to flourish long before "the age of majority," even at moments when our agency tested their last nerve, we thank parents Susan and John Schmehl (Alison) and Ruth and Jay Tichenor (Dan). And, of course, we are especially grateful to our spouses for generously rearranging their schedules to accommodate our unpredictable and disruptive working hours and for being an ear to our incessant ramblings about politics— no easy task over the last couple of years. Alison counts her blessings every day to have Stephanie Axman by her side—loving, supporting, inspiring, and reminding her to take a breath and eat a snack. The two met while working at a youth center and Alison immediately fell in love with Stephanie's goofy sense of humor and her fierce commitment to helping young people thrive—which catalyzed so much of the thinking for this project. Stephanie makes every place a home. Both she and her wonderful parents, Raizie and Michale Axman, have provided Alison with all the key ingredients to a great book: a critical (but loving) ear, neverending coffee, and child care. Above all, Dan's deepest thanks goes to Elaine Replogle, who became the love of his life well before either of them was old enough (legally) to order a drink at a bar. Thirty-six years later, she is, as she always has been, his rock and his heart. She is also the world's greatest pandemic-lockdown pal. He would not have been able to coauthor this book without her encouragement, wisdom, snark, generosity, and love.

Our greatest inspiration as we finish this work are the record numbers of young people stirring up "good trouble" to advance social and racial justice, to save the earth from a harrowing climate crisis, to demand immigrant rights, to fight discrimination on the basis of gender and sexuality, and to seek solutions to gun violence. With our eyes fixed on the more just world these activists aspire to build, we hopefully dedicate this book to our own very independent-minded, generous, and extraordinary children: Eliza and Matias Axman and Natalie, Eric, and Isaiah Tichenor. The world is better and more joyful for having them in it.

1

The Politics Children Make

This continuing indefensible gun violence against children should shame us all. How many more child shootings is it going to take for enough decent people to stand up and say enough and protect every children's right to live?

—Marian Wright Edelman, Children's Defense Fund, 2011

If it's crazy to call for putting police and armed security guards in our schools to protect our children, then call me crazy.

—Wayne LaPierre, National Rifle Association, 2012

My friends and I might still be 11 and we might still be in elementary school, but we know. We know life isn't equal for everyone and we know what is right and wrong. We also know that we stand in the shadow of the Capital and we know that we have seven short years until we too have the right to vote.

—Naomi Wadler, Speech, March for Our Lives, Washington, DC, 2018

Leftists are parading traumatized teens to make an emotional plea about gun control. But we shouldn't let young people make policy for us. . . Children and teenagers are not fully rational actors. They're not capable of exercising supreme responsibilities. And we shouldn't be treating innocence as a political asset used to push the agenda of more sophisticated players.

—Ben Shapiro, *The National Review*, 2018

Democracy's Child. Alison L. Gash and Daniel J. Tichenor, Oxford University Press.
© Oxford University Press 2022. DOI: 10.1093/oso/9780197581667.003.0001

On the evening of Tuesday, September 7, 2021, a local sheriff's department in Pleasant Hill, Missouri, called for police backup to help break up a fight at the local high school. By the next morning, news of the fight had made national headlines. Fist fights in high school parking lots are hardly new. Teenagers are prone to bursts of aggression. On this evening, however, the brawl involved two parents who had just attended a local school board meeting, and reflected a growing national trend of parental hysteria toward COVID regulations. Pleasant Hill School Board members had just heard testimony on a proposed mask mandate when the fight erupted. "People were actually throwing fists and hitting each other," reported one journalist, and one man had to be forcefully removed in handcuffs.[1] Mask mandate meetings in Eastern County, Minnesota, and Lee County, Florida,[2] saw similarly violent outbreaks between opposing parents, and prompted one Eastern Carver County school board member to caution the audience that "our children are watching."[3] These fights are not limited to the COVID crisis. Recent school board attempts to either expand or eliminate K-12 curriculum discussing racism, sexism, or LGBTQIA issues have sparked equally explosive and hostile exchanges among parents. Violence between parents, over issues involving their kids, has become so commonplace that some school boards are limiting opportunities for public engagement to email or truncated windows of public exchange. School board members, too, have been the targets of violence. By the end of September 2021, the National School Board Association and the American Association of School Administrators, two venerable nonprofit organizations representing thousands of local school board members and officials nationwide, had urged the Biden administration to protect educators and school leaders from "threats of violence and acts of intimidation" that they said bordered on "domestic terrorism and hate crimes."[4]

While they remain one of the quintessential forms of local democracy in action, school board meetings have become volatile battlegrounds defined by anger and political division. Whether over guidelines for safe school openings, mask mandates and other health precautions, or the treatment of transgender students, provision of sex education, or the teaching of slavery and racism in US history, board meetings across the country have grown jarringly raucous.[5] By the end of September, 2021 new groups like Moms for Liberty and No Left Turn in Education had seeded and nurtured fears among conservative parents. Seizing on these anxieties, Republican politicians activated this fear by claiming that liberal officials wanted to "silence parents, and prevent them from having a say in their own children's education."[6] Shouting matches, scuffles, staged protests, death threats, long delays, and arrests for aggravated battery and disorderly conduct are an increasingly regular occurrence when school boards enter the partisan fray. Although framed as disagreements over what is best for children, one reporter aptly observes that children "are usually props and symbols in these scenes; this is a parents' war, and they mostly don't want to hear the students speak."[7] In fact, when undaunted young people made their voices heard at volatile board meetings, they were not spared partisan abuse. During a notorious meeting in Murfreesboro, Tennessee, audience members laughed and jeered at a high school junior, Grady Knox, when he described losing his grandmother (a former teacher) to COVID while pleading for more mask wearing. A woman seated behind Knox held up a sign against mask mandates that read "Let Our Kids Smile."[8]

These school board struggles are dramatic, but they are neither new nor isolated. Some of the most important and ferocious conflicts in the public square are struggles between parents, government officials, other adult stakeholders, and young people themselves over how to define and advance "the best interests of the child." Yet, despite their prominence in partisan struggles, we know relatively little about how young people incite, catalyze, or lead political reform. This is a book about children as pivotal subjects and actors in democratic politics. A crucial reciprocal relationship exists between children and politics: young people are constituted by their political environs, but liberal democratic politics in turn are shaped and influenced by their young constituents. Struggles over the welfare of children pervade every realm of public policy, from education and healthcare to criminal justice and environmental protection. Equally significant, but less frequently acknowledged, are the ways young people are mobilized or leveraged in our political life—from the 1963 Birmingham Children's Crusade in which thousands of schoolkids marched for civil rights to the 2018 Trump administration's "family separation" policy using migrant children as bargaining chips in its push for border control. In the most contentious of political conflicts, we also see young people exercising independent democratic agency in battles over climate change, immigrant rights, gun control, police violence, LGBTQIA+ rights, prison reform, and other causes. Ours is a book about the political control, leveraging, and agency of children—a struggle in which young people emerge as important democratic subjects, recruits and activists.

Once again, the coronavirus pandemic provides a glimpse of how the politics of young people permeates almost any issue on the public agenda. Consider, for example, the vast number of child welfare challenges confronting local, state, and national officials during the COVID-19 global pandemic. Decisions to close schools and childcare centers presented a host of questions about the educational and emotional development of children largely confined to their homes. They also intensified disparities in the resources and capacities of children, as educators wrestled with how to address technological gaps for remote learning, food insecurity once ameliorated by school breakfast and lunch programs, and special pedagogical needs. As stay-home orders placed many families in social isolation away from most outside observation, pediatricians and child psychologists warned officials that vulnerable children were at greater risk of abuse and neglect.[9] Administrators of juvenile detention centers nationwide struggled with virus containment in close quarters, while government, child advocate, and victim's rights lawyers battled in courts over the release of juvenile offenders.[10] Meanwhile parents who hosted large parties in defiance of state bans on large gatherings faced charges of child endangerment when minors were present.[11] The pandemic also added new wrinkles to family law as child custody and visitation for parents who are medical professionals or other essential workers met opposition from some former spouses and partners over fears of infection.[12] To enhance social distancing, municipalities imposed curfews on minors, stores banned children under sixteen, and playgrounds and sports fields were closed.[13]

Yet during the coronavirus pandemic, young people were not simply the subjects of control and protection. Indeed, the independent actions of young people—their potential *agency*—in this traumatic pandemic garnered special attention. Early in the global health crisis, stories of students crowding beaches, theme parks, and other vacation hotspots for Spring Break, despite dire warnings of the public health risks posed, dominated the news. Although vacationers of all ages posed risks to their home communities when they returned from leisure trips, young and frivolous Spring Breakers vividly captured the dangers of self-indulgence. "What is happening in Florida with spring break partying-on by students oblivious to the epidemiological implications of their actions is nothing short of tragic," fumed a Yale epidemiologist. "While many of us have been hunkering down to try to break the chains of infection in our communities, these young people have decided the pleasures of the moment are worth bringing back the coronavirus to their friends and family."[14] Less discussed, but readily apparent to anyone ordering takeout or buying groceries during the pandemic, was the large number of teenagers serving as essential workers in the food supply chain. "People need to eat" and "my store needs younger people like me continuing to work," one teenage cashier explained, while nervously adding that "we're soldiers with no training and not enough protective gear."[15] Jayde Powell, a young pre-med student in Nevada, formed a free grocery delivery service for senior citizens called Shopping Angels, spearheading a nationwide army of young volunteers.[16] Moreover, governments weighing how to ease COVID-19 lockdowns considered proposals for millions of young people with low viral death rates to leave their homes first to repopulate depleted workforces and spur economic revival.[17] The prominence of young people as crucial dependents in need of special protection from the coronavirus and its socioeconomic impacts, as reckless "COVID vectors" who might imperil us all, or as resilient essential workers reminds us that they are important political subjects and actors even when our focus may be elsewhere.

Similarly, the Black Lives Matter protests that erupted in cities and towns across the world, in the middle of the pandemic, highlight the significance of young people as activists for change. Just as young people stepped up to deliver food, provide support in COVID recovery centers, or supply critical labor for essential businesses, young protestors have fueled the fight against police brutality—risking COVID exposure and also police violence. In Tennessee, Zee Thomas, aged fifteen, decided two days after George Floyd's death that she had to take action. Thomas tweeted, "If my mom says yes, I'm leading a Nashville protest." A self-described introvert who had never gone to a protest, five days later Thomas led a march of 10,000 through her city, standing atop water coolers to address the crowd. On the other side of the country in northern California, seventeen-year-old Tiana Day led a Black Lives Matter protest across the Golden Gate Bridge for which she thought "something like 50 people would show up." Thousands of marchers, stretching along several miles, joined her.[18] The weeks-long protests—initiated by the televised murder of George Floyd by four Minneapolis police officers—called for immediate recognition of the many Black lives lost at the hands of police officers and an end to unchecked police authority over Black bodies. In so doing, they also highlighted the very police tactics that protestors were attempting to abolish. As several media outlets reported, protestors not only served as voices for change, but as frontline witnesses and victims of police violence. Young protestors who attended the marches to lend their support found themselves being beaten by police batons, battered by rubber bullets and paint balls, or doused with tear gas and pepper spray. Police sprayed seventeen-year-olds Aly Conyers, Chris Owusu, and Naomi Spates with chemical gas or rubber bullets and, yet, the teenagers continued to lead thousands in protests against police violence. Eighteen-year-old Zoe Willcutts sat on her knees with her hands in the air, peacefully demonstrating with a crowd of protestors near Lafayette Square in Washington, DC, when police officers hit her face with a pepper ball—bruising her jaw and burning her eyes to tears. "They're bullies," said the suburban Maryland student about police officers. "They want you to be scared."[19] Fourteen-year old Roberto Rivera marched with a gas mask and an extra water bottle—just in case police used tear gas—and used his spare water to help a woman who had been blinded by tear gas.[20] The struggle for Black lives vividly captures young people mobilizing and leading in social and political transformation.

The epigraphs that open this chapter highlight the unmistakable power of child protection, symbolism, and agency in one of the most contentious realms of US politics: gun control. The first is a call to "protect children not guns" by legendary child advocate Marian

Wright Edelman, the founder and president emerita of the Children's Defense Fund (CDF). The CDF began championing gun control in 1994 after "Chicago inner city children told us their greatest fear was dying from guns" in focus groups, in a Protect Children Not Guns campaign that was stepped up after the 1999 Columbine High School massacre.[21] Collective responsibility to protect innocent children was an inescapably palpable theme after the horrific 2012 mass shooting at Sandy Hook Elementary School that left twenty first-graders and six adults dead. "With their very first cry, this most precious, vital part of ourselves—our child—is suddenly exposed to the world, to possible mishap or malice," President Barack Obama told a heartbroken audience at an interfaith prayer vigil in Newtown, Connecticut, in honor of the Sandy Hook victims. "This is our first task—caring for our children. It's our first job. If we don't get that right, we don't get anything right. That's how, as a society, we will be judged. And by that measure, can we truly say, as a nation, that we are meeting our obligations?"[22]

Officials at the National Rifle Association (NRA) were themselves deeply rattled by the Newtown tragedy. "Everyone was saying, 'Are we doing the right thing here?' " a former NRA employee recalled. Senior leaders understood that most Americans were scalded by the murder of so many innocent children by one assailant with a semiautomatic rifle, and they feared an unprecedented clamor for firearms restrictions. Recognizing that this was not the time to highlight second amendment rights, NRA chief executive Wayne LaPierre announced that his organization was creating a new program—NRA School Shield—to better protect children by "hardening our schools" with armed security guards. If the president's children were guarded by armed secret service agents, he argued, then all schoolkids deserved the same protection.[23] While NRA hard-liners defensively claimed to champion child safety, its Congressional defenders effectively logjammed bipartisan reform proposals despite popular support in 2013. Five years later, eleven-year-old Naomi Wadler addressed a massive crowd at the March for Our Lives rally in Washington, DC, warning lawmakers that she and her elementary schoolmates knew right from wrong, that they were tired of delays that made children victims of gun violence, and that, in seven years, their votes would count. As our last epigraph conveys, conservative NRA supporters like Ben Shapiro worried anew about the influence of young faces and voices advancing gun control, questioning the rationality of child activists and the opportunism of adult reformers. The #NeverAgain movement that emerged in 2018 provides an instructive example of how the welfare, mobilization, and agency of young people can be potent forces in democratic politics.

Parkland and the March for Our Lives

On the morning of March 14, 2018–one month after hundreds of students fled a mass shooting that killed seventeen students and staff at Marjory Stoneman Douglas High School in Parkland, Florida— more than one million children from kindergartners to high schoolers across the United States participated in a National School Walkout to demand government action on gun control. Youth organizers of the student-led movement recorded 3,100 registered demonstrations in all fifty states; yet because calls for the action spread like wildfire on social media among Generation-Z peers (the demographic cohort following Millennials), the total number of protests and participating schoolkids is hard to pin down beyond registered events. Journalists, organizers, and scholars have a better fix on the size and scope of the March for Our Lives demonstrations that teenage activists organized ten days later. Between roughly 1,380,000 and 2,182,000 demonstrators marched for gun regulation and safer schools in 763 US cities and towns. In Washington, DC, alone, the 200,000–800,000 marchers created one of the largest single-day protests in the history of the nation's capital. The reach and momentum of a political insurgency fueled by children jarred many observers. "The emergence of people not even old enough to drive as a political force has been particularly arresting," *The New York Times* reported at the time, "unsettling a gun control debate that has seemed impervious to other factors."[24]

Teenage Parkland survivors like Sarah Chadwick, Jacklyn Corin, Ryan Deitsch, Aalayah Eastmond, X González, David Hogg, Cameron Kasky, and Alex Wind soon appeared as compelling and determined voices for reform on screen, in print, and at rallies. These outraged student activists became overnight celebrities, landing on the cover of *Time* magazine and dominating the airwaves and mainstream media.[25] Thrust into the spotlight, they seized the opportunity to address and channel widespread youth anger and fear about gun violence. Social media was pivotal to their campaign. It began with harrowing tweets and disturbing Snapchat videos posted by terrified Marjory Stoneman Douglas students hiding in closets and under desks during the attack. Millions watched their online videos. Screenshots of texts between two brothers, Sam (eighteen) and Matthew (fourteen) Zeif, trapped on different floors of the school were retweeted over 150,000 times. They began with Sam telling his scared younger brother hiding one floor above him that "we're going to get out of here I promise." Matthew responded, "my teacher died." He then asked, "I'm on the third floor, you think I'm ok?" "Don't do anything," Sam replied. When Matthew didn't respond, Sam texted, "Don't DO ANYTHING." Followed by: "Do you understand?" As time went by with no response: "Matthew." Then: "Please answer me." When Matthew finally responded that he was fine, Sam texted, "Just stay hidden please."[26]

On the evening of the tragedy, Kasky, a self-described "theater kid," was unable to sleep and started writing Facebook posts that led to invitations to write a CNN editorial and television interviews the next day. Corin, the junior-class president, woke up the day after sobbing over the death of her friend, Joaquin Oliver, then began writing Instagram posts demanding "stricter gun laws IMMEDIATELY," before organizing student meetings with elected officials. Two days after the tragedy, Kasky and Corin joined forces to form an activist movement named #NeverAgain with the goal of mandating stricter background checks for gun buyers. Other students who had been posting online and talking to the news media independently about gun control joined #NeverAgain a day later, including Hogg, the school newspaper reporter, Chadwick, whose profanity-laced tweet in response to President Trump's "condolences" went viral, and González, a senior who started talking to reporters because "this is how I'm dealing with my grief . . . the thing that had no right to cause me grief."[27] In the days that followed, their deft use of social media was crucial to fueling widespread organizing behind the National School Walkout and March For Our Lives. "People always say, 'Get off your phones,' but social media is our weapon," Corin explained. "Without it, the movement wouldn't have spread this fast."[28]

The Parkland activists recognized and talked openly about the fact that children of color in urban communities faced much greater risks from gun violence, yet lacked the financial, social, and political privilege to catalyze media attention and public outrage. Aalayah Eastmond, whose quick decision to "look like I'm dead"[29] kept her alive and grabbed the headlines, became an overnight activist when she "recognized the conversation was very one-sided when we discussed gun violence. It was on a national front, but it was only addressing mass shootings."[30] The ordinarily shy teenager from Brooklyn, New York—and one of the few Black students at Marjorie Stoneman High School—joined the executive council of Team Enough and became a leading voice in centering Black and Brown voices in gun violence debates.

I tried to speak out as much as possible but also recognized that I am a young Black woman and oftentimes our voices don't get heard. So not a lot of people care about what I have to say or take what I have to say seriously. I just found myself being unapologetically outspoken and just pushing aside caring about the comfortability of others.[31]

#NeverAgain leaders worked to build coalitions with reformers from communities of color across the country, including Peace Warriors of Chicago and Dream Defenders, a racial-justice group formed after the killing of Treyvon Martin. "We're fighting for the same thing," said Arieyanna Williams, a teenager from Peace Warriors who was invited to Florida with other urban Black activists to coordinate messaging and mobilization efforts. "We found our voice in Parkland." Evidence of these alliances were on full display on March 24 in the diversity of marchers, organizers, and speakers. At the Washington, DC, demonstration, for instance, Naomi Wadler's words electrified the nation. "I am here today to acknowledge and represent the African-American girls whose stories don't make the front page of every national newspaper," she told a cheering crowd, "whose stories don't lead on the evening news."[32] As captured by both Wadler and González in the epigraph at the start of this chapter, these young activist survivors offered a gripping message—#NeverAgain must "make life survivable for *all* young people." Weeks earlier at a gun control rally in Fort Lauderdale soon after the school massacre, González captivated the crowd in a speech that listed the ways the gun industry and their political allies "are lying to us, and us kids seem to be the only ones who notice and are prepared to call B.S." She then provided a defining slogan of the movement by eight times punctuating false gun lobby claims with an indelible refrain echoed by the crowd: "We call BS!"[33]

Adults, of course, figure prominently at every turn of this explosion of grassroots youth insurgency. Parkland teenagers, initially, were encouraged by parents and beloved teachers and administrators. As #NeverAgain mushroomed, it gained financial and organizational support from seasoned gun control advocates and groups like billionaire Michael Bloomberg's Everytown for Gun Safety, the Brady Campaign, Giffords's nonprofit, and Moms Demand Action. "Our mission was to give them the biggest megaphone possible," explains Moms Demand Action founder Shannon Watts.[34] Moreover, hundreds of thousands of adults across generations joined the March for Our Lives, including senior citizens who formed Stand Up for Our Grandkids to support the student gun control activists.[35] Other adults—gun industry leaders, the NRA, and intransigent elected officials—loomed as the student movement's powerful adversaries. Because nearly all #NeverAgain activists could not vote, their influence hinged upon their moral claims as innocents whose welfare is entrusted to others. "Congress needs to get over their political bias with each other and work toward saving children's lives," Hogg declared. "We're children. You guys are the adults."[36]

Gun rights advocates initially sought to duck this Parkland youth challenge. President Trump scheduled a "listening session" in Parkland, at the same time that young activists were meeting with state lawmakers in Tallahassee, wary of crossing paths with angry #NeverAgain leaders.[37] The NRA remained silent for a week as #NeverAgain demanded gun control. Yet the gun lobby soon pivoted when it determined that the student-led groundswell was too dangerous to ignore. NRA spokespersons assailed "opportunists" who "exploit tragedy for political gain," insisting that only expanding the presence of armed security at schools would save children. Resurrecting language he used after the 2012 massacre of twenty first graders and six staff in Newtown, the NRA's LaPierre declared that "to stop a bad guy with a gun, it takes a good guy with a gun."[38] As the March for Our Lives grew dramatically in size and scope, opponents felt compelled to challenge the notion that it was conceived and organized by young people. The conservative website Breitbart, for example, insisted that the insurgency was "directed, promoted and funded by left-wing adults and adult-led organizations."[39] Other far-right critics challenged the credibility of the Parkland activists by desperately peddling a conspiracy theory that the students were paid actors—not unlike conspiracy tropes that the murders of the agonizingly young Newtown victims (most age six) were fabricated.[40]

For some gun control opponents, the best way to stymie the momentum of the #NeverAgain movement was to directly challenge the innocence and integrity of its young leaders. RedState, a conservative blog, falsely claimed that Hogg was not even in school on the day of the shooting. Gun rights advocates created a doctored image of Gonzalez ripping up the US Constitution that circulated widely online (the original photo depicted her tearing up a paper shooting target). Other opponents resorted to infantile and sometimes vicious personal attacks. Leslie Gibson, a Republican candidate for the Maine statehouse, called González a "skinhead lesbian,"[41] while GOP Congressman Steve King intimated she was a communist sympathizer.[42] Conservative media pundits mocked Hogg for multiple college rejections and labeled him a "Damien, Children of the Corn, Hitler-youth type."[43] If one of the most important assets of the Parkland insurgency was the appeal of its earnest young leaders, their opponents sought to derail their message by defaming its most prominent messengers and degrading their image.

The Parkland students wore these attacks as a badge of honor. Gun rights advocates are lashing out "because they know we're strong," the students told reporters, and because "together we kind of form an unstoppable force that terrifies them."[44] On social media, they responded to the onslaught by tweeting Harry Potter references, calling Republican Governor Rick Scott "Voldemort" and likening "this battle to the showdown between Dumbledore's Army and the Death Eaters inside the ministry of magic."[45] Kasky theorized that the power of their insurgency owed much to adult guilt over not doing what they should to protect children from gun violence. "The adults know that we're cleaning up their mess," he told *Time* magazine.[46] By contrast, commentators like Ben Shapiro directly challenged the very idea that teenagers, let alone younger children, are in any position to address the gun policy debate. Indeed, consistent with many traditionalists, he argued that until the age of majority (between eighteen and twenty-one in the United States), young people are not fully rational actors whose preferences and judgments can be taken seriously in weighty government choices.[47]

The burst of collective energy and intense struggle elicited by the #NeverAgain movement only a month after the devastating Parkland massacre highlights three core dimensions of how young people shape and are shaped by the polity. First, like the Sandy Hook massacre in 2012, the March for Our Lives posed the essential question of how government and society address the welfare of children in balance with other demands. The movement fervently underscored the staggering number of US children who are victims of gun violence—a disturbing feature of US exceptionalism—to slam home the point that the nation was failing at what Obama aptly described as its "first task—caring for our children."[48] Second, the widespread appeal of their message reflected the political resonance of young people as symbols or leverage for reform. Just as images of sobbing Newtown parents burying their six- and seven-year-old children left the nation heartbroken, the #NeverAgain movement forcefully drew attention to innocent child victims (and all schoolkids imperiled by the US gun culture). Third, outraged by the intransigence of elected officials in league with the NRA and gun companies, young people took independent action in spearheading nationwide protests and, ultimately, a new movement. The political agency of "the Parkland kids" should remind us of another reform campaign led by young people dedicated to figuratively and very literally cleaning up the mess made by adults: the youth climate movement.[49] Instead of dismissing the #NeverAgain insurgency, gun rights opponents quickly recognized their potential strength and tellingly sought to counterpunch along all three dimensions. They argued that children are better protected by "hardening" schools with armed security, challenged the innocence of the most visible teenage leaders, and contended that youth activists lacked the rational capacity and legitimacy to participate in democratic deliberations or to make demands in the public square. The protection, leveraging, and agency of young people are defining—and powerful—features of democratic politics. This book trains a spotlight on each of these crucial dimensions of the politics children make.

Figure 1.1 X González, Tyra Hemans, Naomi Wadler and Other March for Our Lives Speakers, March 24, 2018.

Source: Photo by Pierre Barlier. Almay. https://www.alamy.com/no-film-no-video-no-tv-no-documentary-emma-gonzalez-a-student-and-survivor-of-the-parkland-shooting-speaks-during-march-for-our-lives-to-demand-stricter-gun-control-laws-on-saturday-march-24-2018-in-washington-dc-usa-photo-by-olivier-doulierytnsabacapress com-image386938726.html.

The Politics Children Make: Protection, Leveraging, and Agency

The March for Our Lives campaign may be an especially dramatic example, yet children are a regular focal point of democratic politics—and a frequent subject of and participant in legal, philosophical, and political conflict. Indeed, the relationship between children, parents, and the state (not to mention other stakeholders) has always been uneasy, and their battles are waged in legislatures, courts, government agencies, and elections, but also in schools, boardrooms, hospitals, churches, athletic fields, and bathrooms. Recent efforts to ban anti-racist or LGBTQIA+-affirming curricula and books in public schools are just one of a multitude of conflicts that have erupted between and among state officials, private actors, and community groups over children's welfare and parental control. At the heart of these conflicts are rival views over state, community, and parental obligations to children, with sharp disagreements over who should govern children, which children are valued, and how to best promote their welfare.

Of course, childhood is a relatively new concept, a product of twentieth-century innovations. During the early twentieth century, few agreed with the notions of childhood play, learning, exploration, and protection that are now the canon of psychosocial development. Indeed, many Progressive Era Americans viewed minors as property of their parents or, to be precise, of their fathers. As we discuss at length in Chapter 2, child labor was readily accepted for most of the country's history as both an entitled source of income for parents and a legitimate means of fueling national economic growth. Alexander Hamilton noted in his 1791 *Report on Manufacturers* that "children are rendered more useful . . . by manufacturing establishments than they would otherwise be."[50] By the 1890s, nearly two million US children (about one in five) provided inexpensive labor that expanded the profits of factories and farms. In 1903, the union organizer and progressive firebrand Mary Harris Jones, aka Mother Jones, noticed that many of the 10,000 textile-mill child laborers on strike in Kensington, Pennsylvania, were badly malnourished and missing fingers and hands. Elected officials paid little heed to the plight of child workers, she concluded, because they lacked the political clout of the adults who benefited from their servitude. "In Georgia where children work day and night, they have just passed a law to protect song birds," Jones ruefully noted.[51]

Traditionalists saw child labor very differently. "When the rights of a father to govern his own family are taken away from him," one Florida lawmaker proclaimed, "God pity our nation."[52] As late as the 1920s, new campaigns to pass a Child Labor Amendment floundered as conservative political, religious, and professional leaders warned that it represented "a communistic effort to nationalize children, making them primarily responsible to the government instead of to their parents."[53] Despite this resistance, the early twentieth century was marked by a transition in how childhood was conceived. "The devotion and sacrifice of parents for children is a sentiment which has been developed steadily and is now more intense and far more widely practiced throughout society than in earlier times," Yale social scientist

William Graham Sumner wrote at the time. "It used to be believed that the parent had unlimited claims on the child and rights over him. In a truer view of the matter, we are coming to see that the rights are on the side of the child and the duties are on the side of the parent."[54]

Although US child labor is now tightly regulated and minors are no longer easily claimed as paternal property, the struggle between parents, state officials, and other adults over control of children remains a defining feature of democratic politics. The issue of control raises several significant questions about the governance of children. One is how to determine the best interests of children when adults disagree. This clash can emerge, for example, when divorced parents favor competing norms, rules, or expectations for their kids or when educational requirements of the state collide with a family's religious beliefs. Another key question is whether and how to arbitrate between the rights and interests of children and those of other groups and individuals when they conflict. This was precisely what set #NeverAgain activists at loggerheads with gun rights advocates trumpeting second amendment freedoms, for instance. Finally, this issue raises an elemental and crucial question: when is exercising control over young people appropriate and when is it not? One might rely on the age of majority (when someone is legally recognized as an adult), but that threshold ranges from ages fourteen to twenty-one cross-nationally and from ages eighteen to twenty-one in the United States. The "age of maturity" varies even more widely when defined in comparative religious or cultural terms. And as we discuss in greater length in Chapter 2, the age of majority is not necessarily the same as the legal ages assigned for driving, sexual consent, voting, smoking, drinking, military service, leaving school, or marriage.

These legal, cultural, and social variations in how childhood is demarcated are precisely why we do not assign strict age parameters on how to define *children* or *young people* in this book. In truth, as will become clear in the pages that follow, a significant portion of the examples analyzed in our project focus on children under eighteen-years-old, thereby conforming to familiar legal definitions of minors who have not yet reached the threshold of adulthood. From criminal sentencing to healthcare dependency, however, cloudiness pervades many efforts to delineate childhood from the age of majority across legal and policy realms. This ambiguity is part and parcel of the political struggle over whether and how to govern children. Fundamentally, as we discuss later in the book, parents and other authorities in liberal democracies are expected to grant children—as adults-in-waiting or future citizens—increased autonomy as their rational capacities for independent judgement and self-determination grow. This presents a key democratic conundrum of how to nurture and respect the rational claims and aspirations of young people before the age of majority, especially in situations where legal guardians strictly limit autonomy.

One of the central aims of this book is to address these questions of control, tracking children's historical shift from parental property to rights-bearing individuals, and illuminating four categories of how children are governed: paternalism, subjugation, membership, and abandonment. But, as we intimate early on, children are more than just subjects of political control. Along with mapping the core principles, laws, and practices governing children, a second key objective of this project is to unpack the ways that children operate as political leverage in our constitutional democracy. For us, the political leveraging of young people addresses the ways in which children are invoked or mobilized for good or ill. A final goal of this book is to better understand the *political agency* of young people. While children are governed by varied adults in their lives and sometimes are appropriated by political actors to advance their agendas, they also have demonstrated an enormous capacity to unsettle the status quo and to remake the democratic order on their own terms.

Our hope is that, taken together, the three core concepts at the heart of this book—control, leveraging, and agency—provide a valuable foundation for understanding children as crucial subjects and actors in democratic politics. In developing these concepts, we draw on both our own research as well as a rich body of scholarship from diverse fields. Of course, entire fields of study and training are dedicated to children, from pediatric medicine and child psychology to community social work and K-12 education. Children also lie at the center of key areas of philosophy, law, history, literature, anthropology, sociology, and other disciplines. However, we are struck by the fact that few works focus systematically on how children have been governed, symbolized, and activated in political life over time.

This gap is perhaps most glaringly evident in our own discipline of political science. Political scientists over the past half a century increasingly have devoted crucial attention to investigating politicized categories and identities such as race, ethnicity, gender, sexuality, religion, economic class, and immigration status. Yet the subject of children and politics only rarely inspires sustained interrogation in our discipline, and it occupies no special subfield.[55] Despite limited attention, several key works provide an important foundation for our book. Political philosophy long has led the way in exploring the moral obligations of the state, society, and parents to children, as our discussion of Hobbes, Locke, Rousseau, Mill, and others captures in Chapter 2. We also draw on contemporary theorists like Elizabeth Cohen, Ronald Dworkin, Amy Gutman, William Galston, Susan Moller Okin, and Michael Sandel to understand competing moral arguments for expanding or constraining the rights of young people. Cohen is particularly helpful to us in capturing the liminal space that children occupy in the context of semi-citizenship.[56]

We also draw on scholarship that interrogates the agentic capacities of young people—particularly in the context of self-advocacy or political decision-making. Scholarly debates regarding children negotiate between the importance of autonomy and agency and the necessity for dependency and protection. Scholars who propose that young people be given co-equal decision-making authority assert that age is a problematic proxy for deliberative capacity. At the very least, they argue, young people should be evaluated on their demonstrated capacities rather than on questionable presumptions about age-based deficiencies.[57] Policy reforms that call for decreases in the voting age or greater veto power in a range of policy arenas have fostered an especially fertile landscape of scholarly inquiry. Scholars proposing "full agency" demand significant reductions in the level of economic, social, and political regulation that young people face,[58] arguing that the central tenet of democratic participation cannot be achieved if young people are left out of the process.[59] Other scholars emphasize the special limitations that young people experience, and push for further reforms to designate them as partial citizens, limiting their liberties but providing a more robust safety net. Scholars question the notion that childhood can or should serve as a bright line that separates dependency from autonomy. In politics, childhood is deployed by policymakers (as with many social and political categories) primarily to parse out which individuals will be fully endowed with democratic rights and liberties and which will require more heavy-handed state protections and limitations.[60]

There is considerable disagreement over whether, at what point, or under what circumstances children should be treated as special or partial citizens, and these debates offer a rich context for significant political conflict.[61] Thus, there is also considerable debate over how democracies understand childhood. Elizabeth Cohen and Ian Shapiro, for instance, have each developed frameworks for describing the restricted space that children occupy in the context of legal rights and status. Cohen argues that children's rights can be thought of as a tradeoff between autonomous and relative rights.[62] Shapiro uses the language of "basic" and "best" rights to capture the difference between essential and optimal resources for children.[63] This scholarship reveals that childhood—both conceptually and in practice—is highly contingent upon setting, subject, and person.

Research on the political socialization and attitudes of young people is another important vein of scholarship that informs this book.[64] More than fifty years ago, Fred Greenstein conducted interviews with New Haven children to assess early feelings toward political authority, the development of political information, and the roots of partisan identification.[65] Several subsequent studies of children's political socialization and attitudes followed in the 1970s and 1980s, from Richard Niemi's *The Politics of Future Citizens* to Robert Coles's *The Political Life of Children*.[66] Since this pioneering work, an outpouring of scholarship has examined youth political socialization and civic engagement from psychological and developmental perspectives.[67] Recently, Jennifer Lawless and Richard Fox surveyed thousands of young Americans and found that political polarization, paralysis, and scandals have dissuaded the vast majority from running for elective office.[68]

Despite the important contributions of this scholarly literature, the reality is that our fellow political scientists have not given broad or sustained attention to the relationship between young people and democratic politics. Yet, as we argue and demonstrate in the pages that follow, children figure prominently in nearly every major political debate or struggle of the past century. In order to build a broader understanding of democratic politics that centers young people as political subjects, symbols, and actors, this book draws upon works from a wide variety of fields and disciplines to weave together crucial examples, evidence, and insights about children and politics.

As noted earlier, pinning down precise ages to define *childhood* is elusive (and maybe even quixotic) due to numerous legal, cultural, and social variations, if not contradictions. Indeed, the governing, leveraging, and agency of children in democratic politics is fueled by these tensions and ambiguities. But there is another crucial element at the heart of childhood's contingent status that this book highlights: the ways in which age combines with other categories of exclusion to further disenfranchise some young people. The concept of "intersectionality" refers to multiple, intersecting pathways of disempowerment—such as racism, sexism, nativism, classism, or Queerphobia—in ways that amplify and exacerbate systems, conditions, and experiences of oppression.[69] Throughout this book, we view the status of "child" as a politically, socially, and legally constructed category, one that often is defined less by chronological age or biological markers than by its capacity to regulate, elevate, and exclude depending on the young person's privileged or marginalized status.

Recent scholarship on white nationalism, for example, highlights how white children are elevated as both subjects and symbols in forums and narratives designed to increase membership and legitimize violence. Sophie Bjork-James's analysis of the white supremacist discussion board *Stormfront* finds that "protecting the imagined future of the white child . . . is a primary motivation white nationalists give for participating in this movement and a primary justification for prejudice."[70] This analysis captures how valorizing white children for supremacist audiences hinges upon denigrating others—most frequently children of color and LGBTQIA+ young people.[71] Legislative efforts to ban books and eradicate course curriculums that discuss histories and legacies of slavery, white supremacy, and race, gender, or sexuality-based inequality are a perfect example. Policy officials and advocates initiating these efforts argue that a curriculum that acknowledges or addresses inequality "divid[es] our children into victims and oppressors and what's a child supposed to do with that?"[72]

Yet, age or youth is an overlooked arena of analysis in the study of identity and power. The chapters that follow highlight the ways in which marginalized young people—those who are saddled with the challenges of racism, sexism, gay-or-transphobia, nativism, classism, ableism—are especially burdened relative to adults and majoritized peers. We explore how policy actors weaponize "youth" as a category of policy reform and political control, to further exclude, subjugate, and demonize. We also take seriously the ways in which young people, as reservoirs of resistance and resilience, are prominent leaders in our centuries-long struggle for equality and democracy.

As the opening to this chapter highlights and as we underscore throughout this book, many young people have eschewed conventional politics in favor of political protest and social movements, from gun control and environmental justice to Black Lives Matter and immigrant rights. Among the most important studies examining the political attitudes of young people are those which highlight their views and experiences of disenfranchisement on the basis of race and class. In *Democracy Remixed*, Cathy Cohen draws on a rich survey of young Black Americans to show that they yearn for what everyone wants—decent jobs, safety, fulfilling lives, respect, and equality—yet regularly encounter marginalization and structural barriers.[73] Amy Lerman and Vesla Weaver's *Arresting Citizenship* underscores how blatantly racist and classist forms of US policing, such as searches, stops, frisks, detainment, invasions of privacy, and violent attacks from law enforcement officials, disempowers and alienates young people whose lives are regularly impacted by the carceral state. As one young man told Lerman and Weaver, being young, Black, and poor meant that he and his friends were certain targets for law enforcement officials: "We got that bull's eye on our back as soon as we're born."[74] And Erin Kerrison, Jennifer Cobbina and Kimberly Bender expose the contingent nature of Black rights through in-depth interviews with Black youth in Baltimore as they navigate the politics of "Black Respectability" as targets of police scrutiny.[75] The ways in which age—and conceptions of children in particular—intersects with race, gender, sexuality, class, immigration status, and other constructed identities are illustrated throughout this book, from border control and criminal justice to education and welfare policy.

Our hope is that this book helps fill important conceptual and theoretical gaps for anyone who studies or cares about children to better understand how young people are governed and in turn, how they shape politics. To this end, the chapters that follow train a spotlight on young people in several key roles—as political subjects, icons, collateral, and agents. In our next chapter, we focus on how children have been governed over time, moving through history from parental property to rights-bearing individuals, demanding special protection from the state until reaching the age of majority. We map diverse laws, policies, and practices according to the degree to which they control or liberate young people and whether they serve "the best interests of the child" or other, potentially conflicting, interests. This framework enables us to illuminate in Chapter 2 the distinctive means and rationales for governing children through four categories: paternalism, subjugation, membership, and abandonment. The theoretical frames developed in this chapter are given form and substance by diverse examples, including child labor, Aid to Families with Dependent Children (AFDC), compulsory education, school prayer, adoption and foster care, gay conversion therapy, free speech, parental consent for abortion, trying minors as adults, driver's licensure, and abuse and neglect laws. In short, the conceptual framework developed in Chapter 2 offers a novel view of traditional notions of state and parental obligations to children—one that recognizes how our democratic political struggles and policies produce child protection and abandonment, as well as youth freedom and subjugation.

After developing in Chapter 2 a conceptual foundation for understanding the core principles, laws, and practices governing children in liberal democracies, Chapter 3 shifts to the political leveraging of young people. Here we concentrate on the ways in which children are deployed as symbols, activist recruits, and bargaining chips for political purposes. As one form of leveraging, the political iconography of children can alter public opinion or mobilize adults to take action in the public square when their images and stories of innocence or natural virtue are effectively disseminated. Sometimes stories about children are enlisted to politically inspire, to symbolize innocence, or to highlight the need for reform on behalf of the most vulnerable and sympathetic members of society. As a second form of leveraging young people for political purposes, children are deployed as activist armies—as they were in Progressive Era labor organizing and the *long* Civil Rights Movement—by those seeking to gain attention and mobilize action by eliciting empathy toward innocents. Yet despite their frequent allure as exemplars of innocence, children also are appropriated as symbols of deviance, threat, and social decay. The *othering* of children has been a familiar frame in US politics from fears of unassimilable "new" immigrant kids at the turn of the century, to wayward counter-culture youth of the sixties, to contemporary so-called "gang-bangers" and "anchor babies."[76] Likewise, political actors have used children as collateral to be leveraged for instrumental purposes such as the Trump administration's policy of separating migrant children from their parents and detaining them as means of discouraging unauthorized border crossings.[77] In summary, Chapter 3 captures the political uses of children as important symbols, foot soldiers, and bargaining chips appropriated to advance often rival agendas.

Chapter 4, our final substantive chapter, provides a crucial twist: the children who are controlled and appropriated in previous chapters emerge as independent political actors who make autonomous demands that transform the political system. We draw important connections between early "Children's Crusades" in the 1900s and 1950s to today's Black Lives Matter, March for Our Lives, Gay Straight Alliances, the Sunrise Movement, and United We Dream. For example, we introduce readers to the ways in which our democratic politics can be transformed by captivating youth leaders—such as Diane Nash, John Lewis, X González, Gavin Grimm, Greta Thunberg, and Naomi Wadler—and legions of activist children mobilizing in ways that often defy the best-laid plans of their elders. In the 1960s, the Student Non-Violent Coordinating Committee (SNCC) launched campaigns that were more radical in their insurgency than preferred by the older guard of the Civil Rights movement. Indeed, SNCC activists were offended by the compromises that Martin Luther King Jr. and his Southern Christian Leadership Conference were willing to accept.[78] Half a century later, young Dreamers rejected the political moderation of older immigrant rights advocates in favor of confrontational tactics that helped pave the way to Deferred Action for Childhood Arrivals (DACA).[79] Although often treated in both law and practice as subjects of protection or control, children have long exercised meaningful agency in our democratic political life.

Democratic politics is replete with struggles of, by, and for young people. The most transformative moments of political reform have been scaffolded by battles over the rights of children. Children have served as messengers and armies of change—as evocations of injustice. They also have reminded us of the pathologies of adult governance, attempting to wrest control from adult leaders and demanding to be legitimized as agents of their own fate. We began this chapter describing young activists like Zee Thomas, who was one of six teenagers who organized Nashville's massive Black Lives Matter march one week after George Floyd's murder. After the protest, fifteen-year-old Thomas was struck by the fact that she and her peers responded forcefully to a crisis whose solution eluded the political establishment. "As teens, we feel like we cannot make a difference in this world," she said, "but we must."[80] Despite their clear importance as subjects, symbols, and activists in our political life, children have received surprisingly little to modest attention from scholars who study politics, policy, and governance. Our primary aim in this book is to make the case—and provide a conceptual framework—for centering children in the study of democratic politics. We hold no illusions that our approach is the only (or best) means of studying the influence of young people in politics. Rather we propose this as a launching point—as a first step in a more complete re-examination of the evolution of democratic politics in general and US politics in particular.

In the pages that follow, as we investigate the political control, leveraging, and agency of young people, it will be analytically useful to conceive of children as more than adults-in-waiting. The historian Harry Hendrick aptly observes that "children are usually viewed from the perspective of *becoming* (growing to adult maturity), rather than *being* (children as their own persons)." He adds that *age* or *childhood* is often overlooked as an essential category of analysis—one that is not on par with gender, race, ethnicity, indigeneity, sexuality, or religion—because "individuals experience childhood for no more than a small part of their lives before growing out of it, unlike members of other 'oppressed' classes."[81] Yet we contend that when children are only conceived as future citizens, their political significance is too easily underestimated. Even as they lack the vote and other vested rights of democratic membership, and despite their dependency on adult authorities, we find that children exercise significant influence in the public square as crucial political subjects, icons, and independent actors. In fact, the child activists we discuss in Chapters 3 and 4 made their presence felt in key democratic conflicts long before they grew out of their constrained political, legal, and social status. But first, let us turn to Chapter 2 and shifting conceptions of children as property and miniature adults to vulnerable dependents requiring control and protection.

2

Governing Children

Paternalism, Membership, Subjugation, and Abandonment

Introduction

In 1620 Virginia, a year after the first Africans arrived in chains to
the fledgling colony, more than a hundred of London's street children
were forcibly shipped to America where they were "bound out" to colonial overseers. Ranging in age from six to nineteen years old, these
unwilling child laborers were seized by London officials at the behest
of the English Virginia Company.[1] The city council openly explained
that it was "especially desirous to be disburdened" of "a superfluous
multitude" of children who had lost their parents through death or
abandonment. When these street children resisted, the English Privy
Council authorized the company "to imprison, punish, and dispose
any of those children" until they could "ship them out" to Virginia
where "under severe masters they may be brought to goodness."[2] In
truth, the New World proved to be a "death trap" for many of these
street children as well as successive waves of forced child laborers
imported to toil in colonies of the South and Chesapeake region over
the next century; an estimated 45–55 percent perished before their
twentieth birthday.[3] Their ordeal was hardly isolated. Parents in colonies south of New England frequently sent their children away by
age ten to toil for other families or employers, and their mortality
rates paralleled those of indentured youth. Those born out of wed-
lock were taken from their mothers and forced to work for various
overseers under harsh conditions.[4] "Sentimentality about children and
childhood, which bloomed in the nineteenth century, was nearly absent in this practical, struggling era," legal scholar Mary Ann Mason
notes. "[I]n the hierarchical structure of the colonial household the

Democracy's Child. Alison L. Gash and Daniel J. Tichenor, Oxford University Press.
© Oxford University Press 2022. DOI: 10.1093/oso/9780197581667.003.0002

relationship between child and father overlapped the relationship between slave and master."[5]

It may be jarring for many of us today to learn that aside from the London street kids themselves, no one in English society particularly cared about their removal and enslavement across the Atlantic. As illustrated by city councilmen and members of the crown's influential Privy Council, government actors were happy to meet the instrumental labor needs of the Virginia Company while ridding the country of unwanted children. The fate of these young people in a menacing new territory that proved lethal to nearly half of all colonial children was of no concern. Indeed, the well-being of these children barely registered in adult deliberations, except perhaps for the Calvinist view that innately sinful children might learn "goodness" under the lash and command of "severe masters."[6] Far from being a cause célèbre, the forced migration and labor of London street children in seventeenth-century England was relatively consistent with centuries-old norms of treating children as property. It is a stark reminder that conceptions of *the child* have been anything but static over time.

In fact, a vigorous debate has raged among historians and other scholars for more than half a century over precisely how ideas of childhood have evolved over time. At the heart of these arguments is a path-breaking book, *Centuries of Childhood*, written by the French historian Phillipe Aries in 1960.[7] This influential work has commanded a large audience for generations, and its power lies in Aries's skill at constructing a captivating and provocative account of childhood history. The very notion of *childhood*, he proclaimed, is a modern invention. Before the eighteenth century, Aries noted, children over seven years of age were thought to be merely "small-scale adults" who shared many the same qualities and capacities as grown-ups. Accordingly, he wrote, children in medieval times were not viewed as requiring any special treatment or protection, and they were subjected to significant exploitation, including hefty work responsibilities, as well limited space for child education, play, and care. Lloyd deMause's *The History of Childhood* (1974) provided a similarly grim view of life for young people in the Middle Ages. "The history of childhood is a nightmare from which we have only recently begun to awake," deMause notes. "The farther back in history one goes the lower the level of child care, and the more likely children are to be killed, abandoned, terrorized, or sexually abused."[8] According to Aries, children began to escape this dark fate during the Enlightenment of the seventeenth and eighteenth centuries, as important historical changes fueled a new sensibility about minors: an increased emphasis on literacy and education, greater privacy for families and concern for child rearing, stronger attention to age as something carefully measured, and the growth of liberal capitalism. From this perspective, the special care and treatment of children is not something shared universally by parents and other adults across time, but instead reflects a modern revolution in thinking about the young—one that created childhood as an exceptional stage of life obligating families and states to meet particular needs and rights.[9]

Aries provides a clear and compelling history of childhood. This undoubtedly explains why his book remains the most cited work in the field, and why his account pervades many contemporary professional and general understandings of children's lives in earlier times. Yet many contemporary scholars question its accuracy. A mountain of historical research has accumulated over several decades that refutes Aries's claims, showing the outlines and development of childhood stretching from ancient to modern times.[10] New scholarship reveals that medieval societies attached enormous importance to childhood, as evidenced in art, literature, religious life, toys, clothing, furniture, food, and family practices.[11] Whereas Aries contends that parents in earlier times were less emotionally connected to their children because of high infant mortality rates, later research challenges his assumptions about parental affection in previous eras.[12] "The love for children cannot be said to have begun at any one point in history," Paula Fass aptly observes, "while the callous treatment of children cannot be said to have ended once modern times began."[13]

What emerges from newer research is a different but no less provocative story of childhood not as a modern invention but as a privileged status reserved for children of elite families in medieval and early modern societies. This meant that the children of wealthy and powerful parents were cherished and protected early on, but the vast majority faced significant perils and were expected to do the work of adult men and women by their teens, long after the Enlightenment.[14] It also reveals something more chilling than Aries's account: powerful grown-ups in earlier times recognized that children were *not* "small-scale adults," but they nonetheless exposed most to a Hobbesian world of perpetual danger. Slave children in the Ancient World and in the Americas during the modern age faced brutal lives, and their parents could do little to spare them.[15] Poor and unwanted children were disposable, and infanticide, physical abuse, neglect, economic exploitation, and other forms of mistreatment were common outside elite circles.[16] Over time, as more children gained access to education and various forms of targeted resources, a variety of childhood experiences became the norm—shaped by differences in class, gender, race, ethnicity, and religion.

In 1762, the French philosopher Jean Jacques Rousseau famously penned *Emile* as an enlightened treatise on education, proclaiming in his preface that "we know nothing of childhood, and with our mistaken notions the further we advance the further we go astray."[17]

Emile was, as Larry Wolfe notes, "a literary and philosophical work on an entirely different scale, with hundreds of pages dedicated to the subject of children. Representing a kind of culmination of early modern attentions to the subject, *Emile* also outlined a new agenda of children's issues that have remained prominent ever since."[18] In addition to education, these issues include the health of children, children's literature, the significance of gender for young people, and the meaning of children's innocence.[19] In his own life, however, Rousseau had his common-law wife leave all five of their infants at the Paris Foundling Hospital, an institution where roughly one-quarter of its charges lived to adulthood. He later explained that poverty compelled him to abandon his children.[20] Long past the dawn of the Enlightenment, a child's fate largely was determined by her family's financial straits.

Another reality for children in ancient and early modern Europe was the dominance of fathers, fortified by the legal principle *patria potestus*—"power of a father"—originating in Roman family law and later finding expression in common law. English common law, for example, granted fathers the right to control the physical custody, labor, and earnings of their children in exchange for supporting and training them. In North America, children comprised a vital element of the colonial labor force. As much as masters saw child slaves, indentured child servants, and apprentices as essential to their bottom lines, fathers recognized the labor of their biological and adopted children as an enormously valuable resource.[21] By the Industrial Revolution, parents continued to exercise nearly absolute control over the labor of their children, which was considered among the family's most important assets; a perspective that prevailed in law and practice for much of US history. During the nineteenth and early twentieth centuries, all but wealthy US children worked long hours in textile mills, coal mines, glass factories, wharfs, farms, and city streets. When numerous girls tragically perished in a Fall River, Massachusetts, mill fire in 1874, including one as young as five years old, newspaper editors and other opinion leaders demanded reform. Consistent with Gilded Age thinking, however, they did not call for children to leave the mills. Rather, they suggested that surviving girls return to the millwork only after better fire safety precautions were established.[22]

From the exploitation and endangerment of London street children in 1620 to young girls toiling in US mills in 1874, one might logically conclude that little changed in the treatment of children as chattel over time. "Historically, the lot of children was often nasty, brutish, and short," note two prominent scholars summarizing research on the subject.[23] Moreover, given the disquieting prevalence of child enslavement, trafficking, neglect, and suffering across the globe today, these craven and dehumanizing traditions seem alive and well.[24] Yet various experts on the history of childhood find that these harsher practices and perspectives did not go unchallenged, discerning especially significant shifts, for example, in how industrialized societies including the United States viewed children in the nineteenth and twentieth centuries. Children in these years came to be valued for their contributions to the productive work of their families and for their capacity to support parents in advanced age. The socialization and education of children became important goals as Americans focused on the development of young people into functioning members of society. Gradually, child-oriented family life emerged, as did a broader collective "belief that children were the essential human resources whose mature form would determine the future of society."[25] As fields like developmental psychology blossomed, reformers from diverse civic and religious associations championed the health and welfare of children. In 1924, the League of Nations adopted a *Declaration of the Rights of the Child* expressing the aspiration that "mankind owes to the child the best that it has to give." Inspired by social reformers who tackled child suffering after the First World War, the *Declaration* underscored a universal responsibility to provide food, shelter, healthcare, education, "relief in times of distress," and "protection from every form of exploitation."[26]

By the 1930s, compulsory education, juvenile courts, child labor protections, and new social welfare programs reflected significant changes in how childhood was governed in the United States.[27]

A crucial engine for these transformations was a new emphasis on the best interests of young people, rather than simply following the preferences of parents or other adults. During the twentieth century, as the moral and legal claims of children advanced, so did the demands and expectations of the state and society on parents and others with authority over young people. Social workers, judges, lawmakers, and other state actors increasingly intervened in family life and other private spheres to protect children. In short, conceptions of *the child* were and are very much influenced by politics. Fresh understandings of children as potential persons with guaranteed rights were both a product and source of important political contention in the United States. At the core of this book, as we discussed in Chapter 1, is a focus on how politics has shaped the ways young people are perceived and governed, and in turn how young people have influenced our broader political life. Our central aim in this chapter is to unmask the politics of protecting and controlling children, a realm animated by competing ideological traditions, preferences, and agendas.

Mapping the Governance of Children: Control, Autonomy, and Competing Interests

Because they are framed in law and policy as adults-in-waiting who lack key capacities for full autonomy, children are a paradigmatic group excluded from the fundamental rights accorded to most individuals in democratic societies. A child's freedom of action thus can be justifiably constrained, establishing an important "paternalistic" standard to, as political theorist Amy Gutmann puts it, "protect children from being harmed and to insure that they be given those goods necessary for making reasoned choices for themselves as adults."[28] This standard is critical for recognizing the dependence of children on the protection and support of adults in their lives, valuably creating moral and legal requirements for parents, the state, and others to meet children's physical, emotional, and educational needs. Yet as Elizabeth Cohen underscores, this paternalistic standard also enables parents, state officials, and other adults to "conflate or substitute" their own interests for those of young people. As a result, children "inhabit an uncertain space" of "ill-defined partial membership," in which some of their most crucial interests and ideals may be extinguished because they lack power and representation in private and public life.[29] In the process, a key liberal paradox emerges: children are denied essential membership rights until the age of majority, and thus they experience democratic exclusion before inclusion.[30] Central to the politics of protecting children are important tensions between the control and autonomy of young people and between the best interests of the child and those of legal guardians and other adults with broad authority over their lives.

One of these important tensions in the relationship between children, parents, and government authority centers on the issue of balancing benevolent control and increasing independence. On one hand, liberal democracies consider individual liberty to be sacrosanct and strive to evaluate people based on their choices, actions, and abilities. Yet, modern societies also believe that children should be protected by their parents, caregivers, and state actors. Nurturing children in democratic societies therefore cuts two ways: limiting minors' decision-making authority to protect them while also providing them with the room and resources for self-governance.

Mapping relevant laws and policies along two dimensions provides a useful means to better understand the politics of regulating children and childhood. Consider, for example, one dimension that focuses on whether a law, policy, or practice primarily serves "the best interest of the child" or the interests of others, with a horizontal continuum stretching from maximum adherence to the best interests of children on the left to maximum emphasis on other interests on the right. Now imagine a second dimension that concentrates on whether a law, policy, or practice advances significant control or autonomy of children, with a vertical continuum that stretches from maximum control over children at the top to maximum autonomy of children at the bottom. As Table 2.1 shows, we can identify from this model four distinctive categories of laws, policies, and practices governing children: paternalism, subjugation, membership, and abandonment.

Paternalism as a category includes a rich variety of policies and programs that seek to shield children from harm and may constrain their freedom "for their own good" (e.g., compulsory education, social welfare assistance, child labor restrictions). Like the centuries-old view that children were the property of their fathers, *subjugation* as a category comprises laws and policies that impose controls on young people that primarily serve someone else's interests. Contemporary examples of this category include the denial of medical care or

Table 2.1. The Politics of Children's Governance: Control, Autonomy, and Rival Interests

	In the Child's Best Interest	*In Others' Best Interests*
Control/ Intervention	PATERNALISM - Compulsory Education - Custody/Adoption/ Foster Care - Juvenile Courts - Sheppard-Towner Act/ Infant Health - Aid to Dependent Children - Child Labor Protection - Child Abuse and Neglect Laws - Children's Health Insurance Program	SUBJUGATION - Children as Property - Stripping Children's Free Speech - Constraints on Reproductive Health Choices - Anti-gay/Anti-trans Therapies - Limits on Same-Sex Parenting
Autonomy	MEMBERSHIP - Free Speech Protections - Religious Liberty - Due Process Rights - Medical Emancipation - Voting Rights at 18 - Reproductive Choice - Driver's Licensure	ABANDONMENT - Parent-Initiated Emancipation - Unregulated Child Labor - Racial Disparities in Trying Children for Adult Crimes - Family Welfare Caps - Trump's Family-Separation Policy at the Border

education to minors in the name of parental religious freedom or youth curfews designed to enhance public safety. The *membership* category entails a range of policies and legal decisions that expand rather than limit the autonomy of young people, with their best interests in mind. Validating the free speech claims of underage students or the reproductive choices of pregnant teenagers are prime examples. Finally, *abandonment* encompasses laws, policies, and practices that strip special protections away from children with little or no regard for their best interest, focusing instead on advancing competing adult, state, or societal interests. For instance, the Trump administration's separation and detention of child migrants was carried out in the name of border security, even after top health and human services officials warned the White House that separating children from their parents would be harmful.[31] The trying of "problem children" as adults, without the protections of juvenile courts, is another apt example.

Although these four categories are helpful for drawing distinctions among the wide variety of laws, policies, and practices aimed at children, it is important to keep in mind that the lines between them are often far from neat and clean. As we discuss later in this chapter, for example, compulsory public education is a prominent example of paternalism because requiring children to attend school clearly serves their long-term intellectual, social, and professional interests. At the same time, as nineteenth-century education reformer Horace Mann argued,[32] universal education also clearly promotes broader state interests in producing good citizens and productive workers, thereby controlling minors in ways that advance others' interests. We would classify this as subjugation. Likewise, adult officials are expected to formulate and implement policies on behalf of minors because children ostensibly lack the rational and emotional capacity to vote or serve in elected office. Absent voting rights, then, children are dependent on the benevolent paternalism of adult officials. Yet far better off is a constituency like the elderly, which votes regularly, mobilizes on behalf of desired programs, and thus has direct and significant influence on policymakers. A comparison between US social welfare programs for children and those for the elderly captures the implications of their dissimilar political status. The poverty rate among Americans aged 65 and older has declined markedly since the 1930s (to 9.2% in 2017), protected by expensive and politically sacrosanct *universal entitlement* programs like Social Security and Medicare. By contrast, 17.5% of children under eighteen years old were impoverished in 2017, and most of their safety net is comprised of underfunded and politically vulnerable *means-tested* programs like Temporary Aid to Needy Families (TANF), Food Stamps, Head Start, and the Supplemental Nutrition Assistance Program for Women, Infants, and Children (WIC).[33] US social welfare politics demonstrates that representation of children during policymaking may be justified by paternalism in theory, but the outcomes often reflect abandonment in practice.

It is hardly surprising that complex issues and policies defy simple classification. Yet even when examples like public education and social welfare policy bleed across categories, the process of evaluating where they fit and where they overlap is revealing. Together paternalism, subjugation, membership, and abandonment illuminate the core political dynamics of how children are governed in our constitutional democracy. Each helps us analyze the presence or absence of protections and controls for young people, and each reflects significant political struggle over rival interests and ideals. Let us explore paternalism, subjugation, membership, and abandonment further in the pages that follow, unveiling how competing claims for child welfare, self-determination, parental prerogative, and other aims collide in the public square. As we shall see, these political struggles highlight the critical and uneasy relationship between children, parents (and other legal guardians), and the state.

Paternalism: Control in the Child's Interest

With two national championships and countless bowl-game wins in its glorious past, Penn State's football program ranked among the royalty of big-time college athletics in 2011, even after a mediocre showing the previous season. Joe Paterno, the team's legendary head coach, served at the helm for a whopping forty-five years and won more games than any other gridiron chief in NCAA history. For a decade, a bronze statue of the iconic coach stood prominently on the campus where he was held in awe and where he wielded enormous power. In the slice of central Pennsylvania that called itself "Happy Valley," Penn State football was king. Then horrifying news broke of a child sex abuse scandal involving one of Paterno's former coaching assistants, defensive coordinator Jerry Sandusky. Especially shocking were revelations that Paterno knew and concealed information about Sandusky's sexual molestation of young boys, and that he pressured university officials not to tell authorities beginning in 2001. The backlash was fierce. Paterno's contract was quickly terminated and his statue taken down. Penn State football was banned from the post-season for four years, fined more than $70 million, lost scholarships, and had all of its victories from 1998 to 2011 vacated. The university's president Graham Spanier was forced to resign, and he and two other high-ranking school officials were charged with failure to report suspected child abuse, obstruction of justice, and other criminal offences.[34] Six years later, a comparable firestorm engulfed US gymnastics and Michigan State University (MSU) when the public learned that hundreds of female athletes were sexually abused as minors by the national team's osteopathic surgeon and MSU faculty member Larry Nassar.[35] Similar charges against a sports physician emerged at Ohio State University (OSU) in 2018, enveloping prominent conservative Congressman Jim Jordan (R-OH), a former OSU wrestling coach who vehemently denied any knowledge of abuse despite countercharges from numerous wrestlers.[36] All of these scandals came on the heels of nationwide horror over a pattern of sexual abuse of minors by Catholic clergy and subsequent cover-ups in large US Roman Catholic dioceses.[37]

These disturbing cases and the moral outrage they triggered reflect a core tenet of *paternalism* as applied to young people: adults are morally and legally obligated to protect children from harm precisely because they are so vulnerable.[38] In each of these scandals, the public fury that resulted was directed not only at the sexual predators who victimized young people, but also toward those in authority who failed to act decisively to guard them from this predation. All US states legally require some form of mandatory reporting of physical, sexual, and emotional abuse of children by relevant professionals and institutions to law enforcement agencies or child protective services. Because children are presumed to be unable to fend for themselves, parents and legal guardians exercise enormous discretion over them as primary caretakers and protectors. But these parental powers are not legally or ethically unlimited: child abuse and neglect laws call for government intervention to remove young people from a home when parents or guardians are either dangerous or ill-equipped to care for those in their charge. In this context, the law intervenes to remove children from the care of parents or other guardians when they suffer abuse or neglect. As the revered South African leader Nelson Mandela put it, "We owe children a life free of violence and fear."[39]

Of course, adults often fail to fulfill this obligation. That disquieting reality may help explain why rescuing children who are abused, neglected, or starved of affection has served as such a powerful theme in popular literature, theater, and film. Charles Dickens's *Oliver Twist* offers a harrowing portrait of a boy subjected to grinding abuse, peril, and poverty in Victorian-era England. Oliver's torments are both physical ("the fist had too often been impressed on his body not to be deeply impressed upon his recollection") and emotional ("one kind word or look had never lighted the gloom of his infant years"). Tellingly, his liberation comes not from state officials—the government-run workhouse is especially cruel to its young charges—but from a kindly man of wealth.[40] Set in Depression-era New York City a century later, the hit musical *Annie* spotlights a scrappy eleven-year-old enduring a "hard-knock life" of abuses with other kids in foster homes and boarding houses. "'Stead of treated, we get tricked! 'Stead of kisses, we get kicked! . . . Empty Bellies, 'stead of full . . . . No one cares for you a smidge, when you're in an orphanage." Like Oliver (and Cinderella), Annie hurdles the great class divide when she wins over a wealthy benefactor who introduces her to elite society.[41] More recently, readers and movie goers drawn into the Harry Potter series learn that the beloved wizard Albus Dumbledore sent his towering but kindly protégé Rubeus Hagrid to rescue one-year-old Harry from the ruins of his home after the sinister Lord Voldemort had murdered his parents in the 1980s. Poor Harry is left in the care of his mother's sister and her husband, Petunia and Vernon Dursley, who openly disdain him while showering affection on their son Dudley. Despite plenty of room at Number Four, Privet Drive, Harry was forced to live in a cupboard under the stairs, where he was often locked in without food as punishment. Dumbledore sends Hagrid to find Harry on his eleventh birthday to tell him that "he'll be goin' to the finest school of witchcraft and wizardry," showing him one of the first kindnesses of his life by sending a birthday cake and forcing the Dursleys to let Harry enter the Wizarding World.[42] In these stories, children exhibiting pluck and innocence are justly liberated from cruel guardians by benevolent and powerful saviors. Tellingly, both the villains and the rescuers of these dramas are adults, all of whom are judged by their fulfillment or desecration of duties to nurture and protect children.

As we hinted earlier, the moral and legal obligations to protect children are also a major focus of philosophical debate. In fact, the very concept of *paternalism* draws its lifeblood from philosophers who have provided its richest articulation over time. English philosopher John Locke, for example, devoted careful attention to how children ought to be governed and what rights they ought to exercise in his *Second Treatise of Government*, penned in 1690. He introduced the idea that all people, including children, are endowed with *natural rights*, which are intrinsic and cannot be violated to serve the interests of others. Locke's position was that children are creations of God and thus are not the property of their parents; he was adamantly opposed to "giving parents a power of command over their children, or an authority to make laws and dispose as they please of their lives and liberties." He argued that parental power is "that which parents have over their children to govern them *for the child's good*."[43] More than many of his contemporaries, Locke asserted that parental dominance is constrained to the extent that their chief obligation is to facilitate the eventual freedom of their children. That is, parents are to control their children's lives until "they can be able to shift for themselves."[44] Young people should remain dependent on adults, he noted, until they demonstrate the capacity to reason and to understand the core principles by which they are governed.

As Locke's formulation highlights, guarding children from nefarious actors and numerous other external threats represents only half of the paternalism equation. Adults also are expected to save children from themselves. The notion that minors need to be controlled in order to serve their best interests reflects the view that they must be, in the words of nineteenth century libertarian John Stuart Mill, "protected against their own actions as well as against external injury."[45] Because they are thought to seek instant gratification and to lack full emotional and intellectual development, children cannot be trusted to make entirely sound decisions about their own best interests. Some minors may prefer to never brush their teeth or to spend nearly every waking moment playing violent video games, but parents and other adults are expected to save children from their worst impulses. William Golding's *Lord of the Flies* imagines just how dark and frightening these impulses can be without strong adult authorities. This story about a group of boys stranded on a paradisiacal Pacific island reveals their potential for savagery in this 1950s-era state of nature. The final scene features an intense death hunt of main character Ralph, whose demise seems certain until he and his frenzied pursuers run into the first adult of the novel, who holds the promise of rescue home. The temper of the boys changes instantly. "The ululation faltered and died away," Golding writes. "A semicircle of little boys, their bodies streaked with colored clay, sharp sticks in their hands, were standing on the beach making no noise at all."[46] The boys were saved from their worst selves. For Mill, the granting of broad liberty to people hinges upon their full development as rational beings.[47] Because the reasoning of minors is not fully developed, so the argument goes, adult interventions limiting the freedom of young people is legitimate so long as the aims are benevolent.

This familiar model of paternalism—justifying well-intentioned adult controls designed to protect children both from themselves and external dangers—undergirds a host of laws, policies, and practices concentrating on young people. Parents and other legal guardians have considerable discretion to regulate nearly every facet of the lives of children under their care, especially when their decisions reflect their vision of their children's best interest. Schools have imposed dress codes in the name of promoting an atmosphere conducive to learning, curbing gang violence, and nurturing the self-esteem of all students.[48] Businesses are legally required to deny children access to alcohol, cigarettes, pornography, firearms, and other products deemed only appropriate for adults. Reformers who sought to prohibit child labor in the early twentieth century framed their arguments in paternalistic terms, underscoring that exploitative work damaged children's physical, mental, spiritual, and social development.[49]

Justified as crucial to future life chances and informed citizenship, compulsory education laws in the US compel children to attend a public or state-accredited private school for a given period of time. Even exceptions for homeschooling involve prescribed levels of educational attainment. In its landmark *Brown v. Board* decision (1954) outlawing racial segregation in public schools, the Supreme Court proclaimed that "compulsory school attendance laws and the great expenditures for education . . . demonstrate our recognition of the importance of education to our democratic society . . . . In these days, it is doubtful that any child may reasonably be expected to succeed in life if he is denied the opportunity of an education."[50] Educational opportunity thereby serves the best of interest of the child as well as crucial ends of the state, including the fostering of civic training and duty and economic productivity. These goals highlight a crucial rationale for guarding the best interests of children, namely, their status as future citizens. In addition to numerous policies designed to protect children from abuse and neglect, social welfare programs often enable parents or guardians who live in poverty to apply for food stamps, Medicaid, housing subsidies, and other forms of public assistance to meet the basic needs of children under their care. With all of these examples, claims of protecting the best interests of children serve as important rationales for diverse laws, policies, and practices. But society's broader interests in nurturing competent economic, social, and political participants also figure prominently.

As discussed thus far, paternalist policies and practices seem readily justified by the core proposition that children lack the physical, emotional, and intellectual maturity to be independent and to engage in reasoned self-governance that enhances their contributions to the collective good. This means that protecting children promotes both their and society's interests. Paternalism, however, faces several important challenges when applied to governing children in modern democracies. One practical problem is that the state lacks precise means to determine when young people are rationally competent to possess specific rights of adulthood. This is apparent in the complex tangle of legal rules governing minors in the United States. Legal definitions of a minor of course hinge upon age, but Martha Minow reminds us that the law ascribes incapacity or competence to different ages depending on different contexts and aims. A boy at age twelve can be held criminally responsible for illegal behavior under federal and state law and be routed into an adult system of prosecution and punishment; but the same child cannot perform most kinds of remunerative work. A fifteen-year-old girl can obtain birth control and other reproductive health services in most states without parental consent, but she cannot miss school in those same states without her parent's permission. Sixteen-year-olds can drive cars but they cannot purchase alcohol or tobacco. Eighteen-year-olds can vote, decide to marry, or join the military, but they still can be considered financially dependent on their parents if enrolled full-time in school.[51] In short, the age at which young people are ascribed rational capacity and treated as rights-bearing individuals varies markedly under law and reflects distinctive and sometimes quite inconsistent purposes. More generally, the age of majority (the threshold for adulthood as established by law) is, as Cohen notes, essentially "an arbitrary point" (typically eighteen years old) that "is convenient for adults" but "bears varying relevance to the actual capacities of children ... to govern themselves."[52] The fact that some proportion of children have rational capacities to deliberate and make choices in a mature and wise fashion beyond expectations for their age introduces a dimension of capriciousness to paternalistic policies. "[E]ven children under ten are capable of some degree of autonomy in particular areas of their lives," the philosopher Amy Mullin points out. "Therefore, we cannot simply assume that actions that thwart their wills are justified" whenever the interventions are undertaken for benevolent reasons.[53] In turn, laws that assign competence to children who in fact exhibit irrationality and immaturity, such as certain determinations to try juveniles in adult courts, also introduce randomness that undercuts the core logic of paternalistic regimes.

Another challenging issue for paternalism is the unsettled and ambivalent relationship between parents and the state in governing children's lives. As discussed at the outset of this chapter, the historically broad ownership rights that fathers (and later both parents) exercised over their children only gradually gave way to significant claims of the state and children in family life. In the United States over time, state interventions on children's behalf often have inspired suspicion if not outright hostility. Consider the seemingly benign Sheppard-Towner

Act of 1921, a public health law championed by Progressive Era settlement-house workers and social workers to reduce high levels of infant mortality that exceeded most other industrialized countries. This bipartisan measure signed by a conservative Republican President provided modest federal grants for state programs to better educate expectant parents and medical professionals about prenatal health and to enhance child nutrition, hygiene, and other forms of infancy care. The law led to the creation of thousands of child and maternal healthcare centers in forty-one participating states, including centers in underserved rural areas, contributing to a marked decline in infant and maternal mortality rates at an annual cost of roughly $1.28 million during the 1920s.[54]

Yet opposition soon mounted against this infant and maternal health reform. When it faced renewal in the late 1920s, conservative women's organizations—like the Daughters of American Revolution and The Woman Patriots—said Sheppard-Towner smacked of Bolshevism that undermined the traditional structure and freedoms of American families.[55] "The Communists and socialists seek every opportunity that cunning can discover to use the 'general welfare' clause of the Constitution," they warned, "plus all the emotion and sentimentalism which modern propaganda methods can associate with the word 'welfare' when coupled with women and children to undermine that which cannot be directly overthrown."[56] They were joined by the American Medical Association, which complained that this intervention into children's health reflected a dangerous form of state medicine that eroded a cherished bond between doctors and parents. By 1929, the Sheppard-Towner initiative was dead. Its demise captures the uneasy, often contentious relationship between the state, parents, children, and other actors that has developed as rival interests have intensified over the past century.[57] Returning to the popular musical *Annie*, fans of the show will recall that the spirited child hero is ultimately rescued not by New Deal reformers but by a Republican tycoon who hates government: Daddy Warbucks.[58]

A final nettlesome issue for paternalism in practice is the reality that significant amounts of independence for children are needed to promote their long-term interests and healthy development into adulthood. As one of the most intemporary thinkers on paternalistic policies, Ronald Dworkin, observes: "paternalism is justified only to preserve a wider range of freedom for the individual in question."[59] This means that guarding the best, long-term interests of children requires adults to loosen controls when possible in order to expand young people's rational capacities and meaningful independence in the future. "Frequent reliance on physical control and psychological control (making threats, invoking guilt, and withdrawing love) can undermine children's development of autonomy, as does behavior that makes children feel they lack the capacities to realize their goals," writes Mullin. "Parents should therefore aim at children's development of realistic self-confidence, accurate self-assessment, and faith in their increasing ability to make strides towards achieving their goals over time."[60] To serve the best interest of the child, then, paternalistic decisions and policies often involve a tough balancing act between protective constraints and calibrated autonomy (something most parents wrestle with regularly).

Subjugation: Controlling Children to Serve Other's Interests

As a middle schooler growing up in Florida during the early 2000s, Sam Brinton came out as bisexual to his parents. Devout Southern Baptists with a background as missionaries and a firm belief that homosexuality was sinful, Brinton's parents forced him to endure two years of so-called gay conversion therapy to "cure" him of a sexual identity they perceived as unacceptable. Conversion therapists claim their treatments can forcibly change someone's sexual orientation or gender identity. During regular conversion sessions with counselors that Brinton described as "emotionally painful," he was told that he was abnormal, that his sexuality was an "abomination," that his faith community would never accept him until he was straight, and that he would inevitably contract HIV and AIDS. At its most extreme, a conversion therapist had Brinton "bound to a table to have ice, heat, and electricity applied to my body" while being forced to watch film clips of gay intimacy. The stated purpose was to have Brinton associate physical pain with images of gay sex and affection. "In the end it didn't work," he later noted. "I would say that it did, just to make the pain go away." As an adult, Brinton declared himself "proudly bisexual and gender fluid" and became a chief advocate for the Trevor Project, an organization dedicated to suicide prevention and crisis intervention on behalf of LGBTQIA+ young people. An estimated 350,000 Americans have undergone conversion therapy as minors. The American Academy of Pediatrics, the American Psychological Association, and the American Medical Association have denounced conversion therapy as harmful to young people. Brinton now helps lead a movement to ban conversion therapy nationwide, galvanized by the fact that many states still permit gay conversion therapy practices by clergy, licensed therapists, correctional boot camps, and parents.[61]

The harrowing experiences of Brinton and other LGBTQIA+ youth coerced into gay conversion therapy exemplifies core features of *subjugation* as a category of laws, policies, and practices governing young people. The practice is a clarion example of forcing young people to do something that is profoundly harmful to their best interests in order to serve what authoritative adults in their lives demand (in this case, to serve homophobic ends). To be sure, proponents of gay conversion therapy insist that they are protecting wayward young people in a virtuously paternalistic fashion. Yet as therapy survivors and public health professionals underscore, the emotional and physical coercion endured by these LGBTQIA+ youth is designed to suppress or erase their desires for intimacy in order to satisfy the intolerant worldviews of adult authorities.

We can discern similar forms of cruelty masked as care in recent efforts to block transgender students from having access to gender-comporting bathrooms, locker rooms, and sports teams or receiving gender-affirming healthcare. As we discussed in Chapter 1, broadening inclusion of marginalized young people long has been a flashpoint for reactionary hysteria from those claiming to defend the innocence of white, cisgender, and heterosexual children. Any imagined threat to their safety—racially integrated schools, gender-positive curriculums, Queer-inclusive policies—inspires a predictably frenzied response. Transgender young people face a mountain of daily challenges—physical and verbal assaults at school, hostility of teachers and administrators, unsupportive families, and the emotional or physical challenges of addressing gender dysphoria. These can produce traumas that increase the possibility of depression or anxiety which can then lead to disengagement from school, substance abuse, or suicidal ideation to quell the pain.[62] Whether transphobic legislation passes or not, bills attacking transgender youth—restricting bathroom access, blocking participation on women's athletic teams, and prohibiting physicians and parents from providing gender affirming hormone treatments—create an atmosphere of hate. Even trans young people living in trans-inclusive states experience these efforts as violent—as attempts to erase their identities.

These campaigns only compound the challenges and suffering of transgender youth. Yet legislative assaults on transgender or nonbinary youth in the name of protecting cisgender kids persist across all political spectrums. Although a staple strategy among conservatives, efforts to subjugate the well-being of transgender young people to serve the interests and preferences of others are not limited to political right. Some self-declared feminists[63] like J.K. Rowling—yes, *that* J.K. Rowling—have become vocal opponents of trans-inclusive policies, publicly demeaning trans girls and women as a threat to cis women's livelihood. As the renowned author of the beloved *Harry Potter* series, Rowling used her high-profile Twitter account and personal website to oppose new rights and accommodations for transgender people and drawing distinctions between cisgender and transgender entitlements. "I want transwomen to be safe. At the same time, I do not want to make natal girls and women less safe," she wrote. "When you throw open the doors of bathrooms and changing rooms to any man who believes or feels he's a woman . . . then you open the door to any and all men who wish to come inside." Rowling's casual and callous reference to male pronouns and male predators to describe transgender women, all the while claiming to care for the safety of trans women, is both demeaning and demoralizing—especially to the many queer and trans girls among her faithful followers. When she took to Twitter to vilify gender-neutral language, she placed a target on the backs of the very trans women she claimed to support. " 'People who menstruate' " she mocked. "I'm sure there used to be a word for those people. Someone help me out. Wumben? Wimpund? Woomud?"[64]

In March, 2021, Arkansas became the first to state to enact a pro-hibition on gender-affirming care like hormone therapies or puberty blockers for transgender youth, and then further condemned trans youth by barring their presence on women's sports teams. By March, 2022, over thirty states had considered similar measures—with ten states passing anti-trans athlete bills and at least four limiting access to puberty blockers. On their own, each bill is an assault. In concert, they obliterate key pathways of trans expression and silence trans identity. Without puberty blockers, which can be a critical resource for trans-gender adolescents, one important pathway for a healthy transition is eliminated.[65] Young people who rely on puberty blockers may scope out internet sources (of dubious provenance) for these therapies or resort to extraordinary measures to hide their developing bodies. In states where puberty blockers are classified as child abuse (like Florida or Texas), parents of trans kids using puberty blockers have to choose between watching their children struggle with the consequences of untreated gender dysphoria (increased depression and suicidality[66]) and the permanence of puberty or risk being charged with child abuse if they continue to pursue these treatments for their children. Transgender athletes residing in states with gendered limitations on team participation are forced to choose between playing a sport that they love and closeting themselves for the duration of their athletic pursuits, or forgoing organized athletics altogether to live openly and honestly. Read in tandem, these initiatives represent a simultaneous strategy of eradication and exclusion for all transgender youth regard-less of their medical status or athletic abilities.

Historically, the subordination of children's well-being to adult interests, like the anti-transgender initiatives just outlined, reflects tra-ditional norms and precepts. The philosopher Thomas Hobbes, writing in the seventeenth century, argued that children had no natural rights and that they resided outside the social contract because they lacked the capacity to enter into or to fulfill covenants between individuals. Accordingly, he concluded that "like the imbecile, the crazed and the beasts, over . . . children . . . there is no law."[67] Hobbes saw the relation-ship between fathers and their children as one founded upon fear in which male heads of households were treated as a sovereign by his off-spring.[68] Following ancient Roman law, he also contended that fathers had the ultimate power of life and death over their children. This absolute power, Hobbes reasoned, reinforces filial compliance because each person "is supposed to promise obedience to him in whose power is to save or destroy him."[69] One century later, William Blackstone, the influential eighteenth-century English jurist, celebrated that English laws were "much more moderate" in rejecting a father's right to kill his children. But he reaffirmed the principle that children are part of a father's "empire" in which he is entitled "to have the benefit of his children's labor" akin to that of his servants.[70]

The traditional premise that children are the property of their fathers may be unfamiliar if not jarring to most readers today, but it was a paternal right firmly established in English common law that was widely accepted in colonial North America and the early US republic. "In labor-scarce America the services or wages of a child over ten was one of the most valuable assets a man could have," notes Mason. "Thus fathers, without dispute, had almost unlimited authority of custody and control over their natural, legitimate children."[71] While these English common law traditions waned over the course of the nineteenth century, the country's appetite for child labor did not until the 1930s. Consider Reuben Dagenhart, who in 1916 was a skinny fourteen-year-old from a struggling family in Charlotte, North Carolina. He worked *sixty hours a week* at a textile mill with his father Roland and younger brother John, bringing home 10 cents a day. He and his brother were among the vast majority of poor US children who toiled sixty and seventy-hour weeks for low pay in mines, mills, sweatshops, and fields across the country.[72] Facing hazardous conditions, these child workers were three times more likely than adult workers to suffer serious injuries.

Reformers and investigative journalists of the time noted that child workers who escaped on-the-job accidents were still physically and intellectually impaired by lack of schooling, exercise, fresh air, and rest. Against this backdrop, the Keating-Owen Act of 1916 was passed by bipartisan majorities in Congress to ban interstate commerce of any goods produced by children under fourteen years of age or involving work by older minors that exceeded eight hours a day or that included overnight shifts. It was a reform that drew stiff resistance from two groups that sought to restore the unregulated status quo ante: industries that relied on cheap, tractable child labor and parents who depended on their children's wages as a means of fortifying their family's overall income. Hoping for relief from the federal courts, the Southern Cotton Manufacturers organization recruited Roland Dagenhart to file a lawsuit claiming that the new federal regulations unlawfully deprived him of his sons' earnings.[73] Lawyers for Dagenhart, funded by cotton mill owners, challenged the law's reliance on congressional powers over interstate commerce. In a 5–4 decision, the Supreme Court in *Hammar v. Dagenhart* (1918) ruled that the federal child labor protections were unconstitutional.[74] Although dissenting Justice Oliver Wendell Holmes fulminated against "the evil of premature and excessive child labor,"[75] Reuben and John Dagenhart soon returned to the Fidelity cotton mill in Charlotte to work long hours for less than a dollar per week.[76] Six years after his father and the cotton mill owners won their case, twenty-year-old Reuben told a reporter that millwork had taken its toll on him. "Look at me!" he declared. "A hundred and five pounds, a grown man and no education . . . I think the years I've put in the cotton mills stunted my growth. They kept me from getting any schooling. I had to stop school after third grade." Undersized and illiterate, Reuben lamented the legal defeat of the Keating-Owen reform six years before. "It would have been a good thing for all the kids in this state if that law they passed had been kept."[77] It ultimately took twenty more years before child labor was successfully regulated and limited in the US.[78]

Like LGBTQIA+ youth forced into harmful gay conversion therapy, the withering labor demands placed on generations of impoverished American children exemplify relatively blatant forms of subjugation, at least by contemporary standards. Whether toiling in textile mills, coal fields, factories, or farms, child workers were placed under stringent adult control in service of various interests far removed from their own. The education and physical health of working-class children were routinely sacrificed on the altar of corporate profits and parental financial needs. When the subjugation of children is particularly cruel, audiences cheer and romanticize the paternalistic rescue of beloved fictional characters like Oliver Twist, Cinderella, Little Orphan Annie, and Harry Potter. Yet the historical reality is that the exploitation of Reuben Dagenhart was anything but unusual, and few were

Figure 2.1 *Breaker Boys*, Children Working in a Coal Mine.
Source: Photo by Schultz Reinhard. Almay. https://www.alamy.com/stock-photo-brea ker-boys-ewen-breaker-coal-mine-industry-portrait-group-coal-co-33044622.html.

rescued from its physical and intellectual damage in the nineteenth and early twentieth centuries. Until the Fair Labor Standards Act of 1938 imposed regulations that cured most of the evils of child labor in the United States, millions of young people as young as seven worked twelve to eighteen hours a day, six days a week to fuel the nation's economic growth.[79] In 1989, the United Nations General Assembly adopted its landmark Convention on the Rights of the Child, which stipulated that children had the right "to be protected from economic exploitation and from performing any work that is . . . harmful to the child's health or physical, mental, spiritual, moral or social development."[80] One decade later, in response to widespread global exploitation of child workers, the International Labor Organization (ILO) passed its own convention against the worst forms of child labor.[81] Today the ILO estimates that there are 152 million child laborers worldwide, of which 73 million are engaged in hazardous work.[82]

Of course, not all forms of harmful and unwarranted control over children are as blatant or harsh as Dickensian-style child labor exploitation or anti-gay therapy regimes for LGBTQIA+ youth. Sometimes the line between paternalistic interventions promoting child welfare and subjugation of their best interests is far from clear. That line can be contingent upon the facts of specific controversies or upon the rational capacities of a minor to make well-developed intellectual or moral choices. The facts in particular controversies are especially relevant, for example, in family law where, as Justice Sandra Day O'Connor put it, "underlying each family law case that reaches us are issues of state law and policy, as well as an actual family with its own dynamics, challenges, and problems."[83]

The Supreme Court's adjudication of rights-claims of fathers is instructive. In *Caban v. Mohammed* (1979), an unwed couple lived together for five years, during which time they had two children.[84] After separating, the mother remarried and sought to adopt the children with her new husband while challenging the biological father's legal claim to the children. The Court ultimately defended the father's continued role in his children's lives not on the basis of his biological connection to them, but because he had demonstrated long-term "care and support" and established himself as a "loving father" whose "affection and concern" rivaled that of the mother. With similar reasoning a few years later, the Court in *Lehr v. Robertson* rejected the claims of a biological father to nullify the adoption of his child because he failed to "demonstrate a full commitment to the responsibilities of parenthood."[85] In short, these important parenting cases rested custodial authority not on any notion of fundamental parental rights based on biological entitlement, but on whether parents fulfill their legal duty to take proper care of their children and to establish constructive and lasting relationships. As constitutional family law scholar Jeffrey Shulman observes, "the Court's cases reveal a willingness, at least implicitly, to tailor the nature and strength of judicial scrutiny to the facts of each family privacy controversy."[86] Along the way, he adds, "the authority of the parent has been treated as a sacred trust, a delegation of state power made on the presumption that it will be employed to promote the eventual enfranchisement of the child."[87] In this way, our legal tradition often frames parental rights as contingent rather than absolute, and it makes the line between justified paternalistic control and unjustified subjugation of children subject to careful review of substantive facts related to their best interests.

For controversial, nonobvious issues, arbitrating the line between paternalism and subjugation can also hinge on the capacity of young people to make well-developed intellectual or moral choices. For example, these capacities lie at the heart of burdens placed on many young women under eighteen who have sought out legal abortions in states with age-related restrictions. As of May, 2022, thirty-seven states require minors to notify or obtain consent from one or both parents to have an abortion. These laws have been deemed constitutional so long as they allow for exceptions to parental notification and consent via "judicial bypass" procedures. Judicial bypass procedures must ensure anonymity and be conducted expeditiously enough that a pregnant minor can receive abortion services. Yet the actual decision to grant a waiver of parental consent or notification rests with judges who are charged under *Belotti v. Baird* to grant a waiver under two conditions: (1) when a pregnant minor is "mature enough and well enough informed to make her abortion decision, in consultation with her physician, independently of her parents' wishes"; or (2) even when she is unable to make a mature and informed decision independently, an abortion is in her best interest.[88] Theoretically, this judicial bypass procedure leaves room for both paternalistic protection and justified autonomy for pregnant minors. In practice, the level of evidence required by young women to demonstrate adequate maturity and knowledge has varied markedly across courts and states, especially since judges have enormous discretion.[89] If significant numbers of young women who are mature and knowledgeable enough to make informed decisions do not find it practicable to pursue judicial bypass, or if they routinely face unreasonable burdens of evidence, then these restrictions fall into the realm of control in others' interest (subjugation).

One of the most contentious debates in the modern public square hinges on the question of how much discretion parents should exercise over their children's education. These conflicts routinely pit interests of the state against claims of parents that they have the right to control their children's educational experience. Two major state interests loom large in its promotion of compulsory public education. The first is that educating children provides civic training for future citizens to participate constructively in the democratic political life of the nation. The second is that a sound public education enables children to become self-sufficient and productive adults. Given the fact that education has an enormous impact on the choices and well-being of individuals in modern society, many parents share a strong interest in seeing their children gain access to the richest possible set of educational opportunities and experiences. Yet not all parents want to expand their children's choices in adulthood, and their conceptions of success and the good life can vary significantly. It is here that significant dilemmas emerge in liberal democratic societies that recognize plural conceptions of the good life and that tolerate diverse belief systems.[90] For instance, deeply conservative religious parents may define the general welfare of a child very differently than secular and progressive religious parents.

The essential needs of children for food, clothing, shelter, physical safety, and affection are uncontroversial. Yet the "best interest of the child" can quickly become subjective when diverse visions of the good life are permitted, if not embraced. That is, pluralistic democracies that protect the freedom to follow one's own beliefs and worldviews might grant considerable parental latitude in choosing among public and private schools or home-schooling. Some parents may seek to exclude their children from educational offerings that professional educators and mainstream society consider valuable, not because they are selfish or malevolent, but because they believe that their children's welfare is best served by steering them toward certain value systems and ways of life over others.[91]

The case of three Amish teenagers who stopped attending public or private school after eighth grade reinforces many of these key tensions over parental authority over education. In 1971, Frieda Yoder (aged fifteen), Barbara Miller (fourteen), and Vernon Yutzy (fourteen) all graduated from a public elementary school in Green County, Wisconsin. Their fathers decided that further education for Frieda, Barbara, and Vernon would compromise their Amish simplicity, viewing a worldly high school education as harmful to maintaining an Amish faith and way of life.[92] These actions violated the compulsory education laws of Wisconsin, and state officials argued in court that denying these young people public education undermined their capacity to participate in the political system and left them ill-equipped to develop into independent, flourishing members of society. Lawyers for the Amish fathers argued that if the children were required to attend high school, these families "would not only expose themselves to the danger of the censure of the church community, but . . . endanger their own salvation and that of their children."[93] Frieda herself testified that she preferred to forego further education in favor of a traditional Amish lifestyle, while Barbara and Vernon did not testify. Eventually the case went all the way to the US Supreme Court, which ultimately decided that compelling the Amish teenagers to attend high school against the beliefs of their parents violated their right to free exercise of religion. Yet critics argued that the vindication of parental liberties constrained the ability of these teenagers to later choose among a wide range of ways of life in adulthood.

If forced gay conversion therapy and unregulated child labor are definitive examples of subjugation because they entail harmful coercion in the interest of various adults, the question of parental oversight of educational choices for their children is more contingent. Good parents might elect to remove their children from one school in favor of another, or to home-school their child, for laudable and sound reasons that promote their best interest. The reality is that parental discretion over educational options can just as easily promote damaging subjugation as virtuous paternalism. Eamon Callan summarizes the tradeoffs well: "If parental choice is thwarted in such cases, we have what seems to many people a violation of freedom of conscience. If parental choice is accommodated, children are denied at least part of the education to which many people will think them morally entitled."[94] These were precisely the two dilemmas that political theorist William Galston highlights in two key works, *Liberal Purposes* and *Liberal Pluralism*; both books advance an ethical resolution favoring more deference for parental authority.[95] However, another influential political philosopher, Amy Guttman, offers a very different understanding of the imperatives of diversity and pluralism in education, arguing that the state plays a critical role in teaching young people respect for different viewpoints and lifestyles. "It makes choice meaningful by equipping children with the intellectual skills necessary to evaluate ways of life different from that of their parents," she notes. According to

Guttman, the Court's *Wisconsin v. Yoder* decision mistakenly "assumes that the welfare of the child is best defined and secured by the freedom of the parents."[96]

This returns us to the intellectual and ethical capacities of young people as a means of distinguishing between paternalism and subjugation in tough cases. As Justice William Douglas noted in his blistering dissent to the *Yoder* majority, the Court assumed that "the only interests at stake in this case are those of the Amish parents on the one hand, and those of the State on the other." But the highest stakes, he pointed out, were borne by the Amish children whose parents' preferences walled them away from foreign ideas, rich experiences, and peers from different backgrounds—they were to be "forever barred from entry into the new and amazing world of diversity."[97] Equally troubling to Douglas was the fact that only Frieda Yoder had the opportunity to testify. Barbara Miller and Vernon Yutzy never had the chance to express their own preference or to demonstrate their own capacity to make life choices for themselves.

Membership: Mature Minors and Ageless Freedoms

Sherry Sotello "divorced" her mother when she was fifteen years old and a high school freshman, not long after she had stopped living with her mother. Sherry and her siblings had moved with their mother from California to Tijuana for a job, but Sherry decided to move back to the United States. On her own, Sotello enrolled in school, found work, and rented an apartment. Despite her proven capacity to live independently, anyone under the age of eighteen, by law and regardless of circumstance, requires an adult co-signer for school registration and rental agreements. She successfully and independently balanced school, work, and keeping a roof over her head, but she lacked one crucial quality—the necessary age. And there was an added wrinkle to Sotello's story. She was pregnant. Paradoxically, this meant that as a parent she could legally make decisions for her child, but still lacked the authority to make decisions on her own behalf.[98] So she sought a divorce or emancipation from her mother for legal autonomy. Emancipation, a legal exception to the rule of minor dependency that permits eligible and qualified minors to be treated as adults for the purposes of decision-making, provided Sotello with the ability to enroll in school, pay taxes, seek rental housing, and care for her child—without the authorization of a guardian.[99]

Despite the tradition of child dependency, US history is replete with instances of minors and their advocates seeking and gaining independence from the strictures of their caregivers or other legal authorities. Among the most prominent is a legal designation first used in the early 1970s allowing minors in some circumstances to be recognized as "autonomous individuals, entitled to the same rights and privileges before the law as adults." The push for emancipation emerged from the twin movements for civil rights and abortion access. As more states began to pass parental consent measures barring pregnant minors from seeking abortions, legal advocates leveraged the momentum of the civil rights movement to argue that children deserved liberties and protections—and authority over their own bodies. James Manahan first floated the idea in 1976 in an American Bar Association (ABA) newsletter asking colleagues to "consider the logical and ultimate step—that all legal distinctions between children and adults be abolished." And there would soon be at least a kernel of Supreme Court support. In July, 1976, Justice Blackmun issued an opinion in *Planned Parenthood v. Danforth* intimating the potential for minors to claim, under some circumstances, a zone of privacy separate from their parents. "Minors . . . possess constitutional rights," Blackmun argued. There will be circumstances under which they "may give effective consent for termination of [a] pregnancy." Buoyed by a burgeoning movement centering children's liberties, child advocates demanded anywhere from full-scale reversal of age-based benefits to a more customized context-based approach to children's liberties—one that acknowledged the "special case" of children without abandoning the rhetoric of equality and rights. It was during the course of this movement that advocates first proposed the notion that a minor, like Sherry Sotello, could "divorce his or her parents." Advocates argued that stories like Sotello's highlight the problems that arise when dependency is the rule and pushed state actors (frequently in court) to recognize that there may be instances or issues where the presumption of immaturity places too many burdens or risks on the capacity of young people to survive. They called for safeguards to allow young people, in some cases, to be considered as full-fledged members of a democratic society, rather than as exceptions to the promise of liberty and autonomy. In their view, age was a convenient but capricious (and potentially burdensome) proxy for rationality—one that must be relaxed when the costs outweigh the efficiencies.[100]

There is good reason to view age as arbitrarily limiting. First of all, as mentioned in Chapter 1, age of majority designations shift over time, are policy contingent, and vary across states and among policymakers. Teenagers in Arkansas and Alaska, for instance, can start driving with a permit at fourteen and receive their full license at sixteen and a half. Those in our nation's capital, however, cannot begin to learn how to drive until they are sixteen—with full licensing privileges postponed until eighteen years of age. Children in Maryland can stay at home alone at eight years of age, whereas minors in Illinois must wait until they are fourteen. Allowing an eight-year-old to walk to school alone in Maine carries a maximum penalty of ten years in prison for the parents, while in other states children are free to walk to school alone without placing their parents in legal peril. Yet all teenagers, regardless of their capacity to drive at a young age, are restricted from serving in the military until they are seventeen years old and cannot vote until they are eighteen. In other words, it is state or region, not maturity, that determines one person's legal authority to drive a car at fourteen or fifteen years of age, stay at home alone, or walk to school. Similarly, it is politics, instead of some objective scientific criteria, that permits seventeen-year-olds to go to war, but nevertheless prevents them from voting.

Second, even if policymakers reach some consensus regarding the magical age that separates the irrational from the reasonable, there are still exceptional circumstances that require a more precise tool for evaluating an individual's decision-making capabilities. For instance, what happens when a minor defies the general presumption of irrationality? Or when parents fail to achieve the expectations of age? Are parents or state actors still permitted to exert authority over young people even when the children in question have the same (or an even greater) capacity for decision-making as adults? The United Nations—ironically through a US-led initiative—developed language to account for this uncertainty and recommends that members create for children "a sphere of autonomy and freedom from control."[101]

"Divorce" or emancipation is an extreme version of legal efforts to endow minors with the power to consent. This legal designation allows minors who are otherwise self-sufficient or on their own to be declared "of age" in the eyes of the law and legally removed from parental care and control. The process is difficult and the cases are rare (the most salient are child celebrities), but minors who wish to live on their own, to make their own decisions, or have some say over who cares for them can ask a judge to waive their dependent status. For instance, some minors, like actress Juliette Lewis, seek emancipation to escape the strictures of child labor laws, which limit underage working hours. Emancipation helped a fourteen-year-old Lewis work the longer hours required to jumpstart her acting career. Others seek emancipation in order to escape an abusive household. The reasons for emancipation vary—and the process is difficult. When a minor petitions the court for emancipation, she must demonstrate that she can financially support herself, that she has the mental and physical capacity to be self-sufficient, and that emancipation—rather than continued dependency—advances her best interests. In other words, she must not only demonstrate that she is the exception to the rule of immaturity, but that this presumption imposes significant hardships.

Emancipation confers upon minors full and irreversible adult status—and, at least on paper, provides minors with most of the same rights and liberties (and imposes on them the same responsibilities) as adults. However, there are numerous instances where minors receive a partial or context-contingent reprieve from the confines of dependency. For instance, children often are entitled to the same free speech and due process rights as adults—even if they are, in all other ways, treated as a dependent. When Mary Beth Tinker, her siblings (John, Hope, and Paul), and friend Christopher Eckhardt decided to wear black armbands to each of their respective Des Moines schools to protest US involvement in Vietnam, they unwittingly launched another, more enduring, campaign—to protect the free speech rights of minors. District leaders caught wind of their plan and gathered together to preemptively invoke a policy barring the armbands. Mary Beth and Christopher were immediately suspended and John was suspended the following day when he continued the protest in the others' absence. Upon learning of the suspensions, the Iowa Civil Liberties Union reached out to the Tinkers and the Eckhardts and filed suit, arguing that the children's free speech rights had been violated. The school district maintained that they had the authority to halt the protest, especially if the protest disrupted other students' capacity to learn. Eckhardt and the Tinkers argued that their armbands were a form of protected symbolic and political expression that should be—and had been in the past—protected within the confines of the school. In a landmark 7-2 ruling, the Court argued that students do not "shed their constitutional rights to freedom of speech or expression at the schoolhouse gate." Students are entitled to the same rights of free speech and expression as adults, so long as they do not "materially or substantially interfere" with the operations of the school or "the rights of other students."[102]

Young people have similar freedoms to reject forced speech—especially if that forced speech or expression violates their religious beliefs. Marie and Gathie Barnett, two Charleston, West Virginia, students, successfully challenged laws established in the aftermath of a 1940 Court decision permitting school districts to require students to salute the flag and recite the Pledge of Allegiance.[103] Students who attended schools in these districts faced expulsion and, in some instances, were "sent to reformatories maintained for criminally inclined juveniles" if they refused to comply.[104] In some regions, parents were punished as well, facing criminal charges and prosecution for promoting juvenile delinquencies. Marie and Gathie were expelled from Slip Hill Grade School for refusing to follow their district's flag salute requirements, even though the practice violated their religious beliefs. The Court overturned its 1940 ruling and the many policies that had emerged in the intervening years, arguing that neither peacetime, nor war, requires "compelling little children to participate in a ceremony which ends in nothing for them but a fear of spiritual condemnation."[105]

The Supreme Court extended these freedoms to school regulations forcing students to engage in prayer or moments of silence. Between 1958 and 1962, Steven Engel, Madalyn Murray O' Hair, and Edward Schempp each brought separate cases to the Supreme Court, arguing on behalf of their children's rights to refuse to engage in forced prayer or bible recitation at school. In a series of key rulings issued in 1962 and 1963, the Court overturned bible recitation and other religious activities based in public schools.[106] Twenty years later, the Court reaffirmed these precedents when Ishmael Jaffree asked that it extend its "wall of separation" doctrine to compelled moments of silence or voluntary prayer. Children bullied and teased Jaffree's youngest son, a kindergartner, when he chose not to pray—significantly hampering his ability to opt out of the school's clear preference for religion. The Court agreed and expanded the scope of children's first amendment freedoms to limit the ability for schools to force or constrain their thoughts and beliefs.[107]

Students and their advocates have scored similar victories in cases involving due process rights. When Dwight Lopez and nine other students were suspended from a Columbus, Ohio, high school for destroying school property in 1971, they sought to appeal the school's decision. However, the district offered no pathway for contesting the charges. The students sued the district and prevailed on the grounds that any limitation of a student's right to a public education without the opportunity for appeal constituted a due process violation.[108] Fifteen-year-old Gerald Gault successfully contested his arrest after he and a friend were confined for making a prank phone call to Gault's neighbor, Mrs. Cook. Shortly after Cook complained to the police, police apprehended the boys for using "vulgar, abusive or obscene language" in the presence "of a woman or child."[109] The police did not inform Gault's mother of his arrest. She learned of the arrest only after reaching out to the friend's family to inquire about her son's whereabouts. During the next day's hearing on Gault's arrest, without aid of an attorney or the opportunity to question the neighbor (she did not attend), Gault maintained that, although he made the phone call, he did not speak Mrs. Cook. Court officers did not record any of the hearing testimony, however, and those in attendance offered conflicting accounts of Gault's statements. During his second, and similarly informal hearing, the judge sentenced Gault to six years confinement in a juvenile facility; a similar charge carried a $50 fine and two years' imprisonment for adult offenders. Gault's parents filed suit, arguing that their son's due process rights had been violated. The Court agreed—mandating that minors facing criminal charges be guaranteed the same due process rights as adults.[110]

Along similar lines, fourteen-year-old Roger S. fought his confinement to a California state mental institution in 1976, arguing that by denying a pre-commitment hearing (in which he could have contested his diagnosis), the state violated his due process rights. Roger's mother claimed that he was psychotic and ordered his confinement. However, several medical professionals, with whom Roger had consulted, attested to Roger's sanity and described him as "a vulnerable youngster who has most of his energy focused on his own self-protection."[111] They urged the state to object to his mother's requests, arguing that Roger "cannot tolerate physical restraint and needs space."[112] Roger eventually prevailed. The state's highest court ruled that, although parents and guardians are permitted to limit the liberties of their dependents in order to protect their welfare, Roger's inability to contest his own potentially erroneous diagnosis constituted a significant infringement on his liberties. Roger was entitled to a pre-commitment hearing and an attorney, in order to question witnesses, testify, and offer evidence on his own behalf.

Healthcare is a particularly thorny policy arena in which the rule of dependency clashes with a minor's needs for self-determination—and where the costs may be insurmountable when their needs are ignored. Jodi Picoult's *My Sister's Keeper* dramatizes exactly this kind of circumstance. In Picoult's story, Kate Fitzgerald has been fighting leukemia since she was a toddler and is in frequent need of tissue and blood donations. Kate's parents "engineer" Ana, Kate's younger sibling, to be a perfect genetic match and donor for Kate. But Kate, now a teenager, no longer wants to receive Ana's genetic material (in this specific instance, Ana's kidney) and convinces Ana to file for emancipation. Once emancipated, Ana could have autonomy over her body and could refuse to consent to participate in the invasive and ongoing medical procedures. Ana takes her story to attorney Campbell Alexander, recalling how she was created for the purpose of providing optimal genetic donations to her ailing sister, and describing the ongoing procedures she has had to submit to (since the age of five) in order to fulfill her filial obligations. As Ana argues "a major decision about me is being made, and no one's bothered to ask the one person who most deserves to speak her opinion."[113]

Picoult's story is fictional, but there are numerous cases of real children seeking and receiving the legal right (often through emancipation) to refuse physician-advised medical treatment. E.G.—a seventeen-year-old girl who, like the older sister in Picoult's book, had acute nonlymphocytic leukemia—sought emancipation in 1989 to escape pressures from physicians to receive blood transfusions (the primary treatment for her condition at the time). Both E.G. and her parents opposed the treatment because it violated their religious beliefs. When E.G.'s parents first refused her doctor's recommendations, the hospital moved to declare E.G.'s parents unfit and were awarded temporary custody over her. Over a two-month period E.G. received approximately ten transfusions and began to regain her strength. But she also regained her resolve. Acting on her own behalf, E.G. continued to reject the hospital's calls for continued transfusions. She testified in court that she "understood the nature of her disease and the consequences of refusing the transfusions," and while she did not want to die, she was more concerned about violating her religion's unequivocal prohibitions against blood transfusions. Eventually, E.G. prevailed. An Illinois court removed her guardianship on the grounds that, as a mature minor and because of the rights at stake, E.G. should have the authority to refuse medical treatment.[114]

Unlike E.G., Billy Best did not have the support of his parents (at least not initially) when, in 1994, he refused physician-recommended treatment for Hodgkin's Disease, a form of cancer that has an 80 percent survival rate if treated with radiation or chemotherapy. Best had witnessed his aunt lose her violent struggle against breast cancer and had already experienced the devastating effects of radiation and chemotherapy. After rejecting the treatment recommended by physicians, he decided to sell his belongings, purchase a bus ticket, move someplace warm, and figure out another, better, way to beat his cancer. He ended up in Houston, Texas. Beleaguered with grief, Best's parents took to the airwaves, telling anyone who would listen about their son's health crisis. With increased media attention came an outpouring of information from individuals who had survived Hodgkin's through alternative means. His parents made a plea to Best and a promise: no more traditional treatments.[115] He returned home and survived his battle with cancer and as an adult became an advocate for other young cancer patients seeking alternative treatments.

Abortion and gender reassignment cases are special instances of juvenile medical consent that have catalyzed policymakers and activists to develop targeted procedures. After all, teen abortion cases set off the initial legal fight for emancipation. In 2017, when Jane Doe, a pregnant unaccompanied minor immigrant who had been detained by immigration officials in Texas, requested to have an abortion, she was required under state law to get parental consent. At the time, Texas had been one of thirty-seven states that required parental notification or consent for pregnant minors seeking an abortion. Texas now bars abortion at six weeks, but some pro-choice states, like Rhode Island, have considered tightening age restrictions by criminalizing any individual who helps a minor seek an abortion out of state. Yet the fight over parental consent mirrors those in many other *membership* debates. Those advocating on behalf of pregnant minors believe that the abortion rights originally granted to pregnant women in *Roe v. Wade* should extend to anyone who is pregnant, regardless of their age. They believe that to do otherwise could pose deadly risks for girls who are desperate to seek an abortion but afraid to tell their parents. For instance, in 1988, state law required Becky Bell to ask her parents for permission to have an abortion. Out of fear of their reaction, she sought out an abortion from an unregulated provider. Bell experienced complications stemming from an infection and, shortly after receiving her illicit abortion, passed away. Bell's parents, Bill and Karen Bell, became strong opponents of parental consent laws because, as much as they wished their daughter had talked to them about her decision, they came to believe that it is impossible for parents (or state actors) to "regulate what [kids] are going to do in a time of crisis."[116] By contrast, parental consent advocates contend that parents have a specific right to be involved in the decision and that states play an important role in keeping parents in the loop in order to protect children.

Historically courts have been critical players in either facilitating or limiting the capacity for young women to receive abortion services— and, therefore, have played an important role in framing debates around children's autonomy. Supreme Court doctrine has not only set the stage for future legislative debates over parental consent; it has also cemented the ongoing involvement of judicial actors in determining youth autonomy. Despite its 1976 ruling in *Planned Parenthood v. Danforth*, overturning a Minnesota law requiring parental consent, the Court revisited this issue less than twenty years later, after parental consent laws had continued to spread.[117] In *Planned Parenthood v. Casey*, the Court upheld parental consent laws as constitutionally valid so long as underage pregnant girls have an option to, instead, seek consent from a judge.[118] This "judicial bypass" requires the pregnant minor to make a compelling argument as to why a substitution of consent is warranted. In Jane Doe's case, parental consent was impossible since she had entered the United States without her parents. Through *Casey*, she had the option to seek out the judicial bypass and received the necessary consent from a Texas judge.

On paper, the process for seeking a judicial bypass seems simple and efficient. File the paperwork, appear in court, and get the consent. And in some regions, this is the reality. In Cook County, Illinois, for instance, pregnant minors file an anonymous request for a judicial bypass and are frequently represented pro bono by attorneys from the American Civil Liberties Union (ACLU) and other nonprofits. According to local attorneys, no minor has ever been denied the bypass request.[119] In other jurisdictions, however, minors are left at the mercy of (mostly male) judges who have the discretion (and inclination) to interrogate and rule in any manner that they want. For instance, the judge who would have presided over Becky Bell's case, had she decided to seek a judicial waiver, had never granted one in the twelve years that he had been a judge. He was an avowed supporter of pro-life principles. One judge in Florida told a pregnant minor that "her mother would understand" after he denied her request for a bypass and sent her back to her mother to receive consent to end her pregnancy.[120] And, of course, the process can be anything but efficient; sometimes it can take weeks for a pregnant minor to receive notification of a judge's intent to hear their petition. Moreover, young mothers often are denied attorneys, especially in communities that are especially antagonistic to abortions, forcing young women to represent themselves in hearings. At the same time, judges in these restrictive jurisdictions have gone as far as appointing attorneys to represent the fetuses—and even given the fetus a name that is invoked during cross-examinations of the pregnant minor.[121]

Despite social and medical advances, many transgender teens are demeaned in their attempts to access gender affirming treatments—especially those addressing gender dysphoria. Increasingly, as we discussed earlier in this chapter, these challenges emanate from state limitations. But sometimes, even in states that permit hormone therapies and puberty blockers, they can face similar if not more daunting challenges from their parents or guardians. In these instances, they face a false choice: pursue puberty-blocking therapy, delay puberty, and risk losing their parent's support; or delay these therapies to accommodate their parents' wishes, but risk a much more challenging transition in the future. Without parental consent, some teenagers have opted to pursue emancipation or custody reassignment in order to begin the process, typically with the backing of healthcare professionals who have been assigned to their case. For instance, a seventeen-year-old transgender boy asked his grandparents to take over guardianship because his parents were religiously opposed to his transition (and refused to recognize his chosen name or gender). Medical professionals supported his custody request in part because they believed delaying hormone treatment would significantly increase his risk of suicidality.[122] A mother in Minnesota attempted to sue her transgender daughter and state officials to have her parenting rights restored after medical professionals in the state declared her daughter emancipated. The mother had declared and demonstrated her disinterest in continuing a relationship with her child which provided sufficient evidence under state law to allow medical professionals to declare the teenager emancipated and initiate hormone therapy at the seventeen-year-old's request.[123]

Stories like these have prompted increasing and significant disagreement about whether age should ever be a proxy for rationality when it comes to medical treatment. Canada does not use age as a bright line but instead enlists evaluative techniques to ascertain a minor patient's maturity, emotional stability, and intelligence in order to gauge the extent to which healthcare providers can or should engage minors in their own diagnosis and treatment options. There is now a growing consensus in the United States among medical practitioners that children ought to be included in the decision-making processes of their own treatment plans. Recently, the American Academy of Pediatrics developed a set of recommendations regarding patient care, advising that it is in the child's best interest if minor patients are actively informed and consulted in their own care.[124] However, young people continue to contend with policies and authorities who believe that children are incapable of making decisions on their own behalf.

The reality is that even where there is an option for minors to be treated as full citizens, those options are fraught with uncertainty. Judicial precedent and public policy provide only narrow spaces of autonomy and agency, and in these infrequent cases minors are at the mercy of judges and other public officials. This is, in large part, due to the fact that children's autonomy—even if it is in their best interest—is the exception to the rule that children are deemed categorically unfit to make decisions on their own behalf. This is obvious in the context of abortion rights, where judges are given the discretion to reject a request for a bypass. But it is also true in the context of free speech and due process. For instance, despite *Tinker*, the Court has since constrained the rights of students to freely express their views and opinions. In 1986, Matthew Fraser publicly introduced a fellow classmate, Jeff Kuhlam, for a student government position. Fraser used what Bethel School District administrators referred to as "vulgar" and sexually graphic language when introducing his friend and was suspended for three days (and removed from a list of potential speakers for graduation). Fraser's family obtained a lawyer and sued the district, arguing that the *Tinker* standard protected Fraser's speech. The Court disagreed. While *Tinker* protected "political speech," the Court reasoned, schools have the right and pedagogical responsibility to limit vulgar speech, especially when it takes place during school activities. The past twenty years has seen schools' restriction of speech in student newspapers or other student activities upheld by the Court as "long as their actions are reasonably related to legitimate pedagogical concerns."[125] In this way, children's autonomy in the context of constitutional rights could be read not as an indication of potential membership and citizenship, but instead as an extension of the paternalism that pervades public policy. The overriding principle in these cases is that children need protection, even when their independent rights-claims are compelling or when adults overseeing their care pose significant risks to their well-being.

Of course, the most essential form of equal membership for political subjects in democratic societies is access to the ballot box. Yet voting rights for minors long has fueled heated debate: between opponents who argue that young people below a given age lack the maturity to evaluate election choices and proponents (including young advocates) who claim that many minors under eighteen have the capacity—and thus the right—to vote as political equals. In Hollywood, the prospect of full youth participation in national political life inspired a campy 1968 drama that generated a loyal following: *Wild in the Streets*. To reviewers, *Wild in the Streets* was a "chilling" film illustrating the "logical result of an over-accent on youth."[126] Shot at a time when youth protest was pervasive and the voting age was a hot issue, the film was a political satire that offered an extreme portrait of how democratic society would be transformed if larger numbers of youth were given access to the ballot box. The movie depicts a political apocalypse of sorts that ensues when a legislator is duped into championing a constitutional amendment reducing the voting age to fourteen. Suddenly armed with the right to vote, young people elect a pop star, reduce age requirements for public office, and quarantine anyone over thirty-five in New Age "re-education camps," where they are permanently dosed with LSD. In effect, under the leadership of teenaged voters, the world turns to chaos.

As a cartoonish and sensational vision of what could transpire if young people achieved voter enfranchisement, *Wild in the Streets* eventually became a cult classic.[127] Yet at the time, the film struck a raw political nerve—particularly among those most resistant to a very real movement to reduce the voting age to eighteen. The subject of age-based voting restrictions first gained significant attention during the Second World War. Large numbers of people who served on the front lines during the war were unable to vote because of age-based voting restrictions which, at the time, limited voting to individuals twenty-one and older. In the immediate aftermath of the war, some politicians issued legislative proposals reducing the voting age, but these efforts were swiftly dismissed. While proponents perceived voting as an entitlement, arguing as President Eisenhower did that "if one is old enough

to fight, one is old enough to vote," adversaries perceived voting as a
privilege that could only be placed in the hands of more seasoned citizens.[128] Skeptical of the decision-making capabilities of young people,
Congressman Emanuel Celler argued that "voting is as different from
fighting as chalk is from cheese."[129] Recurring conflict over youth
voting rights is a predictable manifestation of durable adult resistance
to youth demands for increased autonomy.

Abandonment: "Not Our Problem"

Sixteen-year-old Gideon Barlow left his home and the Mormon
Church after being excommunicated for allegedly watching "forbidden" movies and hanging out with the wrong crowd (other LDS
outcasts).[130] In reality, the church facilitated his departure to help
maintain a workable mix of men and woman to accommodate growing
wife-to-husband ratios.[131] Barlow was one of a growing number of
"lost boys" of the Mormon Church—boys who had been expelled from
the church and from the care of parents or siblings, to preserve desired
gender ratios. Church elders had initially transferred Gideon out
of his father's house when they assigned his mother (and his father's
other wives) to a different husband. His mother's new husband asked
Gideon to, instead, live with older siblings, after which Gideon developed a crippling depression that quickly spiraled into drug addiction,
prompting his excommunication. John Jessop faced excommunication at the age of thirteen, after running away from home.[132] Church
officials removed Jessop from his family's home, and he spent several
years sleeping on the couches of other "lost boys" until he ended up in
juvenile detention.[133] "Lost boy" Sam Icke became the sole provider
for a household full of other excommunicated boys when he turned
nineteen—his $300 a week salary their only steady income. Church
elders had threatened Sam's father with expulsion if he didn't remove
Sam himself. So, Icke left voluntarily.[134]

Despite the growing number of lost boys, states with large Mormon
populations have remained generally unresponsive. The Utah legislature instituted policies to facilitate emancipation so that they no longer
had to seek out parental approval. Yet most states with notable lost boy

populations have done little to help them make the transition beyond the church—to become enrolled in school, or to receive housing assistance and job training. Much of this has fallen to private actors—like Sam Icke. These young people are "abandoned." Where young people like Sherry Sotello seek out and demonstrate their capacity to live independently—and are rewarded with emancipation—abandoned youth are prematurely cut-off from the safety net of dependency.

Courts, again, play a key role in facilitating both membership and abandonment. As the primary location for arbitrating particularistic disputes involving young people and their adult caregivers, courts are imbued with significant power over the treatment of children. In some cases, courts scaffold young people, amplifying their voice and legitimizing their claims. But courts can also be critical locations of abandonment and abdication. The tragic suicide of Abrielle "Abbie" Bartels while a student at Milton Hershey School (MHS) provides a glimpse into the capacity for courts and caregivers to cast aside young people and abdicate accountability. MHS is a nonprofit boarding school located in the chocolate capital of the United States. The school's namesake—a rags-to-riches candy magnate—had been an orphan and had always felt a pull to care for young people in need through the power of education. In addition to providing its young scholars with a free education, MHS also places its students in family homes so that they can continue their studies in a stable and supportive home environment.

In many ways, Bartels had grown up at MHS, joining the school when she was in kindergarten. For most of her time there she was a happy student with a promising record. But as she approached adolescence she began to struggle with anxiety and depression, which quickly escalated to suicidal ideation. Bartels received medical help, first from a physician at the school's health center and then from a nearby psychiatric hospital called Philhaven, where both Bartels and her physician concluded that her family was the primary source of her continued depression. After her first discharge from Philhaven, on June 5, 2013, the treating physician suggested that Bartels return to school "to help build her sense of belonging to a community and strengthen her self-esteem." The physician cautioned that without school "it is possible that Abrielle could decompensate and require future hospitalizations."[135]

Bartels returned to school and continued to improve, but shortly after a brief visit home, her depression re-surfaced, and she again sought treatment from the school's medical staff. In consultation with a psychiatric consultant the school physician encouraged Abbie to check into the Pennsylvania Psychiatric Institute to receive continued care. This second hospitalization had the potential to trigger an MHS policy that would mandate Bartels's removal from campus. If during their residence at MHS a student experienced more than one hospitalization for mental illness they would be, possibly permanently, removed from the school and sent home. Bartels understood that her second hospitalization may result in some time away from MHS, but she and her physician had hoped it would be temporary. After a few days at the hospital, receiving stabilizing treatments, she had come to terms "with going to a different school for a year and then returning to [MHS] after she is stable."[136] Bartels returned to her family home on June 19, 2003, excited to attend the school's eighth grade graduation and the barbeque hosted at her school home. But the school had decided to cut ties with her, permanently barring her from the school and from any school-based events. Ten days later Bartels hung herself in her bedroom closet.

Abbie's parents sued MHS arguing, among other things, that their decision to deny Bartels access to the party at her school home because of her mental health struggles violated the Fair Housing Act's (FHA) proscription against disability-based discrimination. The FHA outlaws discrimination "in the sale or rental, or to otherwise make unavailable or deny, a dwelling to any buyer or renter because of a handicap." While she did not pay rent (room and board were included in the scholarship), Bartels did complete chores as part of her residential obligations. Attorneys for her parents reasoned that her service in exchange for housing entitled her to FHA protections. A third circuit district court judge disagreed and granted summary judgment to MHS, expressing special antipathy to the notion that Bartels held any fair housing rights. Because she received housing as part of a gift of free education at MHS, the court likened Bartels to a "tramp" who has received the gift of free clothing as a kindness from a benefactor, but must "go around the corner to the clothing shop" in order to receive "[the benefactor's] credit."[137] In this scenario, explains the court, walking is not payment for the clothing, but merely a condition for receipt. As such, the court argued, her "chores are analogous to the tramp's short walk to the store," nullifying coverage under the Fair Housing Act. The court also ruled that MHS could not be held liable for her decision to take her own life as she was no longer a ward of the school (of course by the school's own doing). Through this decision, the court abandons Bartels and others like her who are struggling with mental illness. By upholding a school policy that effectively triggers expulsion when students seek out mental health treatment, students are required to choose between their mental health and their intellectual and social development: pursue treatment for mental illness and risk losing housing and school support; refuse treatment and continue to endure the trauma of mental illness.

Courts may also facilitate abandonment by fostering pathways for emancipation that benefit parental rather than dependent interests. The process of adult-initiated emancipation can look similar to those in cases where young people pursue emancipation proceedings: the minor is self-sufficient, no longer lives at home, and agrees that emancipation is the best option. But dig a little deeper and one can see that the decision to emancipate is driven by parental, not filial, desires. Some parents nudge children to seek emancipation—or argue "implied emancipation"[138]—in order to reduce child support, relocate for better job prospects, or in other ways reduce or eliminate their parental responsibilities. In 1993, for instance, the Idaho Supreme Court ruled that economically self-sufficient minors can be declared emancipated regardless of age, thereby liberating parents of child support obligations.[139] In other instances, parents endorse emancipation for minors because of challenging or unmanageable behavior.[140] Examples like these make many child advocates wary of emancipation laws and procedures. As legal scholar Tia Wallach argues, "statutory emancipation serves less to empower mature minors than to enable their parents to abdicate their caretaking responsibilities."[141] Even youth-initiated emancipation proceedings may be the product of adult exploitation, caution scholars. Regardless of whether the minor appears to desire their freedom, advocates worry that adult caregivers use statutory emancipation to pressure young people into releasing parents from their caregiving obligations. In the end, emancipation may do little to improve the livelihoods of "mature minors," but will certainly relieve caregivers of their fiscal and legal obligations.[142]

Children may also find themselves being treated as adults outside of the context of emancipation. Children in the criminal justice system, for instance, are sentenced as if they are adults, not because they demonstrate the characteristics of adulthood but because they exhibit behaviors that, the state contends, require adult penalties. In these instances, children are stripped of the protections of childhood for reasons that have little to do with age. Racial biases abound in this regard, as Black children and other nonwhite minors are far more likely than their white counterparts to be stopped by police, arrested, and incarcerated.[143] It is a prime example of how the intersection of youth with attributes like race, class, and growing up in a high crime neighborhood make some young people instant targets and suspects of law enforcement officers and criminal justice structures. As legal historian Tera Eva Agyepong deftly chronicles, the criminalization of children who are poor and nonwhite has a long history in the United States. Progressive Era reformers fought to transform a criminal justice system that punished children as adults, insisting that the inherent innocence of minors warranted fundamentally different treatment.[144] Yet even as these advocates won juvenile justice reforms, "racialized notions of innocence and delinquency" meant that Black children of the early twentieth century faced harsh sentences and confinement. The early criminalization of Black children, Agyepong argues, created the ideological and practical foundation for mass incarceration as the "new Jim Crow" decades later. "This notion of 'super-predator' children—Black children—who were so vicious and irredeemable in spite of their youth," she writes, "was used by both liberal and conservative politicians in the late twentieth century to argue that only the most punitive measures a criminal justice has to offer, like life imprisonment and even death, were rational and just responses to childhood delinquency."[145] Here the slipperiness of *childhood* as a contingent category remerges, one that reflects political, social, and legal constructions of *who* should be granted the status of "child" and thereby gain specific protections. Conceptions of child innocence, vulnerability, and redeemability are thus shaped not simply by chronological age, but also by other attributes such as race, religion, gender, sexuality, and class.

The place where children grow up also has a significant impact on criminal sentencing patterns for young people. In particular, like the driver's license regulations described earlier, region (rather than science) plays a decisive role in determining the relationship between age and criminal punishment. In thirteen states, for instance, there is no minimum age to receive an adult penalty.[146] In these states, children as young as ten have been tried as adults—even if, in other areas of law and public policy, these children would be far too young to receive the benefits of adult status. Individual prosecutors hold significant power, too—making the determination of whether or not to try a child as an adult both subjective and political. Trying a child as an adult vastly increases the options of where, how, and for how long the minor defendant can be punished. It also enables prosecutors who try children as adults to frame themselves as "tough on crime."

States also vary significantly in the penalties applied to juveniles who have committed violent crimes. Nineteen states permit life without parole for minors who have committed serious crimes, while the remaining states do not have anyone serving a life sentence before legal adulthood. From 2005 to 2016, the Supreme Court issued a series of decisions that sought to limit how harshly minors can be sentenced for serious crimes. Swayed by research showing that the brains of juveniles are not fully developed and that they often lack impulse control, Court majorities ruled that minors are less culpable for their criminal acts than adults and that their youth raises greater hope for rehabilitation.[147] By a 7–2 margin, the Court ruled in 2005 that juveniles cannot be sentenced to death. Five years later, it prohibited sentences of life without parole for minors not convicted of homicide. In its 2012 *Miller v. Alabama* decision, the Court decided that mandatory life-without-parole sentences are unconstitutional for juvenile offenders. The *Miller* majority argued that mandatory sentences that failed to take account of a young defendant's age violated the Eighth Amendment's ban on cruel and unusual punishment. "Mandatory life without parole for a juvenile precludes consideration of his chronological age and its hallmark features—among them, immaturity, impetuosity, and failure to appreciate risks and consequences," Justice Elena Kagan wrote for the majority.[148] Finally, in 2016, the Court determined that its *Miller* ruling could be applied retroactively. By 2021, however, a new conservative majority on the Court made a dramatic U-turn in *Jones v. Mississippi* by affirming the discretion of states to issue sentences of life without parole to minors as "both constitutionally necessary and constitutionally sufficient." In a blistering dissent, Justice Sonia Sotomayor pointed out that states like Louisiana "imposed L.W.O.P. [life without parole] on an astonishing 57 percent of eligible juvenile offenders," and that 70 percent of youths sentenced to die in prison are nonwhite. Unbound by *Miller's* reading of the Eighth Amendment, Sotomayor concluded that the new conservative Court majority was giving child offenders "no hope" for rehabilitation and "no chance for fulfilment outside prison walls."[149]

Unaccompanied minors, and other child refugees, have been similarly abandoned by government actors and treated as adults. Rather than being handled like children—and given the protections of due process, guardianship, or fundamental resources like food and clothing—state actors often have left child refugees to fend for themselves. Indeed, the United States has a long-documented history of treating children like adults when it comes to determining refugee status. During the Second World War, for instance, Congress rejected desperate appeals to lift sweeping restrictions on immigrant and refugee admissions that would have allowed twenty thousand unaccompanied Jewish children fleeing Nazi Germany to enter the country. Despite support from prominent celebrities, artists, clergy, and academics, nativist lawmakers made no effort to hide their anti-Semitic motivations in rejecting the proposal, stating plainly that "twenty thousand charming children would all too soon grow into 20,000 ugly adults." Tellingly, large majorities in both houses of Congress *did* open the gates to tens of thousands of British (mostly Protestant) children to provide safe haven while war raged overseas.[150] Once again, child protection or abandonment hinged on young people's connection with other constructed categories like race and religion.[151]

Since that time, the United States has adopted similarly draconian policies when it comes to child refugees. Unaccompanied minors who enter the country seeking asylum are subjected to intense interrogations and court proceedings, all without the guarantee of legal assistance. A federal judge in California ruled in 2018 that immigrant children seeking asylum are not entitled to free legal assistance during their asylum hearings—even if they are just infants or toddlers.[152] During these hearings, judges still must follow the typical protocols even when the children are barely out of diapers. For instance, judges are required to make sure that asylum seekers "understand the pro-ceedings." This places judges and lawyers in the absurd position of having to explain the intricacies of immigration proceedings to their toddler clients. As one judge admitted to a lawyer regarding their one-year-old client, "I'm embarrassed to ask it, because I don't know who you would explain it to, unless you think that a 1-year-old could learn immigration law."[153]

Children have become frequent targets of immigration reform in the United States. Under its so-called zero tolerance policy, the Trump administration separated migrant children from their parents at the southern border and detained them in camps. Under these conditions, the federal government treated separated children as *de facto* unac-companied minors in asylum proceedings. It also demonstrated little to no concern for the welfare of these migrant children during their detention. While in the camps, according to legal documents, children were explicitly ignored—as a matter of policy. Camp guards were under orders to resist engagement with the children except under emergency conditions—and subjected some child detainees to debilitating levels of drugs to pacify them during their detainment.[154] During hasty im-plementation of the policy, government officials also neglected to doc-ument the location of these migrant children, making reunification all the more challenging for family. As we discuss in detail in Chapter 3, these "zero tolerance" policies were designed explicitly to create strong disincentives for Latin American asylees to enter the United States, ef-fectively collateralizing migrant children to discourage unauthorized entry. These policies also provide a clear example of abandonment, not by migrant parents, but by Trump administration officials who deployed unilateral executive authority to set aside commitments to child welfare in order to preserve, what they characterized as, core na-tional interests.

When US officials forcibly separate children from their parents to satisfy national security interests, they are engaging in abandonment—regardless of whether it is at the border or within US communities. When the US government deploys federal agents, for instance, to deport the undocumented immigrant parents of children who may be US citizens, legal permanent residents, or themselves undocumented they do so without accounting for the interests or well-being of the children who are left behind. Under US immigration law, despite their citizenship and their dependency, the minor citizens or legal residents of immigrant parents are not permitted to sponsor their parents for a path to citizenship. This leaves children from families with an undocumented parent in a continued state of potential abandonment. A 2016 report by the Migration Policy Institute notes that roughly five million children living in the United States (80 percent of whom are citizens) have at least one undocumented parent. US immigration agents make regular and frequent use of raids to deport undocumented adults often at worksites, and even occasionally at schools and day care centers when immigrant parents pick up their children. Annual deportations have ranged between 300,000 and 400,000 during the past decade.[155] An Migration Policy Institute study finds that the parents of more than 500,000 US child citizens were deported between 2011 and 2013.[156] In some instances, these children were placed in the foster care system. But in many cases, they were left to fend for themselves—and had been prepared by their parents to live on their own, or with designated caregivers, should the need arise. More recently, researchers found that one in five US children being raised by extended family members— such as grandparents, aunts, uncles, or cousins—are from immigrant households in which parents have been arrested, deported, or otherwise separated from their offspring. This research also indicates that so-called immigrant grandfamilies face significant hurdles: traumatized children, inadequate access to educational programs and social services like Medicaid and food stamps, and social withdrawal.[157]

Racism, sexism, classism, Queer/transphobia each play a central role in these stories of abandonment. When young people are devalued by their age and disenfranchised by hate or ignorance, they are more vulnerable to being forced into expedited adulthood—and denied the special protections that are often reserved for children. Discretion in criminal justice proceedings means that arbitrary factors such as race, ethnicity, income, or disability can drive adjudications of minor offenders. For instance, of the 75,000 minor offenders tried as adults in 2015, over 50 percent were African-American.[158] In Oregon, a Black offender under the age of eighteen is almost fourteen times more likely than a white minor to be treated as an adult in criminal proceedings. In Missouri, despite accounting for only 40 percent of juveniles who are arrested, Black children comprise 72 percent of youth offenders who are transferred as adults. With ten thousand kids serving time in adult prisons on any given day (3,000 of whom are serving life sentences), the arbitrariness of age comingles with the enduring legacy of racial bias to stunt entire communities of young people.[159] Children who are members of a fringe religious sect, as in the case of the "lost boys" described earlier, are involuntarily elevated to adulthood by their church and by the state, absolving the state of any obligation to provide services or supports. Jewish refugee children were turned away during the Second World War—and ultimately returned to Germany to meet their fate—while English children were welcomed by US officials. "Zero tolerance" policies separated primarily Latin American migrant children from their parents and treated them as adults for the purposes of expediting deportation hearings. And Brown children living in the country with undocumented parents are the most common victims of immigrant policies that force their parents to leave them behind if arrested, detained, and deported. When children carry the markers of those who are most vilified, the state no longer invests in them as dependents—or as innocents requiring or deserving protection and guidance. Instead, state actors treat these children as unworthy burdens and implement methods to bypass age requirements and create a special class of premature and deserted adults.

Conclusion

Children are a significant focal point of US law, politics, and governance. Whether in response to the problems of child labor, demands for free speech, the shifting sands of the American family, the increased integration of church and school, or fights over financial or bodily autonomy—questions about young people, and the state's role in policing young people, have played a starring role in the most pressing public policy battles. Of course, this should come as no surprise. After all, much of the work of the state involves taking care of its dependents.

As this chapter demonstrates, there is no greater dependent—no more compelling recipient of state attention—than the child. Yet, what is surprising, and what we reveal in this chapter, is that the patterns of state intervention and the motivation for policy action are not simply to protect and nurture. Rather, the US political fixation with child regulation is complicated and serves a host of hidden interests that are not obvious when read in isolation. By locating these patterns within the context of child-centered policies, we can read these policies as a collective expression of specific interests and motivations—rather than isolated examples of dependent care.

We start with the premise that many child-centered laws and policies are what they seem—established to protect the welfare of children. Driven by assumptions that there is a magical age of maturity, and that children fall somewhere below that bright line, policymakers create programs and incentivize private actors to take responsibility for their development. The motivation here is simple: if we nurture our children and keep them safe, they will become healthy and productive adults. Classic examples of protective policies, such as Aid to Dependent Children (ADC) and Child Labor Laws, are designed explicitly to serve the best interests of children by advancing their welfare and protecting them from harm. And these are the kinds of initiatives that come to mind when we consider how policies consider children.

Dig a little deeper, however, and we find numerous laws, policies, and practices that do not fit this protective mold. Conversion therapy, constraints on student speech, limits on bodily autonomy—while these policies may be presented as protective, our analysis suggests that these controls on children serve other, more politicized, interests. Once we discover that protective policies may be driven by different masters, or pitched for different markets, we can begin to question whether policy actors use other devices to advance the interests of children or employ child-centered policies to serve other ends. Subjugation looms not only in earlier times when children often were treated as the property of their parents, but also in persistent contemporary struggles over education, health, sexuality, and other facets of young people's lives, in which adults seek control for reasons that elevate *their* choices and aims over those of children. We also find that, while some policies may press for control, others may call for autonomy, independence and, in some cases, abandonment. Fights over medical emancipation, procedural due process, and religious liberties reveal the possibility that serving children's interests sometimes requires expanding, rather than constricting, children's freedoms (or at the very least providing more precise mechanisms for identifying children or circumstances that are the exception to the rule of dependency). Especially compelling, however, is the revelation that, when read in context, instances of expedited adulthood may actually serve adult or state interests at the expense of children's welfare (particularly for children who are doubly burdened by the strictures of bias). A more judicious evaluation of child-centered policies reveals a far more complex interaction of policy approaches, motivations, and interests.

The benefits of our conceptual framework extend beyond a simple accounting of interests and mechanisms. Our categories of paternalism, subjugation, membership, and abandonment reveal how laws, policies, and practices governing children—and the interests they serve—are better understood as dialogic and contingent rather than fixed. For one, our approach helps to explain how two opposing orientations toward a similar policy can be understood as child-centered but also as serving different interests. Among the most obvious are initiatives involving LGBTQIA+ families. Both the proponents and opponents of same-sex marriage and parenthood employ the language of protection in their appeals for support. But a closer look at the rhetoric and the context for social action reveals starkly different motivations for these opposing, but nevertheless child-focused, viewpoints. Advocates for same-sex parenthood argue that the children of LGBTQIA+-headed households are entitled to, and require, the same protections as children raised in heterosexual households. These arguments echo the textbook appeals we see in traditional protective or paternalistic policy arguments. On the flip side, however, opponents take up the interests of children in heterosexual households—and of society at large—when they argue that same-sex marriage, same-sex parenthood, and homosexuality in general, should be eradicated. Their argument: gay children, and the children of gay parents, need to be fixed or controlled to protect morality and society.

Equally important, our approach demonstrates how the same policy mechanism can be used to promote different interests. Emancipation provides a telling example. Unlike the case of LGBTQIA+ family policy—in which proponents and opponents offer starkly different approaches to the care of children—emancipation calls for the same approach to be used for very different ends. Children who seek and achieve emancipation (whether complete or limited to medical care choices) are doing so on their own behalf and (we hope) to serve their own interests. When emancipation is imposed by adults, however, the cover of children's interests is blown, and we find that the primary motivation is abdication or punishment, rather than care. More broadly, our conceptual framework provides a space and a language for understanding not only how public policies are the culmination of a clash between interests and mechanisms, but also how the same policy can serve vastly different purposes when read against the backdrop of intention and in the context of institutional and societal bias.

Yet, as we underscored in Chapter 1, young people are far more than subjects of policies or recipients of state protection. They are also political players in their own right. They operate as especially critical fixtures in contentious policies—as icons, cautionary tales, activists, and bargaining chips. Their stories, images, bodies have been used to catalyze the reticent. Their significance—as innocents or future threats—is used to galvanize action and amplify risk. In short, young people both rely on and transform the policy world.

3

Leveraging Children in Democratic Politics

Symbols, Armies, and Collateral

Introduction

"Let the world see what I've seen," commanded a shattered Mamie Till
when her fourteen-year old son Emmett came home from his 1955
summer vacation in Money, Mississippi, in a pine casket. His body was
grotesquely disfigured, identifiable to loved ones only by the signet ring
he had always worn, passed down from his deceased father. Emmett
had been beaten, shot, and left for dead in a river near his uncle's house.
He had committed the sin of whistling at a white woman, the wife of
a storeowner, and had paid the price with his life. But when Mamie
Till made the decision to "let the world see," she compelled a nation of
waiting activists and advocates to stand up and fight for racial justice.[1]
Emmett's tortured body—immortalized by Black newspapers and
magazines across the nation—became a rallying point and a permanent reminder of the depravity of racial violence. As historian Elliott
Gorn explains, "Till is to America what Anne Frank is to Germany, a
child martyr to a national evil. His torture and murder symbolize the
regime that brutalized his people for decades. Like Anne Frank, he was
an innocent, destroyed by 'adult' hatreds and institutions."[2]

Over half a century later, eager to highlight the Trump
administration's "zero tolerance" for unauthorized border crossings,
Attorney General Jeff Sessions announced in April 2018 that his Justice
Department would fully prosecute all undocumented immigrants—
no matter their age or parental status—seized at the US border with
Mexico. This meant that migrant children, even infants, would be
separated from parents awaiting prosecution, marking a dramatic

Democracy's Child. Alison L. Gash and Daniel J. Tichenor, Oxford University Press.
© Oxford University Press 2022. DOI: 10.1093/oso/9780197581667.003.0003

departure from past policies of keeping families together at detention centers.[3] Sessions flatly rejected criticism that migrant children would be harmed. "If you don't like that, then don't smuggle children over our border," he said. "We are dealing with a massive influx of illegal aliens across our Southwest Border. But we're not going to stand for this."[4] When pressed by reporters if it was acceptable to use children as collateral in the administration's enforcement efforts, White House Chief of Staff John Kelly candidly explained that "the big name of the game is deterrence."[5] Within two months more than 2,400 children, including infants as young as four-months-old, were separated from their parents and kept in mass detention centers where they endured "squalid conditions" and neglect that the United Nations High Commissioner for Human Rights described as "a serious violation of the rights of the child."[6] One year later, the Inspector General of the Department of Homeland Security reported that hundreds of migrant children were still being held in "unsanitary and inhumane conditions."[7] While Trump officials compared the detention conditions for separated migrant children to "summer camp," court-appointed lawyers who visited the detention facilities in July 2019 reported that children of all ages (including toddlers) slept on concrete floors and were denied food, hygiene, and exercise. "We saw no windows in the warehouse," one lawyer told reporters, "and the children reported that they seldom get to go outside. One child reported that the highlight of their day is that when they come in to clean the cell, the children are able to go out in the hallway. And that's the highlight of their day."[8] Meanwhile, Trump officials argued in court that access to hygiene products like soap and toothbrushes were not necessary to provide "safe and sanitary" conditions, and conservative pundits argued that "it's better than what they had."[9]

Emmett Till's open casket and Trump's family separation policy—one launched by an anguished mother determined to expose the horrors of racial oppression and the other by a president hellbent on punishing unauthorized migrants—capture two of the contrasting ways in which children can be deployed for political purposes. In Chapter 2, we explored how children have been governed, changing over time from parental property to young people endowed with significant individual and group rights. At the heart of the contemporary politics of child protection is an ongoing battle between parents, the state, and other actors over the control and welfare of young people. As we have already discussed, it is a struggle fueled by diverse interests and ideals, one that has yielded laws, policies, and practices that fall into contrasting categories of paternalism, subjugation, membership, and abandonment. This chapter trains a spotlight on how and why children are leveraged—for good or ill—as powerful political icons, foot soldiers, and bargaining chips in democratic conflicts. Whereas Chapter 2 focused on distinct conceptions and rationales in policies that regulate or center young people, this chapter concentrates on how children, in turn, may impact democratic politics as potent political symbols, participants, and collateral.

Sometimes images and stories of children are enlisted to politically inspire, to symbolize innocence, or to highlight the need for reform, especially when reflected in the suffering of society's most helpless members. As we shall see, children often provide a riveting focal point amid warfare, economic depression, health crises, and other challenges. More generally, young people provide compelling faces of public problems across the political agenda, from poverty to gun violence. Galvanizing symbols showcase children as either innocent bystanders or unexpected victims of adult inaction, ineptitude, or ambivalence—or highlight children whose bravery and heroism command our attention. As with Emmett Till, images of children as victims or heroes can shock, shame, anger, and inspire—in large part because they stoke our natural instincts to protect and nurture the innocent and incapacitated.

However, young people can just as easily be appropriated as symbols of deviance, threat, and socio-cultural decline. Ronald Reagan launched his political career in 1966 by targeting student peace activists at California universities. At a time when most voters supported the US war with Vietnam, Reagan decried the "morality and decency gap" among campus youth and called for the expulsion of "spoiled" and "filthy speech advocates."[10] In fiery speeches, George Wallace similarly castigated the "little pinkos" protesting against the war during his presidential bids in 1964 and 1968, declaring that the only four letter words insurgent youth did not know were "w-o-r-k" and "s-o-a-p."[11] Moreover, the "othering" of certain children is almost

as familiar in political life as the frequent allure of young people as
icons of innocence. In distinctions drawn between "our" kids and
"their" kids, the children of ethnic, racial, and religious minorities
long have been cast in menacing or undeserving terms. Symbols that
are intended to alarm audiences about "outsider" children—children
who are minoritized (because of racism, sexism, homo/transphobia,
classism, or other forums for exclusion)—are either framed as threats
to "our" safety or as cautionary tales.[12] These narratives are meant to
astonish or frighten people into action by asking audience members to
set aside their beliefs in the innocence of children (at least in reference
to these "outsider" children) or to acknowledge the possibility of children as deviants. Time and again, for instance, nativists have portrayed
the children of "new" immigrants to the United States as unfit for our
society and threatening to the nation's future.[13]

The distinct ways in which children are depicted and framed in
democratic debates regularly have a potent influence on our political life. But as we have already suggested, this represents only half the
equation concerning the political leveraging of children. Just as important in this regard are efforts by political leaders and government
officials to use young people as recruits or foot soldiers in pursuit of
their goals. Sometimes reformers call upon young people in their own
ranks, groups, or families to mobilize on behalf of a critical cause. In
1903, the legendary labor organizer Mary Harris "Mother" Jones led
46,000 textile workers in northern Philadelphia to rally for a fifty-five-
hour work week. Many child textile workers joined the strikes led by
Jones, inspiring her to organize a "Children's Crusade" to march from
Philadelphia to President Theodore Roosevelt's summer home in
Sagamore Bay, Long Island, in the name of labor protection.[14] Sixty
years later, civil rights leaders uneasily mobilized thousands of African
American school children in Birmingham, Alabama, to march for civil
rights. In this second "Children's Crusade," movement leaders worried
deeply about the well-being of these young people, but ultimately concluded (correctly) that media coverage of police officers assaulting unarmed young protestors with fire hoses and vicious police dogs would
shock and outrage most Americans.[15]

But, while adults like the civil rights leaders in Birmingham struggled over the dangers faced by the young activists they organized,

other political actors have had no qualms about using children as bargaining chips or collateral regardless of the harms they might face. As we noted earlier, this was exactly the orientation of former Attorney General Sessions and other Trump officials who zealously advanced family separation and child detention no matter what conditions these young people endured. This chapter discusses both forms of youth exploitation—those used by reticent civil rights leaders to catalyze supporters and those employed by zero tolerance adherents to threaten immigrant families. The former highlights how ambivalent movement leaders may calculate that children on the front lines—because of their vulnerability—have the capacity to expose oppressors, shame adults within movements, and arouse the broader public. The latter shows how political leaders and government officials in this camp view particular young people—such as the children of undocumented immigrants, of the welfare-receiving poor, or of other groups deemed deviant and undeserving—as expendable. Policymakers who collateralize children are, essentially, either disregarding them or holding them ransom to coerce policy subjects into submission. From this standpoint, disempowered children can be sacrificed for political purposes in order to compromise, deter, punish, or otherwise leverage specific behaviors from parents, guardians, or other adults who care about them.

As we focus in this chapter on the deployment of children as political symbols, foot soldiers, and bargaining chips—what we call the political leveraging of children—a clear divide emerges. On the one side are views of children as innocent and cherished. On the other, children are treated as inferior, deviant, and expendable. This dynamic of pitting "our kids" against "their kids" thus highlights two rival political orientations toward using children for political purposes. Let us begin with efforts to deploy children as icons and foot soldiers imbued with innocence and designed to trigger inspiration in, empathy from, and action by adults.

Innocence and Engagement

During bruising political battles over healthcare reform in the spring of 2010, the Obama Administration and Democrats in Congress worried about how to make their Patient Protection and Affordable Care Act (ACA) relatable to a majority of Americans. The problem was that the ACA was an elaborate, complex legislative proposal hard to explain to voters, while conservative critics offered withering caricatures of Democrats' blueprints. The solution, they determined, was to provide human faces for the young president's signature reform plans—people who could capture the need for health insurance access in stark terms. Senate Democrats found a compelling case in Marcelas Owens, an African American eleven-year-old from Seattle, who headlined a Capitol Hill press conference with a gripping account of his mother losing her job, then her health insurance, and ultimately her life. "I am here because of my mom," Marcelas told a packed room of reporters. "I don't want any kids to go through the pain my family has gone through. My grandmother and I want Barack Obama and Congress and everybody to get together and to help get the health care bill passed."[16] Owens soon was making the rounds of cable news shows and granting dozens of media interviews on behalf of healthcare reform, becoming known as the ACA's "poster child" and the "Obamacare kid." Conservative pundits like Michelle Malkin complained that Democrats were using Owens as a "human kiddie shield" for their reform. Dressed in a suit and tie matching President Obama's, Owens was in the front row at the White House when the president signed the ACA into law.[17]

The practice of using "poster children" harks back to early twentieth-century print advertisements featuring appealing young people afflicted with a disease or illness or other condition to solicit donations for particular charities. Theodore Roosevelt was one of the first politicians in the United States to recognize the power of the "poster child" to shift political winds. During his presidency, Roosevelt understood the political value of his six children—Alice, Theodore, Kermit, Edith, Archibald, and Quentin—and allowed a hungry media to record their antics at the White House. The public loved to follow the adventures of Roosevelt's mischievous kids—often frozen in photos—playing sports with their powerful father, trying to sneak their favorite pony onto the White House elevator, frightening visiting notables with a four-foot King snake, or dropping water balloons on White House guards.[18] Politicians and campaign strategists could not ignore the cache of the Roosevelt kids. Today children are standbys in campaign ads, rallies, and efforts to "humanize" politicians. Yet as the deployment of Marcelas Owens as "the Obamacare kid" highlights, children are also often invoked as the transfixing faces of significant political problems or causes. "Poster children have proliferated in media coverage of political crises in recent years," culture reporter Josephine Livingstone noted. But she astutely added that the dynamics of how adults react to children who symbolize political crises may be timeless: "Perhaps the 'poster child' media syndrome will always function as a catalytic stage. First, we see the baby; the baby's cries then connect to some animal part of our hearts, which in turn activates the conscious parts of our minds."[19] In other words, spectacles and narratives of child suffering are politically powerful because they trigger adult empathy and activism.

The political potency of children in trauma is so formidable that defenders of the political status quo may be unwilling to accept the authenticity of the "poster child's" suffering—and may even strive to delegitimize their victimhood. In 1972, for instance, Associated Press photographer Nick Ut snapped an iconic image of a wailing nine-year-old Vietnamese girl, Phan Thi Kim Phuc, running naked among other fleeing children burned by napalm. Like H.S. Wong's famous "Bloody Saturday" photo of a crying Chinese baby amid bombed-out ruins in 1937, Ut's "Napalm Girl" image graphically captured the horrors of war, and particularly those of the Vietnam War. Kim Phuc, who was among a group of children mistaken by pilots as enemy soldiers, endured third degree burns and the loss of family and friends in the bombing.[20] Ut's photo ran on the front page of *The New York Times* the next day and was featured in newspapers worldwide, later winning the Pulitzer Prize. President Richard Nixon was vexed by the photo when he perused newspapers on June 12, 1972. During a meeting with his chief of staff, H.R. Haldeman, Nixon had difficulty accepting its authenticity. "I'm wondering if it was fixed," he mused on unauthorized White House audiotapes. When he heard Nixon's doubts, Nick Ut commented that the photo "could not be more real. The horror of the Vietnam War recorded by me did not need to be fixed."[21]

Another haunting, iconic Vietnam War-era image, frozen in a black-and-white still photo two years earlier, captured fourteen-year-old Mary Ann Vecchio kneeling over the body of Kent State University

Figure 3.1 *Napalm Girl*, Kim Phuc Escaping Napalm Attack.
Source: Photo by Nick Ut. AP Images. http://www.apimages.com/metadata/Index/Nap
alm-Girl/9788660b3cd64f75b34b2665e11761d1/48/0.

student Jeffrey Miller. Miller was one of four Kent State students shot
down by National Guard troops during anti-war protests, which had
reached a fevered pitch after Nixon ordered an invasion of Cambodia.
Anguished as life drained from Miller, Vecchio is pictured at the center
of the photo crying out for help with her arms raised in horror. The
photographer was John Filo, a senior at Kent State working on the student newspaper, who won the Pulitzer Prize for his coverage of the
massacre and later became head of photography for CBS. Filo ultimately concluded that the power of the photo flowed from Vecchio's
teenage response. "It was *because* she was 14, because of her youth, that
she ran to help, that she ran to do something," Filo said. "She was a kid
reacting to the horror in front of her. Had she not been 14, the picture
wouldn't have had the impact it did." The photo, which appeared on the
front page of newspapers nationwide and across the globe, shocked the
collective conscience, capturing as it did the fact that authorities were
willing to kill their own children to suppress anti-war protests. Yet the

very power of the photo elicited outrage from those who resisted its message, leading them to lash out at the young figures on either side of the lens. Filo received death threats and was interrogated and surveilled by the FBI. Vecchio was thrown into juvenile detention, became the target of conservative political attacks, was regularly heckled in public, and was maligned by the governor of Florida (where she lived) as "part of a nationally organized conspiracy of professional agitators" who were "responsible for the students' death." Even students at Kent State questioned her authenticity—complaining that she wasn't a protestor, her fame undeserved. Her whole life has been hijacked by the fact of this photograph and by the widespread derision it induced. Even decades later she faced intense harassment from local police and has spent most of her life trying to keep a low profile.[22]

Decades later, the mass shooting and murder of twenty first-graders and six teachers at Sandy Hook Elementary School in 2012 became a source of frequent denials and conspiracy theories by right-wing extremists. The Sandy Hook tragedy stunned the nation and turned parents into fierce advocates who took to the streets, the state capital, Congress, and the courts, to hold gun manufacturers accountable for gun violence, particularly mass shootings. But radical gun-freedom defenders insist that the Sandy Hook murders never happened. "The whole thing is a giant hoax," proclaimed right-wing internet and radio talk show host Alex Jones. In a four-hundred-page book called *Nobody Died at Sandy Hook*, conspiracy theorists insisted that Sandy Hook parents fabricated their children's death certificates.[23] Tellingly, deniers like Jones and Congresswoman and Q-Anon zealot Marjorie Taylor Green (R-FL) win few followers. "Though the Ann Coulters of the world claim that children can 'act' on screen to manipulate the public," notes Livingstone, "this is not true. A four-year-old cannot act. The power of this kind of media lies in that authenticity."[24] Seven years after the massacre, the issue of gun manufacturer liability is still being litigated in court—with judges scrutinizing the culpability of the gun industry. Sandy Hook parents also have won defamation suits against deniers like Jones. Yet, as farfetched as allegations of forgery are, disbelief of children is a powerful tool in the arsenal of child-focused politics. These accusations delegitimize horrors like Sandy Hook and demean the profound grief of children and parents, but they also turn the tables on movements that seek to publicize child-focused tragedies. In the case of Sandy Hook, while gun-control advocates hoped to translate the tragedy of youth fatalities into a plan for tighter gun regulations, gun rights advocates villainized "liberals" for exploiting children for personal gain.

Images that Galvanized a Movement: The Murder of Emmett Till

As Ut's epochal Napalm Girl highlights, stirring pictures can be central to the influence of children in politics. Indeed, some of the most enduring—and politically powerful—images of the past century are those which hauntingly capture the suffering of innocent and helpless children. These include Lewis Hine's unsettling pictures of children working in Progressive Era factories; Dorothea Lange's photographs of desperation and hunger during the Great Depression; Wong's "Bloody Saturday," Ut's image of Kim Phuc, and harrowing photographs of starving Ethiopian children in the 1980s.[25] More recently, the tragedy of the Syrian civil war and its ensuing refugee crisis hit home for millions who saw Nilufer Demir's 2015 image of a lifeless two-year-old Syrian boy, Alan Kurdi, who had drowned in the Mediterranean Sea and washed ashore on a Turkish beach. Demir later explained that she took pictures of Kurdi "to express the scream of his silent body."[26] The scream of a silent body is exactly what compelled Mamie Till to act in 1955.

When Mamie Till made the decision to have an open casket, she understood that her son's story—as told through his body—had the power to catalyze people out of silence and into action. Mamie had sent Emmett, an outgoing and charming boy from Chicago who was unaccustomed to the violent and visceral racism of Southern culture, to visit her brother in Mississippi in the summer of 1955. Three days after his arrival in Money, Emmett and his friends stopped into Bryant's Grocery & Meat Market for soda pop and candy. Emmett lingered in the store a bit. Worrying for Emmett's safety, one friend went back inside the store to check on him. Emmett "just didn't know the Mississippi rules," recalled the friend, "and [we] felt that someone should be with [him] at all times."[27] Within a few minutes, Emmett had paid for his purchases and exited the store—friend in tow. Carolyn Bryant, the white owner's wife, emerged from the store a few moments after Emmett. As she walked to her car, according to a friend and eyewitness, Emmett let out a loud whistle. Emmett had intended to simply entertain his friends (he was frequently described as "fun-loving" and "mischievous" with "no sense of danger"),[28] but in doing so he had violated a central tenet of Southern white power. A few nights later, Bryant and his brother-in-law abducted Emmett from his uncle's house, beat him beyond recognition, and dumped his body, bloated and riddled with bullets, into a local river.

Emmet Till's grossly disfigured body returned to Chicago, to his mother, on September 6, 1955—with instructions from Mississippi authorities to bury the casket "unopened, intact, and with the seal unbroken."[29] At first, Ahmed Rayner, the funeral director, resisted the grieving mother's demands to open the casket; but he finally conceded to her request and the casket remained open at her insistence. Over 50,000 visitors laid eyes on Till's swollen body over a four-day period and *Jet* magazine dispersed his image to African American families nationwide. Emmett's indictment of US racism, embodied in photographs of his unspeakable transformation from dapper young man to grotesque and disfigured corpse, propelled the outrage that powered a national movement. These haunting images and their story of white terror continue to serve as a visual reminder, an emblem, of the brutality of racism. Yet, despite their prominence in the weeks that followed his death, white America remained largely quarantined from the imagery. In addition to *Jet*, other Black publications like the *Chicago Defender* and the *Amsterdam News* had published the photos. Mainstream (white) publications, however, had, initially, refused to transmit the photographs and story, leaving most of the nation unaware of Till's visual legacy. It was not until decades after his death—after marches, sit-ins, protests, and assassinations had compelled judges and legislators to acknowledge the scourge of white racism—that the image of Till's disfigured face made its way into the homes of white Americans.

Henry Hampton, filmmaker and founder of Blackside, Inc., recalls his experience of seeing photographs of Emmett Till, when he was a boy in St. Louis, Missouri. Having grown up a stone's throw from Money, Hampton knew that what made Till's homicide so tragic was the frequency with which cases like Till's were ignored. It was Mamie Till's instinct to organize an open-casket funeral, and the ongoing publicity that followed, that fueled mass protest. Hampton carried the memory of Till's ruthless murder, and the anger that it had incited, with him through adulthood.[30] After founding Blackside, Inc., one of the earliest and largest minority-owned production agencies, Hampton embarked upon Eyes on the Prize, a multi-series biopic of the civil rights movement. The first hour would be devoted to Emmett Till's life and brutal death, iconizing the two faces of Till—one in hat and tie, the other unrecognizable—as symbols of racial violence. Hampton's renewed attention to Till's murder cemented Till's place in history as a potent symbol of the innocent casualties of hate. His original casket now rests at the Smithsonian in "quiet sanctuary."[31]

Shifting Discourse: Ryan White and the AIDS Epidemic

Transfixing images and stories about children can be powerful engines for political mobilization and reform. The innocence of young people, and their dependence on adults, amplifies adult outrage when tragedy strikes children and increases pressures for policy reform. Emmett Till, Phan Thi Kim Thuc, Marcelas Owens, Alan Kurdi, and the Sandy Hook victims—all were unimpeachable because of their age and, therefore, unmatched in their ability to capture public attention. When children struggle, when they are the targets of violence or the victims of ignorance or inaction, communities feel responsible and can be galvanized by grief, shame, or outrage. As such, children can provide a unifying lens for policy proposals that might otherwise be perceived as benefitting the "undeserving."[32] Ryan White, a teenage hemophiliac, provided exactly this kind of mediating influence on an otherwise polarized battle for federal AIDS funding. Ryan's foray onto the public stage shifted the discourse on AIDS victims from demonization to empathy and galvanized federal funding.

"It was Ryan who first humanized the disease called AIDS," recalled Reverend Ray Probasco of the young man whose tragically shortened life altered the discourse on AIDS funding and research. "He allowed us to see the boy who just wanted, more than anything else, to be like other children and to be able to go to school."[33] White received his AIDS diagnosis in 1984, shortly after undergoing surgery to remove portions of his lungs, which were compromised by pneumonia. By this time, policymakers had acknowledged the mysterious illness that had quickly taken the lives of over two hundred, mostly gay and male, patients who had received minimal federal attention. On the whole, members of the public who were aware of the illness perceived AIDS as "nature's revenge on gay men" and drug users,[34] thereby turning victims into culprits. During its early years, few in Congress even knew of the disease. Ignorance, coupled with steep cuts in the federal healthcare budget, paralyzed efforts to fund AIDS research. Senator Henry Waxman (D-CA), a lone voice of support in Congress for AIDS victims, was informed of the illness by a physician in Los Angeles whose practice had been inundated with victims of the still to be identified virus.[35] In 1982, concerned about the disease's mysterious origins and high mortality rate, Waxman called for Congressional hearings in the hopes of securing federal funding for research. Public officials responded by chastising the victims, using the illness to further an ongoing war on gay men and people of color. Dogged in his commitment, Waxman secured some early (albeit small) victories, but only by slipping the funding request in as a line item in legislation targeting Toxic Shock Syndrome and Legionnaires Disease.[36] Publicly, the gay community continued to bear the brunt of both the physiological and political assaults brought on by AIDS. These political attacks, in turn, delayed life-saving research and licensed egregious acts of discrimination and violence against members of the gay community.

Ryan White had contracted AIDS from a routine blood transfusion to treat hemophilia—a disease, often afflicting boys, that makes it difficult for blood to clot—and started exhibiting AIDS symptoms in 1984. AIDS-related research was then in its infancy, and the medical community had yet to develop protocols that would require donated blood to be tested for the virus. After his diagnosis, Ryan initially remained at home; his doctor had given him a grim six-month life expectancy.[37] But Ryan miraculously recovered and desperately wanted to return to school. Yes, AIDS would shorten his already truncated life, but he wanted to live out his remaining days or years as a "regular boy." In response, his parents explored the possibility of enrolling Ryan at the local high school in Kokomo, Indiana, so he could attend middle school with his friends.

Ryan and his parents understood that his attending school might be a thorny subject. With little known about the illness, except for its high and rapid mortality, enrolling Ryan at school set off a maelstrom of opposition. His parents were careful about Ryan's re-entry to public life; they consulted with their local attorney and sought approval from local health administrators, and were given the green light to move forward with Ryan's enrollment.[38] Community members, however, were less willing to give Ryan a chance. Parents, teachers and administrators vehemently protested Ryan's enrollment, prompting school officials to expel him from the school citing concerns about the health risks posed to fellow students. Even after he had gathered support from his own physician and had sought recommendations and feedback from AIDS-focused epidemiologists, misconceptions about the transmission of AIDS persisted. Ryan and his family took his expulsion to court and, although they prevailed, elected to move to nearby Cicero and enroll him in a new school.[39] At his new school he encountered little protest and remained there as a student until his death in 1990, at the age of eighteen.

Although his life was short, Ryan White exerted a lasting influence on the trajectory of AIDS and the rights of AIDS victims. Through his own legal battles, he helped remove legal barriers for individuals with AIDS. Ryan forced family, friends, and community members to confront their own beliefs and presumptions about the transmission of AIDS. Perhaps most importantly, he changed the face of AIDS debates, by adding a recognizably sympathetic narrative to an epidemic whose victims had been largely disparaged or ignored.[40] Where gay rights groups, like ACT UP, engaged in a wide array of public and disruptive protests, designed to force a largely indifferent heterosexual public to contend with the growing reality and tragedy of AIDS, Ryan White challenged the rhetoric of blame and required individuals to imagine their own son or daughter becoming afflicted with the illness. By staging "installations" of protestors lying prostrate in train stations, post offices, and other public spaces, ACT UP pressured the public to see AIDS and to experience the costs of silence. Nevertheless, these tactics did little to shatter the negative stereotypes about the illness's most visible victims.[41] And this public ambivalence about (or aggression toward) AIDS victims held hostage any headway in negotiations over federal funding. Ryan White's rising fame as the ordinary boy who was expelled from his school because he had AIDS, provided a pitch perfect lever for reform.

Ryan's story offered an elixir for the tenacious partisan and ideological discord over AIDS funding. When his story hit the headlines, Senator Orrin Hatch (R-UT)—a stalwart conservative and key vote in Congressional talks over AIDS funding—embraced the game-changing symbolism that Ryan's story provided and suggested renaming the AIDS funding bill that had been circulating after the young icon.[42] Upon his death, Ryan's mother lobbied for her son's legislation and convinced over twenty senators who had previously been opposed to lend their support. With his story as the central theme, politicians could recast funding for AIDS research as supporting innocent children who, through no fault of their own, contracted the illness and died far too young. The Ryan White Comprehensive AIDS Resources Emergency Act of 1990 marked the largest federal investment in AIDS research and the first time that Congress had devoted legislation to a single disease.[43]

The Hypothetical Child: "Saving the Children" through Mythic Narratives

The idea of a child suffering is so powerful that activists need not enlist the symbolism of real children, as political activists and policymakers did with Till and White. If delivered through a convincing and fear-provoking narrative, the mere possibility of child endangerment, no matter how remote, can propel policymakers and voters into action. These mythic appeals tend to play out in two ways: warnings about the risks of "exposure" and "children-first" narratives. Each of these framings provide potent catalysts for policy reform even for the most reticent voter. Consider, for example, "exposure narratives" that connect any gay rights question to the welfare of children, even if children are not directly implicated in the policy domain. This "slippery slope" argument—that any gain in gay rights would lead to gay adults raising or "recruiting" children—thwarted the attainment of even modest gains in employment protections and general non-discrimination by gay rights advocates. Anita Bryant, former orange juice poster girl and anti-gay advocate, became an exemplar of this strategy in the 1970s when she led efforts to defeat a Miami-Dade County ordinance that would have outlawed discrimination against gays and lesbians. Bryant rose to fame in 1977 after gay rights advocates in Florida had successfully lobbied Miami-Dade officials to amend the county's nondiscrimination ordinance to include sexual orientation. Under Bryant's leadership, conservatives in the county banned together and formed Save our Children to enlist voters to overturn the Florida ordinance. "As a mother," said Bryant, "I know that homosexuals cannot biologically reproduce children. Therefore, they must recruit our children."[44] This imagery of a predatory community seeking out innocent children activated a latent gay panic that existed just below the surface of what many had hoped was a growing tolerance for lesbians and gays. Bryant's efforts were fruitful. Voters defeated the nondiscrimination bill and, compelled by Bryant's "bogeyman" imagery, Florida lawmakers enacted legislation barring anyone living in a household with an individual who identified as lesbian or gay from adopting or fostering children.[45]

Inspired by her swift and significant success, conservative groups in other states enlisted the help of Bryant and Save our Children to strike down nondiscrimination ordinances in their communities.[46] Anti-LGBTQIA+ advocates have recycled this approach many times, most recently through Promise to America's Children, founded in 2021 to market a widespread legislative assault on transgender young people. But earlier and more prominently, Save Our Children inspired a broader arsenal of child-focused narratives intended to scare the public away from marriage equality. Rather than focusing simply on the recruitment rhetoric though, anti–marriage equality activists argued that any positive movement toward marriage equality for gays and lesbians would, necessarily, render schools (and homes) into recruitment centers for attracting young people to the "gay lifestyle." As with Bryant's efforts in Florida, activists sounded an alarm that any child—not simply those raised by gay or lesbian parents—could be harmed by marriage equality progress.[47] As Gary Bauer cautioned in Senate hearings, if gays and lesbians were permitted to marry, "[c]hildren would necessarily be taught in schools that homosexual relations represent the moral equivalent of marital love."[48] These appeals were especially prominent in moderate or liberal states where voters (and especially parents) were reticent to believe that gays and lesbians posed a risk, but were nevertheless concerned about their own children's safety and sexuality. For instance, California's campaign to outlaw same-sex marriage through a constitutional amendment largely hinged on these kinds of appeals. Proposition 8 proponents cautioned parents that their children "will be taught about gay marriage unless we vote" to ban same-sex marriage,[49] and that "parents will have no right to prevent their children" from learning about gay relationships.[50] These "exposure" narratives helped pave the way for a close, but significant, victory for anti-gay advocates in California. Despite a state court decision supporting marriage equality for gay couples and ample polls predicting the amendment's defeat, voters passed Proposition 8 with over 52 percent of the vote.[51]

The battles over same-sex marriage also show us how "children-first" frames provide an equally potent means for political activists to build broad coalitions to support their agendas. Advocates of traditional marriage rely on children's innocence to foster an image of tolerance and to recast the debate from discrimination to child protection. Rather than showcasing their aversion to LGBTQIA+ individuals, compassionate conservatives in the 1990s argued that they were simply safeguarding time-honored principles of good parenting.[52] In 1993, shortly after the Hawaii Supreme Court became the first court in the United States to support same-sex marriage, Congress held hearings to explore legislation that would: (1) explicitly permit states to bar same-sex couples from marrying; and (2) establish a federal definition of marriage that excluded same sex couples. In his opening remarks before one of multiple hearings on the Defense of Marriage Act (DOMA), Congressman Charles Canady (R-FL) echoed Anita Bryant as he reminded the public of dangers posed by challenges to "traditional" marriage. "Marriage exists so that men and women will come together in the type of committed relationships that are uniquely capable of producing and nurturing children," he explained. "In the history of our country marriage has never been anything less."[53]

During hearings, DOMA supporters implored members of Congress to focus on "the education of the children" and the "inescapable fact that . . . only a man and a woman can beget a child."[54]

Opponents invoked children's welfare to distance themselves from explicit anti-gay rhetoric that had begun to lose favor among political moderates.[55] DOMA supporters cast themselves and state policies as first and foremost immunizing children against what they characterized as the risks and dangers of raising children in gay households. By focusing on children's welfare, DOMA supporters could fight back against allegations of "hatemonger[ing]" and instead refocus the question on whether "children deserve a mother and a father."[56] In so doing, they shifted the terms of the debate to more pragmatic—and ostensibly child centered—concerns about custody and adoption rights. DOMA supporters warned of the capacity for gay couples to wield marriage as "a mighty tool" for adopting children,[57] casting same-sex marriage as a zero-sum game that equated "compassion for gays" with "noncompassion for children."[58]

Congress swiftly passed DOMA in 1996, securing the role of child-centered advocacy as a mainstay of anti-gay campaigns. States followed suit, with mini-DOMAs that were overwhelmingly passed through voter-driven ballot initiatives, powered by "children's welfare" appeals. Between 1996 and 2002, over forty states passed statutory bans limiting marriage to between a man and a woman. By 2006, most of these statutory bans had been converted to constitutional bans—again to protect children against the whims of activist judges and gay rights supporters. Ban supporters decried gay rights advocates as obstructing the "rights of children to live in a culture that . . . affirms the role of marriage to give them a mom and a dad."[59] Ballot proponents asked voters to consider the "emotional well-being" of children when deciding whether to limit marriage, statutorily or constitutionally, to heterosexual couples. Campaign materials implored voters to think about the effect on a child as they searched for "a missing mother or father"[60] and described the "uniquely powerful contribution that fathers and mothers make in their child's life."[61] These appeals described marriage equality as an initiative designed to "intentionally subject" children to "a vast, untested social experiment."[62] Campaign ads also featured parents who decried the attacks on heterosexual parenthood implied in marriage equality. They dismissed as heresy any argument that downgraded the importance of both genders when raising children. "Anyone who insinuates that healthy children don't need both a mother and a father," admonished one father of three, "has little understanding of what is required to develop healthy families."[63]

To sell this children's welfare argument as fact, rather than panic, marriage equality opponents launched a widespread effort to scientifically expose the threats that same-sex marriage poses to children. Buoyed by research conducted, initiated, or supported by anti–marriage equality groups, ballot and litigation campaigns referenced statistics to highlight both the opportunity costs and burdens faced by children who were not raised by a mother and a father. Literature in an Oregon-based campaign to adopt a constitutional ban on same-sex marriage described children raised in so-called traditional households as:

> less likely to be on illegal drugs, less likely to be held back in a grade, less likely to drop out of school, less likely to commit suicide, less likely to be in poverty, less likely to become juvenile delinquents, and for the girls, less likely to become teen mothers. They are healthier both emotionally and physically, even thirty years later, than those not so blessed with traditional parents.[64]

These (debunked) studies, they argued, are demonstrably clear in their results: "children do better with a mother and a father."[65]

The "children first" narratives—and the accompanying statistics marshalled by opponents—formed the foundation for opposition efforts in court. Despite mountains of social science data collected over decades concluding that children raised by same-sex couples fair just as well as children raised by heterosexual couples, and amicus briefs from the American Pediatric Association and other children's welfare groups supporting marriage equality, lawyers and judges defending marriage bans remained committed to children's welfare arguments.[66] For instance, in oral arguments for California's Proposition 8, Antonin Scalia cautioned that by "redefin[ing] marriage to include same-sex couples, you must permit adoption by same-sex couples, and there's considerable disagreement among sociologists as to . . . raising a child in a single-sex family, whether that is harmful to the child or not."[67] These narratives, and the statistics that had been marshalled on both sides to support and rebut children's welfare arguments, became so central to marriage equality cases that judges spent significant time interrogating experts to identify what, if any, child welfare costs would ensue if marriage equality were legalized. A Sixth Circuit judge, for instance, asked lawyers representing same-sex couples and the state of Michigan to demonstrate how children fare with same-sex parents. Rather than focusing exclusively on questions of constitutional interpretation, the judge in this case interrogated child-welfare experts to pinpoint whether concerns raised by anti-gay advocates had any grounding in reality.[68]

Innocence arguments have become a mainstay in US public policy. Hypothetical children facing imagined risks play on the emotions of adults. By centralizing even far-fetched or worst-case scenarios involving innocent children, advocates can drastically alter the outcomes of policy debates. Even when policy options have little to do with children, the mere whiff of impropriety toward or risk for children has the potential to move a public toward a given policy position. This is especially true when policy debates take up issues that relate to already "suspect" populations—communities who must battle unyielding and long-held stereotypes and biases in order to partake in the essential elements of a functioning democracy. The "mythic child" narratives highlighted here played on already deep-seated stereotypes regarding gays and lesbians as predatory. By pairing children's innocence and victimization, these hypotheticals supplied voters and public officials with the imagery to catalyze anti-gay stereotypes into action.

Recruits: Young People as Democratic Armies

Of course, policy debates that reference young people through two-dimensional narratives and images cannot compare to campaigns and movements with real children as central actors in democratic political battles. Young people are more than just stories, images, or icons in policy debates; they come with a phalanx of loyal followers, cheerleaders, and advocates. Movements of varied stripes draw on the energy and appeal of young people, who shout from the rafters, take to the streets, and demand change. Political leaders and policy advocates also rely on young people as recruits—as bodies to push for change, voices to spread the word and as leaders-in-waiting.

From Classroom to CPAC

Liberal arts colleges and universities have long been fertile grounds for youth protests, making them an ideal setting for catalyzing anger and publicizing policy conflicts. But they also provide critical locations for identifying and training leaders. And while college campuses are regarded as engines of progressive politics, conservative groups also perceive them as pivotal investments for effecting significant policy reform in the belly of the liberal beast. In the 2010s, conservative leaders saw universities as advancing an explicitly liberal ideology that marginalized conservative students and began to make explicit investments in building a more permanent college presence. Student-led and student-centered groups like Turning Point USA played a big role in this strategy. Turning Point opened its doors in 2012 when retired marketing strategist Bill Montgomery attended Benedictine University's Youth Government Day and heard eighteen-year-old Charlie Kirk deliver a speech that Montgomery described as "practically Reaganesque."[69] Montgomery encouraged the young Kirk to delay college and devote his time to political activism. Together they founded Turning Point USA, a group that works to "identify, educate, train, and organize students to promote the principles of freedom, free markets, and limited government."[70]

The group focuses on establishing conservative beachheads on even the most liberal college campuses, generating increased political engagement for conservative students, and calling out colleges and universities for purportedly normalizing leftist and socialist principles. The group grew in notoriety with the creation of its Professor Watchlist—a student-generated alert system (similar to ratemyprofessor.com) that "unmask[s] radical professors."[71] By the end of 2016—less than one year after the website's launch—200 professors had been added to the list, many of whom research identity-based discrimination or are themselves the targets of gender, race, or gay/trans-phobic bias.[72] Unlike ratemyprofessor.com, the list did not simply affect enrollments or provide momentary anxiety for maligned scholars. The list prompted and, some argued, licensed real threats. Faculty on the list received emails detailing threats of rape, violence, and death.[73] Some suffered physical assault. Some feared administrators would use the list to suspend or expel faculty—especially those at lower ranks in the academic hierarchy or instructors with temporary positions.[74] The implications of landing on the list, at least when it first rose to fame, compelled 1,500 faculty from around the nation to ask that their names be added in a show of solidarity for their targeted colleagues.[75]

With its increased visibility, Turning Point campus chapters expanded under Trump. The organization claims to have inspired over 1,000 chapters and bills itself as the "fastest growing conservative student organization in the country."[76] As of 2017, there were 400 registered organizations on campus and the group had garnered significant national buzz.[77] The organization's focus on "making conservatism cool to millennials" attracted big-name donors with deep pockets.[78] Campus chapters—and national leaders—boasted a marked success in helping to nurture the next wave of conservative leaders, to generate campus-based events, and to create a concentrated social media presence showcasing millennial conservatism. One of the organization's most successful initiatives, Campus Victory, leveraged financial and organizational support to develop a more muscular conservative presence on campus. Taking a page out of past Republican efforts to create a concentrated conservative presence on school boards and expand the pipeline of conservative candidates, Turning Point recognized the potential for generating young leaders to run as conservative candidates for elected campus offices. Although there were few electoral victories, Turning Point candidates who did win challenged the politics and policies of their colleges and universities. For example, one student leader backed by Turning Point at the University of Wisconsin, Max Goldfarb, questioned the university's funding for the Muslim Student Association (MSA) at budgeting meetings, arguing that the group did not meet the university's eligibility requirements. An argument ensued—with a more liberal student leader accusing Goldfarb of using "a conservative student PAC to get on this committee."[79] Goldfarb publicly denounced the comment as a smear on his professionalism, gained media attention for what he described as an unwarranted ideological attack that had nothing to do with budgeting issues, and ultimately extracted an apology from his liberal critic. Campus Victory targeted student campaigns at major universities across the country, focusing like a laser on "[h]ow many seats we're winning in student councils and government councils and presidents of student bodies."[80] In fact, Turning Point's fiscal sway in campus elections has prompted several colleges and universities to create campus versions of campaign finance restrictions to limit the power and prevalence of outside sources in student races.

Turning Point has also recognized the social media skills of young students and has enlisted conservative high school students to troll accounts on Facebook and other social media sites. In 2020, for instance, the organization paid students in Phoenix to create Facebook accounts and plant misinformation about Democratic candidates and election fraud. This move provided conservatives with, as political communications expert Kathleen Hall Jamieson described, "an army locally situated in a battleground state, having them up and online and ready to be deployed."[81] Alliance Defending Freedom, a leader in conservative attacks on Queer rights, has also tapped into colleges and universities to expand their supply of conservative advocates. The group focuses primarily on litigation—and on crafting policies for state legislatures that will ultimately be tested in court. They see young people, recent college graduates, and law students in particular, as legal crusaders-in-waiting and provide opportunities to nurture their training in conservative causes. The group has organized two specific initiatives focusing on young recruits: the Law School Prep Academy, for students just beginning law school, and the Young Lawyers Academy, for recent law school graduates and newly minted attorneys. The programs focus on gathering "like-minded Christian students" from around the country to help incoming law students "excel in law school" and new attorneys to "effectively advocate for religious liberty, free speech, the sanctity of life, and marriage and family."[82] Campuses have always been ground-zero for the politics of protest. Young people—college students in particular—provide the textbook bogeyman for older generations lamenting liberal causes and rule breakers. Yet, these initiatives, geared toward scoping out potential conservative warriors on college campuses suggest that political players of all partisan stripes understand the untapped power of youth idealism and are doing their best to harness it to their advantage.

Children as Heroic Warriors

When children are mobilized to participate in political struggles, to serve as activist armies in causes larger than themselves, their engagement is captivating and sometimes even transformative. The Children's Crusades of 1903 and 1963 engaged young textile workers and Birmingham schoolchildren as foot soldiers in democratic reform. But sometimes children are *literally* foot soldiers. During the Civil War, the bloodiest conflict in the nation's past, historians estimate that one in every five soldiers was under age and that more than 100,000 Union soldiers were boys under fifteen. Although soldiers had to be at least eighteen-years-old to enlist, younger fighters were lionized in newspapers, magazines, songs, and plays of the era. Hundreds of these underage warriors received the Congressional Medal of Honor and other military honors for their bravery in battle.[83]

One of the most popular Civil War-era stories that circulated among Union ranks and across Northern states was the saga of "The Drummer Boy of Shiloh." According to the legend, a young drummer boy at the Battle of Shiloh threw down his drum in favor of a musket when Union fortunes began to flag during intense fighting. As the story goes, General Ulysses S. Grant kept his troops from retreating by pointing to Johnny's courage. "Johnny won't run," Grant proclaimed. "Are you going to let a boy and his general stand and fight here alone?"[84] In this invocation of children in war, Johnny stands not as a helpless victim but as a brave fighter despite his obvious vulnerabilities. Folksongs, plays, and poems cemented the tale. One of the period's most popular songs memorialized Johnny's imagined last words on the battlefield:

"I've loved my country as my God.
To serve them both I've tried."
He smiled, shook hands—death seized the boy,
Who prayed before he died."[85]

Like Grant's imagined challenge to retreating troops, the implications of Johnny's final words were straightforward: If a young boy could demonstrate courage and devotion to God and country, grown men could at the very least do the same. Interestingly, wartime journalists avidly searched for real-life Johnny Shilohs, turning Union drummer boys like eleven-year-old Johnny Clem into national celebrities.[86] The devotion of underage Civil War soldiers could be deployed as especially *authentic* symbols of the righteousness of the Union cause, and had the power to shame adults into making similar sacrifices on behalf of the nation. A century later, the legend of Johnny Shiloh found new life in a short story by Ray Bradbury and a made for TV Disney film.[87]

Of course, long before Johnny Shiloh there was Joan of Arc. Yet, whereas the legendary drummer boy stood for thousands of underage Civil War soldiers, Joan of Arc is a singular heroine. Jeanne d'Arc was a peasant girl born in Northeastern France in 1412 during the Hundred Years War between France and England. As a young teenager, she began hearing voices and believed that God had chosen her to save France by leading its armies against occupying English forces. With the permission of crown prince Charles of Valois, Joan of Arc at age seventeen led a French army to liberate the besieged city of Orleans in 1429. According to lore, she did so in gleaming white armor atop a white horse, scoring a momentous victory over the English occupiers. Two years later, she was captured and executed by French nobles allied with the English. In death, Jeanne d'Arc became a popular and mythic figure, inspiring generations of writers, painters, sculptors, composers, and filmmakers. She was named a national symbol of France in 1803 and was officially canonized by the Roman Catholic Church in 1920.[88] Centuries before Jeanne d'Arc there was Hua Mulan, the warrior heroine of fifth-century China who inspired the animated 1998 Disney blockbuster film *Mulan* and the 2020 live-action adaptation. In the animated film, Mulan is a sixteen-year-old girl who steps in to take the place of her ailing father in the Imperial Army to defend the country. Historical evidence suggests that Hua Mulan is more the product of Chinese folk tales than reality.[89] Centuries and continents apart, Joan of Arc and Hua Mulan are celebrated girl warriors who are integral to stories of

French and Chinese peoplehood, respectively. *Game of Thrones* fans may be reminded of the small but fierce Lyanna Mormont, a girl clad in armor who leads her house at the Battle of Winterfell and slays a white giant before succumbing to her injuries.

During the Second World War, young people took part in anti-Nazi resistance across occupied Europe. Sometimes the resistance involved minor perils, such as when Norwegian school children forced to watch Nazi propaganda films organized mass coughing fits or Ukrainian kids defiantly sang national anthems. But often their contributions involved grave danger. Children put their lives on the line as scouts, couriers, smugglers, spies, saboteurs, and guerillas. Many of these underage warriors followed the lead of their parents, other family members, or friends. As one French woman who joined the resistance at age nine explained, her parents taught her

very, very young to fight for freedom. Fight for your country. Fight for humanity. Stay on the good side. Never be scared to lose all of what you have, if it's for good cause. Go ahead with courage, perseverance, and your head up. And never be scared. And when you are 14, you have the spirit of little Joan of Arc, starting immediately.[90]

Grownups who led resistance efforts recall that despite obvious physical and emotional limitations, children were needed particularly because of one notable advantage: they were less suspect than adults. These children who risked their lives later told interviewers that they did not need to be prodded to do so. Most expressed certainty that they had to do their part in an existential struggle against Nazi occupiers: "Resistance was the most natural thing to do"; "we knew what we were on earth for"; "a cause to devote your life to"; "my motivation was ironclad." Children of the anti-Nazi resistance were recruited and directed by adults, but their testimonials after the war indicate that they embraced the urgency and rightness of the cause. "I followed my ten-year-old conscience," one grade-school saboteur explained. "Not everyone can be a general, but each of us does what we can."[91]

Children as Foot Soldiers for Democracy: The Little Rock Nine and Ruby Bridges

Like youth warriors before them, children were on the front lines of the Black struggle for racial justice in the United States following the Second World War. One reason why children were so prominent from the start of this postwar struggle against Jim Crow segregation, discrimination, and violence was because public education was an early and crucial battlefront. During the 1940s and 1950s, Charles Hamilton Houston and Thurgood Marshall of the NAACP won a series of major victories in the federal courts against racial segregation in public schools. In its landmark, unanimous 1954 *Brown v. Board of Education* decision, the Supreme Court plainly stated that "in the field of public education, separate but equal has no place."[92] Of course, the Civil Rights Movement's triumph in the courts would have to be realized—on an everyday basis—by the Black students who would integrate schools that had been exclusively white.

Nine Black students, the "Little Rock Nine," enrolled at Little Rock Central High School in Arkansas as part of their city's "gradual integration" plan in September 1957. In anticipation of the abuse and challenges they would face, each of these students—Minnijean Brown, Elizabeth Eckford, Ernest Green, Thelma Mothershed, Melba Patillo, Gloria Ray, Terrence Roberts, Jefferson Thomas, and Carlotta Walls—were carefully recruited and screened by civil rights organizers led by Daisy Gaston Bates, president of the Arkansas NAACP and publisher of a prominent Black newspaper. The nine students participated in extensive training and counseling sessions before the school year to help prepare them for a hostile environment. Two days before the first day of school, Arkansas Governor Orville Faubus gave a televised address warning that Black attendance at Central High School would be met with violence and bloodshed. Organized by segregationist groups like the Mothers' League of Central High and Capital Citizens' Council, angry white crowds screamed and spat at the nine Black students as they approached their new school. The Arkansas National Guard, following orders from Governor Faubus, blocked the Little Rock Nine at the school entry. In the weeks that followed, President Dwight Eisenhower quietly but unsuccessfully negotiated with Faubus. On

September 20, federal judge Ronald Davies ordered the removal of National Guard troops, and the nine Black students entered Central High three days later under local police escort. A violent white mob responded by rioting and storming the school. Police evacuated the Little Rock Nine through a back door.[93]

The next day, President Eisenhower sent federal troops to guard the nine students and their new school for the duration of the academic year. Even as order was restored on the perimeters of Central High, the Little Rock Nine endured vicious attacks from white students within the school. They were kicked, beaten, pushed down stairs, and had acid thrown in their faces, while enduring a steady torrent of insults and racial epithets. Results from contemporaneous Gallup polling found that 95 percent of Americans were aware of what was happening in Little Rock due to intense coverage by the news media, with sizeable majorities approving of Eisenhower's handling of the situation and supporting integration of Central High. The numbers in favor of Eisenhower's response and school integration were particularly lopsided when subtracting Southern whites who opposed both by roughly two-thirds.[94] "One of the things that was significant in '57," recounts Elizabeth Eckford, one of the Little Rock Nine who was fifteen-years-old at the time, "was that that was the first time that the public saw events in the context in which they happened . . . .By that time, there had been a violent mob, and both still and television pictures showed people being beaten."[95] The New York Post editorialized at the time that the television footage and newspaper photos of vicious white mobs from Little Rock showed "quiet, resolute Negro children defying jeers and violence and sadism."[96]

One of Norman Rockwell's most famous paintings depicts a small Black girl in a white dress carrying schoolbooks and a ruler, flanked by four tall, white US marshals. On the wall behind them is graffiti— the n-word scrawled in large crude letters—and the smashed remains of a tomato that had been hurled at her.[97] Appearing as a centerfold in Look because it was too controversial for Rockwell's usual venue, The Saturday Evening Post, the painting's young protagonist is Ruby Bridges. Born in the same year that the Court handed down its 1954 Brown decision, in 1960 six-year-old Bridges was the lone Black student who sought to attend the all-white Frantz Elementary School a few blocks from her home in New Orleans. Each day she was escorted by US marshals through angry crowds to her school, where administrators mollified irate white parents by isolating Ruby from other students. For an entire year, she was a class of one for the only teacher who would accept her, also compelled to eat lunch and have recess alone.[98]

Bridge's determination (she never missed a day of school) amid constant abuse and violent threats troubled and inspired the renowned child psychiatrist and Harvard professor Robert Coles, who visited her and offered counsel during the ordeal. She figures prominently in his five-volume *Children of Crisis* as well as later works. In *The Moral Life of Children*, for example, Coles draws on his work with Bridges and other Black children on the front lines of desegregation to underscore an insight missed by most colleagues in his field of child psychiatry: the ability of even relatively young children to exercise moral strength and leadership in response to issues and circumstances in their everyday lives that they perceive as unjust. In *The Political Lives of Children*, Coles finds that the political and moral behavior of children merge as their political thought and action is shaped by parents, peers, and communities with whom they strongly identify. Reviewing hours of taped interviews from his research on school desegregation in 1960, Coles was struck by the ethical and political expressiveness of "boys and girls who were, after all, involved in a dramatic moment of history."[99] Once more, six-year-old Ruby Bridges was a powerful guide. As Coles recounts:

> She once told me she felt sorry for those people who were trying to kill her. I asked her, "You feel sorry for them?" And she looked at me and said, "Well, don't you think they need feeling sorry for?" Talk about wisdom! And talk about moral intuition. I sat there stunned. I was applying standard psychology, trying to help her realize that she was maybe angry at these people, and bitter and anxious, and she was telling me that she prayed for them. I was struck dumb and I was silent, because I had to reflect upon this child's wisdom. She was smart enough to understand, without taking courses in the social sciences or other fields of inquiry, what happens to people's sense of morality.[100]

When Coles probed what makes for a moral life, as opposed to moral reflection and argument, he was again drawn to the view that Bridges took from her parents that she should be like those "who just put their lives on the line for what's right, and they may not be the ones who talk a lot or argue a lot or worry a lot; they just do a lot!"[101]

The Ethical Dilemma of Mobilizing Kids: "Double D-Day" in Birmingham

Like the children of Occupied Europe's anti-Nazi resistance, the young civil rights activists of the 1950s and 1960s ardently believed in the urgency and rightness of their cause. Yet they differed from their anti-Nazi counterparts in two key respects. First, while young people of the anti-Nazi resistance during the Second World War were frequently recruited by parents and other family members, most underage civil rights activists were recruited by peers and movement organizers against the wishes of parents who wanted to shield them from harm (in this respect, the Little Rock Nine and Ruby Bridges were unusual to the extent that most of their parents were as determined as they were to desegregate all-white schools despite ugly reactions from white supremacists). Second, whereas young people of the anti-Nazi resistance in Europe were chosen for perilous jobs because they were less suspect or noticeable than adults, children of the civil rights movement were mobilized not only because they swelled the ranks of protestors, but also because their presumed innocence and vulnerability commanded attention amid the violence of white mobs and officials. This is exactly what movement leaders had in mind during the pivotal 1963 civil rights campaign in Birmingham, Alabama. Yet it also presented a profound ethical dilemma that troubled Dr. Martin Luther King Jr. and his colleagues. Mobilizing children could be justified on the paternalistic grounds that their recruitment advanced a struggle that was crucial to their long-term welfare. But drawing children into an activist army also entailed exploitation and grave danger.

In 1963, the Southern Christian Leadership Conference (SCLC) led by King came to Birmingham to help local civil rights leaders in their efforts to desegregate the city's retail businesses and jobs. King described Birmingham as "probably the most thoroughly segregated city in the United States,"[102] where African Americans comprised 40 percent of its population of 350,000 yet with no Black police officers, firefighters, bus drivers, bank tellers, department store salesclerks, or cashiers. The city shut down many public facilities rather than integrate them, and its sinister record of white violent oppression, often bombings, after the Second World War earned it the nickname, "Bombingham."[103] Through nonviolent sit-ins, boycotts, and marches, civil rights activists hoped that "direct action" would "create a situation so crisis-packed that it will inevitably open the door to negotiation."[104] By the middle of April, however, King and other civil rights protestors had been arrested during marches and remained incarcerated. Movement leaders had hoped to fill jails with demonstrators, but many Black adults were unwilling to make this sacrifice. The city's major Black newspaper, *The Birmingham World*, reflected the view of many established African Americans that the direct actions were "wasteful and worthless," calling for Birmingham's racist policies to be challenged in the courts rather than on the streets.[105] With flagging media attention and few adult demonstrators willing to risk arrest, the SCLC's Birmingham campaign was in crisis.

With King in solitary confinement, the SCLC called on two veterans of the Nashville Student Movement, James Bevel and Diane Nash, to help lead mass meetings and to try to recruit more demonstrators. The Nashville insurgency, three years earlier, was fueled by Black college students like Bevel and Nash, who launched sit-ins at the city's lunch counters, leading to concessions by white political and business leaders.[106] After the success of this mobilization, activist students, with support and guidance from the SCLC's Ella Baker, formed the Student Nonviolent Coordinating Committee (SNCC).[107] Nash, Bevel, and other student activists were pivotal in the 1961 Freedom Rides through the Deep South. In Jackson, Mississippi, Bevel gained experience working with child demonstrators. Young people, Bevel and Nash concluded, were the key to invigorating the SCLC's flagging Birmingham campaign.[108] They started by organizing a daily 5 p.m. youth meeting, two hours before a regular adult mass meeting and called upon popular Black student leaders and athletes to spread the word. The youth meetings featured inspirational messages on racial justice, workshops on nonviolent resistance, music, and stirring footage of Nashville students marching en masse, calling for integrated lunch counters and libraries. The youth meetings soon were packed beyond capacity, in contrast to modest attendance at adult gatherings. When King and his associates were released on bond from jail and addressed followers at the usual 7 p.m. meeting on April 23, there was standing room only at St. James Baptist Church because students had remained after their earlier session. Most of these young activists stood when King exhorted the crowd for volunteers to march and risk jail for the cause. After commending them for their devotion and courage, King asked the young people to sit down, telling them that city jails were no place for children.[109]

The problem, however, was that few adults volunteered for marches and possible jail time. Fewer than fifty local adults stepped forward to march. Behind closed doors, various SCLC and local leaders debated Bevel's proposal to deploy children on the front lines of the campaign. Initially, nearly all were adamantly opposed on ethical grounds. Yet Bevel argued that it was time "to stop the age-old custom in black homes of trying to shield black children from something for which there was, finally, no shield." In truth, he insisted, young people had not and could not be shielded from white oppression. Bevel pointed out that children had spent "their entire lives struggling against racism in some form or another," and his experiences in Nashville and Jackson convinced him that children were willing to disobey their parents and to put their lives on the line in the fight for freedom. The spectacle of young, respectful demonstrators being attacked by white segregationists, he added, would fuel a media frenzy and popular outrage. With considerable ambivalence, King and other key leaders in the Birmingham campaign eventually were swayed. "Black children get hurt every single day by the cruel discriminatory practices of racist whites," King acknowledged, so they should be allowed to risk getting hurt in pursuit of their fundamental rights. It was a decision that mingled the paternalism of enabling children to pursue "their fundamental rights" with their exploitation as an activist army facing enormous peril. Bevel and Nash ultimately were given the green light to organize young people for a fresh round of demonstrations. While Bevel, Nash, and student volunteers recruited an army of young marchers, SCLC leaders informed the national press that they would decisively challenge Birmingham's white segregationists with "a nonviolent D-Day" on May 2. Bevel, Nash, and other SCLC leaders continued training young activists in the philosophy and techniques of nonviolent protest at evening workshops.[110]

On the morning of May 2, as planned by organizers, a popular disk jockey for a local radio station signaled to young activists by declaring on air that there was "a party at the park; bring your toothbrushes" (meaning the march was on and participants should expect to spend time in jail). African American kids responded by walking out of school and streaming to the Sixteenth Street Baptist Church, headquarters of the campaign. "You could see the students coming from every direction," one witness observed, "from high schools and some elementary schools to take part in the demonstrations." Inside the church, one child activist recalls being inspired by the movement's leader: "Rev. Martin Luther King stood right beside me. He said, 'I think it's a mighty fine thing for children, what you're doing because when you march, you're really standing up; because a man can't ride your back unless it's bent.'"[111] At one o'clock, the doors of the Sixteenth Street Baptist Church opened and fifty children emerged walking in two rows, singing "freedom songs." Waiting outside were news reporters, spectators, and a large detachment of police under the command of Public Safety Commissioner Eugene "Bull" Connor. Connor had a well-earned reputation as a racist thug who the SCLC thought "could be counted on in stupidity and natural viciousness to play into their hands" by responding violently to their peaceful protests. On cue, Connor's officers arrested the fifty children and loaded them into waiting paddy wagons. Another fifty young marchers then came out of the church, and then another. Police quickly were overwhelmed by the numbers of child marchers, ranging from teenagers to six-year-olds, as paddy wagons were filled and school buses were called in to transport arrested students to jail. Stray lines of child demonstrators made it all the way to the business district before police could arrest them. By nightfall, nearly 1,000 children were arrested and filled Birmingham's prison, juvenile detention center, and a temporary outdoor prison at its fairgrounds. As the historian Taylor Branch chronicles, many African American adults were deeply moved watching the arrests. "Not a few

Figure 3.2 *Integration Protest Birmingham*, Birmingham Children's Crusade, 1963.

Source: Photo by Bill Hudson. AP Images. http://www.apimages.com/metadata/Index/ Associated-Press-Domestic-News-Alabama-United-S-/3276bdfadfe6da11af9f0014c 2589dfb/49/0.

of the onlookers in Kelly Ingram Park were dismayed to see their own disobedient offspring in the line," he writes, "and the conflicting emotions of centuries played out on their faces until some finally gave way. One elderly woman ran alongside the arrest line, shouting, 'Sing, children sing!' "[112]

The next day an estimated 2,000 students left school and massed at the Sixteenth Street Baptist Church. That morning the principal of Parker High School locked the gates from the outside to keep students in their classrooms, but they responded by tearing down a chain-link fence to join the marches. With no room left in city jails, Bull Connor's strategy for the second day was to disperse, rather than arrest, the demonstrators. When new lines of child marchers respectfully stood their ground, Connor ordered the fire department to turn high-pressure fire hoses on the demonstrators, knocking children off their feet and spinning them down the street. Connor also ordered his K-9 unit to unleash police dogs to tear into the children's disciplined march lines. News reporters and photographers were on hand to capture these events as they unfolded, and the story and images of police violence dominated the evening news, the front pages of newspapers, and magazine covers across the nation and the world. President Kennedy described the scenes as "shameful" and said that the news photographs made him "sick." Senators like Oregon's Wayne Morse compared Birmingham to South Africa under apartheid, and *The New York Times* editorialized that Connor and his police department were "a national disgrace." Birmingham's African American population was unified in its outrage toward Connor and was, as one community leader put it, "instantaneously consolidated behind King." That evening, King preached to a packed church of more than a thousand about the sacred work child activists were doing "not only for themselves but for all of America and for all of mankind."[113] Calling on the faithful to intensify pressure on Birmingham's political and business establishment, large numbers of adults now pledged to join young people as marchers. "Now yesterday was D-Day," King proclaimed, "and tomorrow will be Double D-Day!"[114] The Children's Crusade of Birmingham, as *Newsweek* called it, ended in the middle of May when an agreement was reached between civil rights leaders and the city's white business establishment on desegregating lunch counters, bathrooms, fitting rooms, and water fountains and on hiring more Black job candidates.[115]

The decision to deploy an army of child marchers in Birmingham drew fire not only from the city's white mayor, but also from some critics within the civil rights movement. As Malcolm X scornfully observed, "Real men don't put their children on the firing line." The idea of placing children on the front lines of racial violence cuts against innate (and paternalistic) conventions to shield them from harm. Yet Bevel, Nash, and eventually King, believed the movement needed to mobilize children en masse despite the obvious perils. King emphasized their critical role in a greater cause. Moreover, Bevel and Nash perceived something crucial that Malcolm X's natural reaction failed to reckon with: the political agency of young people (the focus of our next chapter). As we have seen, parents and other adults did not necessarily have the ability to stop Black children from joining the Birmingham demonstrations. "I was told not to participate," sixteen-year-old Jessie Shepherd recounted of joining the nonviolent D-Day protest. "But I was tired of the injustice."[116] Indeed, as the mother of a jailed son told a Birmingham judge during the May confrontations, her son's generation was unwilling to tolerate the oppression that their elders endured. "And I know this, Judge," she declared, "these younger people are not going to take what we took."[117] The political awakening of many children in the movement came when they saw the horrifying images of Emmett Till's mangled corpse. Southern Black children like Anne Moody later recounted that "Emmett Till's murder" made "a new fear known to me—the fear of being killed just because I was Black."[118] As former activists and historians explain, pictures of Till "took racism out of textbooks and . . . showed its true dimensions," inspiring "many Black children of his generation to fight the discrimination surrounding them in the 1960s."[119] Many adults, including Malcolm X, may have wanted to shield their children from dangerous confrontations with white supremacists, but as the principal of Birmingham's Parker High School learned, the activism of young people was not easily fenced in. As scholars like Ellen Levine note, there were "thousands of southern Blacks who were young and involved in the civil rights movement," most of whom are not famous.[120] Over time, King and other civil rights leaders came to understand—like organizers of other movements and causes—that mobilizing large numbers of young people was pivotal to their nonviolent insurgency. They learned that sometimes children can propel political change and seize a nation in ways that adults cannot.

Deviance and Subjugation

Thus far, we have discussed how and why the innocence and political engagement of children can have a profound democratic impact. When young people are perceived or invoked as vulnerable and unimpeachable, their mistreatment or victimhood elicits outrage and their courage inspires awe and emulation. We also have surveyed children as warriors and political activists, mobilized by leaders to fill their ranks while also drawing special attention, energy, and sympathy. Children are not always depicted or treated as possessing universal worth, however, or as deserving of sympathy and protection. Here once again the status of "child" looms as a politically, socially, and legally constructed category, one that often is defined less by chronological age or biological markers than by its intersection with other attributes possessed by children. Some young people, as we have seen, are denigrated because they challenge powerful actors or structures, such as the gun lobby, oil companies, presidents, the military-industrial complex, or Wall Street. Other children are held up for public scrutiny as malevolent deviants because of stereotypes stemming from the economic class, religion, ethnicity, race, or sexual preference into which they are born. Like adults, children can be disparaged and marginalized along the same pathways of exclusion that have polarized societies for centuries. Consequently, as much as leveraging children as symbols, narratives, or activist armies serves to trigger the public's protective instincts—to "save our kids"—it also relies on the "othering" of children. Whereas some children are deemed worthy of protection, others are bargained away or rejected out of hand by government officials and other political actors to promote their policy preferences or reform agendas. In this way, young people can be used as collateral to leverage behaviors or punish parents and other adult caregivers. They also can be depicted as "bad seeds," "problem children," and the unassimilable offspring of parents deemed unfit for our society.

Children as Social Deviants: Cautionary Tales

Although children are regularly invoked as symbols of innocence and virtue, their darker side is also a prominent theme in both popular culture and politics. William Golding's 1954 novel, *Lord of the Flies*, famously imagines the savage and murderous potential of boys aged 6–12 when loosed from the rule of law on a desert island. More than four decades later, Philip Roth's *American Pastoral* vividly captures a seemingly idyllic US family whose fulfillment of the American Dream is destroyed by a teenage daughter bent on bombing and other acts of terrorism to protest US involvement in the Vietnam War.[121] Stories about "good children gone bad" are chilling precisely because of the expectation of innocence that is associated with youth. A deviant child shocks society far more than a criminal adult. Narratives of deviance describe or allude to young people as having developed their bad behaviors at an early age, rendering them as irredeemable—and as omens of a society in distress.

In many instances, of course, these deviant young people have done nothing more than to challenge adults in charge—to demand change and reform. For instance, in 1968, the Black Panther Party, a group of young Black activists focused on reducing police brutality in their community, started a free breakfast program for students of color in Oakland. Their goal was well-meaning: to combat the scourge of malnourishment that sent many Black students to school hungry, fatigued, and unable to concentrate. Teachers and principals saw the program's favorable effects immediately, recalls a breakfast program volunteer. Once nourished, the children "weren't falling asleep in class, they weren't crying with stomach cramps," and teachers noted "how alert they were."[122] The program spread quickly, feeding thousands of children every day across multiple cities and improving student performance in school. Because of its unmitigated success and the continued need, the program became a required offering at each of the roughly forty-five Panther chapters in cities nationwide.[123] It also became an immediate target of the Federal Bureau of Investigation (FBI). Responding to internal debates about the danger of the Panthers, FBI Director J. Edgar Hoover issued a stern warning to agents who had been moved to leniency toward the Panthers because of the breakfast program.

You state that [the bureau should not attack the breakfast program] because many prominent "humanitarians," both white and black, are interested in the program as well as churches which are actively supporting it. You have obviously missed the point. The BPP [Black Panther Party] is not engaged in the "Breakfast for Children" program for humanitarian reasons. This program was formed by the BPP for obvious reasons, including their efforts to create an image of civility, assume community control of Negroes, and to fill adolescent children with their insidious poison.[124]

Under Hoover's direction, FBI agents acted quickly to urge varied community groups to reject the program. In Richmond, Virginia, they warned parents that Panther members were using the breakfasts to teach Black children to "hate white children."[125] In Philadelphia and New York City, agents claimed that Panther members were poisoning the breakfasts or were using them as training grounds for "teaching children to kill." And in San Francisco, parents and children were warned that the free breakfasts were "infected with a venereal disease."[126] In Chicago, one Panther member recalls, "The night before [the first breakfast program] was supposed to open . . . the Chicago police broke into the church and mashed up all the food and urinated on it."[127] These tactics worked. Despite its widespread success, the program ended as quickly as it had begun. Panthers served their last breakfasts in the early 1970s.

Of course, as we now know from historical records, Hoover's FBI were determined to villainize many young activists beyond the Panthers. Members of the Students for a Democratic Society (SDS) were subjected to similar forms of FBI surveillance and sabotage. Today, young activists who attempt to pursue voting rights, champion immigrant inclusion, advocate for gay rights, decry sexual assault, or fight against policy brutality (as the Black Panthers did) are often disparaged as much as their predecessors were. For instance, the efforts of high schoolers to establish Gay Straight Alliances have come under fire from some officials in Utah expressing "serious concerns about the group's moving into recruitment of fresh meat for the gay population,"[128] and from talk radio's Dr. Laura Schlessinger, who insisted that "we don't want it in schools, and we don't want it to be recognized on the same level as heterosexuality."[129] Student-heavy groups like Black Lives Matter have been labeled "Black identity extremists" by members of the intelligence community and described by critics as racists or terrorists in public debate.[130] Attempts to denigrate these young people and their efforts have been a staple of adult-initiated backlashes against youth activism and play on latent fears about youth-led insurrections. Deviance frames—whether used to discredit youth activism or to highlight young criminals—send an important message: young people cannot be trusted and must be controlled.

School shooting narratives offer a distinctive window onto the ways in which children can operate as both innocents and deviants depending on the child and the context. When children are the victims of adult evil, we can mourn the children without compromise; we grieve the loss of young lives and the pain of those forced to bear witness to violence. When adults are the perpetrators of these violent acts, our expectations of and belief in youth innocence remains intact. When young people commit child violence, however, this assumption of innocence is upended—and so too is our faith in our collective child-rearing capacities. If young people are capable of adult violence, what does that imply about the special place that children occupy? What does that say about the quality of the nation's caregiving? If young people are capable of violence without remorse, is society truly able to control its dependents or instill a strong moral code?

We can see some of these tensions in the differing narratives describing white victims or perpetrators of school shootings and those involving students of color. In 1999 Columbine High School seniors Eric Harris and Dylan Klebold, murdered twelve students and one teacher (while injuring twenty-one others) in what was then the deadliest school shooting in US history. In the aftermath of this tragedy, pundits and journalists scrambled to develop theories to explain why the two boys, who committed suicide during the attack, could have performed such a horrifying act of violence. They speculated about the role of poor parenting, bullying, inept teaching, and the boys' alleged membership in an allegedly subversive "Trench Coat Mafia." But investigators later found that these theories did little to explain the boys' shocking violence. As journalist and author Dave Cullen later observed, "We were so anxious to answer that burning question for you that we jumped to conclusions on tiny fragments of evidence in the first days, even hours."[131]

Of course, in the decades since the Columbine tragedy, mass shootings committed by young people have become far too frequent. Parkland, Virginia Tech, Sandy Hook are just a few in a long list of shootings that have claimed the lives of young people and have chipped away at myths of youthful innocence. Still, as the examples rack up, we continue to search for the *reason* these young perpetrators commit such monstrous acts. Reporters, parents, and fellow students cited Nicholas Cruz's attention deficit hyperactivity disorder (ADHD) and autism in the early days following the Parkland High School massacre, during which seventeen were killed. In their interpretation of why

Adam Lanza murdered twenty-seven first-graders and staff at Sandy Hook, journalists and expert commentators focused on his obsession with violent video games, Asperger's syndrome, anxiety disorders, and his mother's gun enthusiasm. In each of these incidents, and dozens more like it, the public is quick to try to identify an explanation for this deviation from the norm, and almost always the ready explanation is mental illness. Of course, the notion of child violence as an aberration is to be expected. For one, statistically, school-age children are not traditionally the regular perpetrators of acts of deliberate or calculated violence.[132] What is noteworthy, however, are the varied narratives and reactions that emerge when certain kinds of kids commit these crimes.

Columbine is often seen as the first of its kind—a dire inflection point signaling countless school tragedies to follow.[133] Yet, gun violence at school is hardly a new phenomenon. In 1993 alone, as many as thirty-five instances of gun violence at school were reported—resulting in an estimated thirty-seven fatalities.[134] Gun violence remains the second most frequent reason for youth fatalities, second only to motor vehicle accidents.[135] Gun violence against children of color is especially prolific. Black youth are more than ten times more likely to die from firearm homicide than their white peers.[136] When these racial disparities are separated by gender, the gap is even more pronounced. Black boys are seventeen times more likely to perish by gun violence than are their white counterparts.[137] Yet when shootings primarily involve children of color, we see a different kind—and frequency—of collective handwringing.[138] Some of this may hinge on public sympathies for the victims or the degree to which shootings are perceived as either extraordinary or newsworthy. Scholar Wanda Parham-Payne describes the attention deficit regarding Black victims as perpetuating "the perception that crime is simply the cultural norm in urban areas facilitating a notion that the shooting deaths of children or minors in urban areas are an unfortunate manifestation of that norm."[139]

And while white males are frequently the perpetrators of mass shootings[140]—including those at schools—treatment of them in news coverage and by public officials reveals a continued collective shock but also a need to seek out how this could have happened. Rarely does the perpetrator's race become a factor in media coverage when the perpetrator is white. Far more frequently, journalists center their inquiry on mental illness or some other potentially mitigating factor—something to explain how a presumptively good white child could commit such a heinous act.[141] When young people of color are the perpetrators, however, race frequently seems to be the first, and sometimes the only, factor considered.

A study comparing the shooting at Virginia Tech with Harris and Klebold's massacre at Columbine observes that, "although the two incidents were more similar than different, . . . media coverage of the VT [Virginia Tech] incident as a whole consistently exhibited one attribute—race—that Columbine coverage had been criticized for overlooking."[142] While the Virginia Tech shooter's race and immigrant status were especially prominent throughout peak coverage of the shooting, in Columbine coverage "there was never any mention of the race of the killers . . . none of the [news media] even made mention of . . . the fact that there were 12 other school shootings initiated by young White males."[143] This finding is all the more surprising when we consider the prominent role that race *did* play in the backstory of Columbine. Harris and Klebold had, specifically, scheduled the shooting to occur on the 110th anniversary of Adolf Hitler's birthday. Harris had fixated on Nazi Germany in his schoolwork and interactions, writing papers discussing "the Jewish race" and using Nazi salutes to greet friends. Nevertheless, the role of race, anti-Semitism, or even hate more generally is downplayed in coverage of Columbine. Instead, Harris's Nazi sympathies are described as a "fascination for the German language, culture and history."[144] Cynthia Willis-Chun finds that regional fixations can also play a role in the treatment that perpetrators receive by journalists. In her study of Columbine coverage, she finds that journalists made frequent reference to urban centers as the more typical venues of violence, because of "drugs and gangs." Willis-Chun argues that in these instances "'urban' functions as code for racialized and financially unstable, suggesting that the violence at Columbine High was all the more shocking because it defied American assumptions about both whiteness and middle-classness."[145]

Deviant children narratives inject powerful (and dangerous) counterfactuals into policy debates that center on presumptions of children's innocence and dependence. Democratic societies often rely on the notion that children are innocent. Entire policies and institutions are erected in support of this conception. When children are perceived as violating this rule, they not only dash these expectations, they delegitimize the hallmarks of public policy and compel abdication of state support. If innocent children awaken armies of supporters or protectors, deviant children send the public running for cover.

The Outsiders: Children Unfit for Our Society

Many of the most negative depictions of children in politics have nothing to do with their individual beliefs or behavior. As noted earlier, young people can be demonized by influential political actors simply based on their economic class, place of origin, race, ethnicity, religion, or sexual preference. Once again, the status of being a child intersects with other social identity constructions to produce systems of discrimination and oppression. Because they belong to groups deemed by certain social and political elites as undesirable and even unworthy of national inclusion, some children are treated as less than others. Their status as outsiders, in this rendering, justifies their marginalization and subjugation. Consider, for example, the experience of India's Dalit children. For generations under India's historical Hindu caste system, Dalits were "untouchables" because they were considered outside caste and thus excluded altogether. Marginalized from nearly all facets of Indian society, Dalits endured centuries of oppression and cycles of poverty. Despite contemporary Indian and international laws that bar discrimination against Dalits, "untouchable" children struggle for education, food, water, and healthcare. Dalit children attending government schools endure discrimination and violent attacks; most give up on education before they are eleven years old. The hit 2008 British film, *Slumdog Millionaire*, features the story of a boy named Jamal growing up in the Juhu slums of Mumbai, presumably as one of about 170 million Dalits. Jamal and his brother beg and steal to avoid being forced into slavery. Their desperation is not far removed from reality. "Dalits are widely abused," explains the author of a sweeping study of India's untouchables, "and they live lives of constant humiliation, indignity and violence . . . . It really is a kind of institutionalized, slow genocide."[146]

In the United States, the children of "new" immigrant groups typically have inspired particularly negative depictions by nativists over time, including an emphasis on their presumed inferiority and the alleged dangers they pose to society. In the early twentieth century, for example, the restriction-minded Dillingham Commission charged by Congress to study immigration's impact on US society followed this pattern. The commission issued sweeping findings on "the children of immigrants in schools" that purportedly showed that the intelligence of and "rate of progress" for offspring of northern and western Europeans far outpaced those of southern and eastern Europeans, Asians, Mexicans, and Africans.[147] Tellingly, the social scientists authoring this study as commission staffers failed to control for variables such as duration of residence in the United States, language, or parental education or class. Indeed, they concluded that the children of immigrants from non-traditional European source countries (such as Russia, Italy, Greece, Poland, and Hungary) and the offspring of all nonwhite, non-European newcomers represented a grave threat to the nation's well-being. Other Dillingham studies associated children of "new" immigrants with higher levels of criminality, insanity, and public welfare dependence.[148] Nativist lawmakers seized on these findings about immigrant children to help justify codifying a literacy test, an increased head tax, a national origins quota system, and an Asiatic-Barred Zone in federal immigration policy.[149] Protests from social reformer Jane Addams and anthropologist Franz Boas notwithstanding, the Dillingham Commission's depiction of new immigrant youth as inferior and ultimately corrosive to US society was largely unchallenged until after the Second World War.[150]

Contemporary immigration debates have featured comparable efforts by nativists to cast the children of undocumented immigrants, especially those from Mexico and Central America, as outsiders who are undeserving and dangerous. Anti-immigrant political leaders, right-wing media, and restrictionist organizations like Numbers USA and the Federation for American Immigration Reform (FAIR) have painted unauthorized immigrants as competitors for jobs and scarce resources, threats to national security and the rule of law, and cultural "others" who will tear apart social cohesion and national unity. As Leo Chavez has observed, these contemporary immigrant threat narratives almost invariably focus on the perceived perils of Latino newcomers.[151] In 1994, California's Proposition 187, popularly called the Save our State (SOS) initiative, aimed to deny social services to undocumented immigrants and to prohibit their children from attending public schools. A few years later, House Republicans and the GOP platform endorsed the Gallegly Amendment (named for its chief sponsor Edward Gallegly, a nativist House member from California) that would block birthright citizenship (*jus soli*) for the children of undocumented parents.[152] At the heart of this proposal to fundamentally alter US constitutional and citizenship law was a deep-seated resentment that the children of unauthorized immigrants gained the same rights and privileges as anyone else born in US territory. Border hawks warned that these "anchor babies" presented opportunities for their undocumented relatives to gain legal status.[153] In contemporary struggles over immigration, nativists like Representative Steve King (R-IA) describe the children of unauthorized Latinx migrants as both menacing and deviant. Challenging narratives of undocumented Dreamers as among the nation's "best and brightest," King and other nativists portray these young people as violent drug runners, gang-bangers, and terrorists.[154]

In the panhandle of Florida from 1900 until 2011, thousands of Black boys considered juvenile delinquents were required to do time and forced labor at the Dozier School for Boys (originally the Florida School for Boys). Most were aged 9–16, and they were largely viewed as expendable by state officials and school staff on account of their race, economic class, and demonstrated "incorrigibility." In truth, the offenses that sent boys to the Dozier facility ranged from violent crimes and theft to minor infractions like school truancy, cigarette smoking, or running away from home. The Dozier School also made profits from the forced labor of their charges, compelling boys as young as seven to work in the fields, harvest crops, tend and slaughter livestock, and cut down timber. "There are many different faces of slavery because it disguises itself," explains genealogist and peonage expert Antionette Herrell.[155] Dozier also became notorious for a staff that beat, raped, and tortured boys who were deemed essentially disposable. When allegations of cruelty and abuse at the juvenile reformatory surfaced every few decades, the state launched investigations and installed new school leadership. Yet the beatings and torture persisted. "You didn't know when it was coming," recalls Jerry Cooper, who attended the school in the late 1950s and nearly died after being lashed more than one hundred times. "These were not spankings. These were beatings, brutal beatings." When the Dozier School was finally closed in 2012, forensic experts were called to the school to analyze unmarked graves scattered across its sprawling campus. They soon discovered evidence of children from different generations who had been murdered and buried outside the school's designated graveyard.[156] What happened at this infamous Florida juvenile reformatory serves as an inspiration for Colson Whitehead's novel, *The Nickel Boys*. The book's protagonist, Elwood Curtis, is sent to a Florida juvenile reformatory called the Nickel Academy, which promises to transform delinquent boys into "honorable and honest men." Yet in reality, Nickel Academy is "a grotesque chamber of horrors where the sadistic staff beats and sexually abuses the students, corrupt officials and locals steal food and supplies, and any boy who resists is likely to disappear 'out back.'"[157] The expendability of poor Black boys imprisoned in cruel juvenile reformatories—whether the fictional Nickel Academy or the actual Dozier School—could not have been more literal.

Collateral: Leveraging Children as Bargaining Chips

The idea of using children as political collateral will resonate for anyone with even a passing knowledge of the *The Hunger Games* trilogy of books and films. In the dystopian, futuristic world created by the author Suzanne Collins, the nation of Panem is ruled by a wealthy and technologically sophisticated Capitol city in the Rocky Mountains surrounded by twelve poorer districts. The story's narrator and protagonist is a teenage girl, Katniss Everdeen, who lives in District 12 amid scarce resources and starvation. As punishment for a failed rebellion against the powerful Capitol in the past, a boy and girl (aged between twelve and eighteen) are selected by lottery from each of the twelve other districts. These twenty-four "Tributes" are forced to participate in a televised annual pageant called the Hunger Games, during which all citizens must watch these Tributes struggle to survive in a large, wild arena filled with menacing animals and dangerous traps. Each year, the twenty-four Tributes ultimately must fight to the death until one victor remains. In addition to exacting regular retribution for the past rebellion, the Hunger Games provide entertainment for residents of the Capitol. Chillingly, these young Tributes also are leveraged to remind subjects of poorer districts of the Capitol's might and ruthlessness in maintaining authoritarian control.[158] Collins tells interviewers that she drew inspiration for the "reaping" of her Tributes at annual Hunger Games from the Greek myth of Theseus in which the King of Crete forced Athens to pay for past crimes by giving seven boys and seven girls each year to the Minotaur, which hunts them down in a terrifying labyrinth. Of course, the use of children as political collateral is not confined to novels and films.[159]

Family welfare caps offer another glimpse of children being leveraged for political purposes. The idea of family caps on public assistance caught fire in the 1990s at a time when welfare reform was popular and elected officials in both parties sought to encourage greater self-sufficiency. Policymakers were particularly interested in fostering greater "personal responsibility" among the nation's dependent poor, railing against out-of-wedlock births and preaching the virtues of mandated work requirements. Determined to reign in "waste, fraud, and abuse" of what was then Aid to Families with Dependent Children (AFDC) and later Temporary Aid to Needy Families (TANF), some reformers argued that dependent adults were "milking" the system by having additional children to collect more cash assistance. These efforts were consistent with a long-standing preoccupation of officials with the reproductive behavior of the poor, as well as familiar racial stereotypes about "welfare queens" draining public coffers by having more children.[160]

New Jersey led the way in capping payments in 1992 as part of its "Work First" program, establishing a Child Exclusion Law that denied additional assistance (less than $100 extra per month) for poor parents who had more children. Two years later, Arkansas, California, and Massachusetts followed suit with their own "maximum family" laws. During the 1994 midterm election, Republicans helped stage an historic takeover of the House of Representatives by calling for a "Personal

Responsibility Act" that prominently sought "to discourage illegitimacy and teen pregnancy by prohibiting welfare to minor mothers and denying increased [benefits] for additional children on welfare—to promote individual personal responsibility." Federal welfare law ultimately granted states the option to impose caps on maximum family payments. "Families must face more directly whether they are ready to care for the children they bring into this world," Senate Majority Leader Robert Dole (R-KS) proclaimed. As Congress and the White House worked together to pass major bipartisan welfare reform in 1996, a parade of family cap laws passed in states in every region. By 2003, twenty-two states denied additional public assistance to low-income mothers who have more children while receiving welfare.[161]

Family cap laws were designed to dissuade poor women dependent on public support from having more children. But they clearly did so by leveraging the well-being of *all* children living in these households (both newer children who were technically excluded and older siblings who were covered), since capped incomes for growing families obviously imposed economic pain far beyond the penalized parents. In other words, the de facto logic of these family welfare caps is that creating disincentives for "irresponsible mothers" outweighs the financial merits of a modest per capita increase in cash assistance dedicated for each new child. As such, these policy blueprints make poor children bargaining chips in their efforts to encourage personal responsibility.

In practice, family caps had no effect on the size of families receiving welfare (10 percent of households with more than two children received public assistance in 2012, as had 10 percent in 1990). But they did have a significant impact on poor children. After more than two decades of their implementation, various experts found that family welfare caps increased the deep poverty rates of children by more than 13 percent, placed sanctioned families at greater risk of homelessness, food insecurity, and hospitalization, and impeded the learning and development of impacted children.[162] In Massachusetts, for instance, a study undertaken by researchers and pediatricians at Boston Medical Center found that "families of infants, toddlers, and preschoolers who were subject to the family cap had more household and child food insecurity and poorer health among children."[163] Similar studies in California led state legislators to question the original assumptions and logic of the policy. "I don't know a woman—and I don't think she exists—who would have a baby for the sole purpose of having another $130 a month," said state Senator Holly Mitchell (D) in 2016. "That makes no sense."[164] Back in New Jersey where the policy had begun, experts found that the maximum family grant rule made no difference in the size of families on welfare—but the cap did exclude 20,000 children from direct coverage. "It didn't have any effect on their birthing choices," one policy analyst concluded regarding New Jersey's mothers receiving public assistance. "But it has a huge impact on impoverishing the child."[165] Despite these findings, Republican Governor Chris Christie vetoed a repeal of New Jersey's family cap in 2016 based on the original argument that increased support for additional children created perverse incentives for welfare mothers. In the end, New Jersey repealed its family welfare cap in 2018, two years after California and one year before Massachusetts—although more than a dozen states still have family caps in place.[166] This policy experiment—fueled by well-worn myths of "welfare queens" and a familiar preoccupation by reformers and officials with the reproductive behavior of poor people—offers a vivid portrait of children as political collateral.[167]

The Trump administration's explosive "family separation" policy on the US-Mexican border provides one more prominent—and polarizing—illustration of how children may be intentionally used as political collateral or bargaining chips. As we noted earlier in this section and at the beginning of this chapter, new immigration has long inspired nativists to denigrate the offspring of newcomers as unfit for our society—drawing invidious distinctions between "our" native-born kids and "their" forever-foreign kids.[168] At the end of 2017, officials leading federal immigration enforcement efforts during the Trump presidency developed a plan for discouraging unlawful border crossings by putting migrant children in the crosshairs of a draconian crackdown. Troubled by reports of a marked increase in unauthorized entries, three key figures—Customs and Border Patrol Chief Kevin McAleenan, Acting Immigration and Customs Enforcement Director Thomas Homan, and Citizenship and Immigration Services Director L. Francis Cissna—presented a drastic policy response to their boss, Secretary of Homeland Security Kirstjen Nielson. At the heart of their proposal was the notion of creating a huge disincentive for those entering US territory without permission: the guarantee that, if caught, their children would be taken away while they faced criminal prosecution. In December 2017, Nielson rejected this plan for separating migrant children from their parents as too extreme. It was not the first time that Trump appointees closely aligned with nativist and immigration restriction groups sought to turn migrant children into key bargaining chips of a new deterrence policy. Nielson's predecessor at the Department of Homeland Security (DHS), John Kelly, had rebuffed similar efforts to advance family separation as a dramatic means of discouraging migrant parents from unlawfully entering the country.[169]

While first Kelly and then Nielson stymied family-separation blueprints at DHS, they found a receptive audience at the Justice Department in 2018 when they came to the attention of Attorney General Jeff Session. For two decades as a Republican senator from Alabama, Sessions was a fierce border hawk and a darling of the immigration restriction movement. During his second year as attorney general, Sessions and his advisers sought to assert themselves more forcefully on immigration control matters. One limitation on US border enforcement was a consent decree from a 1997 federal court decision, *Flores v. Reno*—which became known as the Flores settlement—which prohibited Customs and Border Patrol (CBP) from detaining children caught unlawfully crossing the border with guardians for more than twenty days. For years, under Democratic and Republican presidents, CBP officials responded to the Flores settlement by swiftly processing and releasing adult immigrants who unlawfully entered the United States with their children.[170] Yet DHS officials like McAleenan, Homan, and Cissna, as well as restriction-minded Justice Department officials, argued in 2017 and 2018 that separating migrant parents and children—sending the children to the Department of Health and Human Services (HHS) as "unaccompanied alien minors"—would allow CBP to detain adults for much longer periods of time. If this family-separation policy were implemented broadly and unflinchingly, they reasoned, it would create a powerful disincentive for migrant families contemplating entry without authorization and a strong punishment for those who were caught doing so.[171]

Sessions embraced the plan and set the wheels in motion by announcing the Justice Department's "zero tolerance" for unlawful border crossers in April 2018. Existing law makes it a criminal offense to unlawfully enter the United States without proper inspection at a port of entry (unauthorized physical presence in the country is a civil violation rather than a criminal infraction). A first offense for "illegal entry" is a misdemeanor under the federal code, punishable by a fine, up to six months in jail, or both. For decades, migrants caught entering the United States without authorization usually were charged with misdemeanors and quickly released. However, Session's "zero-tolerance" meant that all unauthorized border crossers would, in his words, "be met with the full prosecutorial power of the Department of Justice." And the prosecution of all unlawful border crossers boxed Nielson into a corner, since CBP would be required to refer all such cases to the Justice Department and to separate adults from their children while the parents awaited prosecution. By the end of April 2018, Nielson approved recommendations from McAleenan, Homan, and Cissna on how DHS could coordinate with other executive officials on new zero-tolerance and family-separation policies.[172]

As we discussed at the outset of this chapter, the consequences of these administrative initiatives were traumatic for migrant families, especially separated children. By the end of May 2018, six weeks after Sessions' zero-tolerance policy was rolled out by DHS and the Justice Department, more than 2,000 migrant children from toddlers to teenagers were torn away from their parents and held under conditions that violated longstanding standards established under the *Flores* settlement. Judges, advocates, and reporters soon learned that few migrant parents were informed about what was happening, that many children were taken away by CBP officials under the pretense that they would soon return after being fed and cleaned, and that other officers forcibly separated parents from wailing children with no explanation. Days and weeks after separation, anguished parents hauled into courtrooms for prosecution pleaded to know where their children were and when they would see them again. Government officials offered no answers— and few could provide information to desperate parents even if they wanted to. The inspector general for the HHS found that none of the responsible federal agencies had developed a centralized database to track the location of migrant children or to match them with separated parents. Moreover, the administration never established a plan for reuniting migrant parents with children taken away by CBP officers. In the rush to implement the zero-tolerance policy, Trump appointees paid no heed to warnings from other officials that more preparation was needed. The Trump administration revealed in a court filing that the government had deported hundreds of parents for illegally entering the country, while their children were still held somewhere in the United States.[173]

While some of these children were placed with foster families far from the US-Mexico border, most endured mass detention in tent centers or deserted big-box stores. The US public quickly learned about what was happening to these migrant children from graphic news coverage as well as heart-wrenching images and audio smuggled out of detention centers. Despite a strong partisan divide over immigration issues, an overwhelming majority of Americans told pollsters that the family separation policy was "unacceptable."[174] Some administration officials were unapologetic about the results. Attorney General Sessions, as we noted earlier, made no bones about the fact that these policies were designed to leverage children and punish parents—"*if you don't like that, then don't smuggle children over our border.*"[175] Yet the White House, under fire at home and abroad for a crisis of its own making, sought to quell the backlash in the summer of 2018 by sending DHS Secretary Nielson before reporters to justify the policy. Nielson's press conference did nothing to quiet the storm, as she struggled to answer a barrage of questions that highlighted the innocence and unfair victimhood of detained children: "Have you seen the photos of children in cages? "How is this not child abuse?" "Have you heard the audio clip of these children wailing?"[176]

President Trump ultimately issued a 2018 executive order that signaled—albeit vaguely—that it was ending its family separation policy. In truth, both court-appointed lawyers and the DHS inspector general found one year later that hundreds of migrant children were still enduring prolonged detention under "inhuman" conditions, in violation of the *Flores* settlement. Revealingly, the trauma endured by roughly 2,400 migrant children under this policy elicited strikingly different reactions. On the one side were a sizeable majority who were outraged by the suffering and who saw these children in universal terms. On the other were a notable minority who minimized the ordeal (mass detention was "like a summer camp")[177] and who perceived the migrant children as undesirable "others." As the family-separation policy was implemented, former First Lady Laura Bush wrote a high-profile opinion piece for *The Washington Post* denouncing the policy as "cruel" and "immoral." President Obama similarly described the plight of these migrant families in terms of broad collective values: "Are we a nation that accepts the cruelty of ripping children from their parents' arms, or are we a nation that values families, and works to keep them together?" Yet others fervently defended Sessions' hardline approach, drawing well-worn distinctions between *our* children and *their* children. "Like it or not, these aren't our kids," Fox & Friends host Brian Kilmeade told viewers, while Iowa Congressman Steve King (R) tweeted that many detained children "are old enough to be tried as adults and are prime MS-13 gang material."[178] Using children as political collateral or bargaining chips ultimately requires proponents of these policies to challenge the equal worth of the young people being leveraged. Indeed, doing so is inextricably tied to political and social categorizations of race, ethnicity, class, and immigration status that create overlapping systems of discrimination and oppression for particular groups of migrant children.

Conclusion

Whereas Chapter 2 provided a foundation for understanding the core principles, laws, and practices governing children in liberal democracies, our task in this chapter has been to focus on the ways in which children are invoked or manipulated politically for good or ill. In particular, we have considered the deployment of children as potent political symbols, participants, and collateral—what we call the political leveraging of children. Sometimes images and stories about children are enlisted to inspire politically, to symbolize innocence, or to highlight the need for reform on behalf of the most vulnerable and sympathetic members of society. In other instances, children are leveraged as activist armies—as they were in Progressive Era labor organizing and the "long" civil rights movement—by those seeking to gain attention and mobilize action by eliciting empathy toward innocents. But, despite their frequent allure as exemplars of innocence, children also are appropriated as symbols of deviance, threat, and social decay. The "othering" of children has been a familiar frame in US politics from fears of unassimilable "new" immigrant kids at the turn of the century, to wayward counter-culture youth of the sixties, to contemporary so-called "gang-bangers" and "anchor babies." Likewise, political actors have used children as collateral to be leveraged for instrumental purposes such as the Trump administration's policy of separating migrant children from their parents and detaining them as means of discouraging unauthorized border crossings. In short, children have been leveraged as politically potent symbols, activists, and collateral to advance often rival agendas.

As much as adults have sought to structure and shape the ways children are invoked and mobilized in political life, young people are not always willing to follow the well-laid plans of their elders. Indeed, children have the capacity to lead and inspire in ways that belie their age. We caught glimpses in this chapter of how democratic politics can be transformed by determined and independent-minded young activists like those who marched in the "Children's Crusade" of 1963 Birmingham. Only a few years earlier, one of the most important young organizers of the Civil Rights Movement, Diane Nash, had defied Kennedy administration officials when she and other activists refused to end Freedom Rides on public buses through the Deep South despite enormous dangers. At the instructions of his boss, Attorney General Robert Kennedy, John Seigenthaler called Nash in 1961 to "let her know what is waiting for the freedom riders" and to urge her to end the campaign. Nash's response stunned Seigenthaler:

She would not be moved and I felt my voice go up another decibel and then another and soon I was shouting, "Young woman do you understand? You're going to get somebody killed!" And there's a pause and she said, "Sir, you should know we all signed our last wills and testaments last night before we left. We know someone will be killed but we cannot let violence overcome nonviolence." That's virtually a direct quote of the words that came out of that *child's* mouth. Here I am an official of the United States government, representing the President and the Attorney General talking to a student at

Fisk university and she, in a very quiet but strong way, gave me a lecture.[179]

As we shall see in the pages that follow, Nash is one of many captivating young leaders who have made powerful claims on the political system. Thus far, we have explored how children are subject to diverse forms of protection, control, depiction, and appropriation. In the next chapter, we train a spotlight on how children have the potential to emerge as independent political actors and leaders, exercising meaningful agency in our democratic political life.

4

The Political Agency of Young People

We are building the DREAM Movement action-by-action, city-by-city, and campus-by-campus. In the spirit of the Freedom Rights and Chicano movements of the1960s, we have decided to put our bodies and lives on the line. Repeatedly, undocumented youth have risked the threat of physical violence, incarceration, and deportation by engaging in acts of non-violent direct action in order to push the immigrant rights movement forward . . . Our progressive allies insist on imposing their paternalistic stand to oppose the DREAM Act and tell us that this is not the "right" choice for us to acquire "legal" status in this country. We wonder: Who are they to decide for us?

—Open letter from Dreamer activists Neidi Domingues Zamorano, Jonathan Perez, Jorge Guitierrez, and Nancy Meza, September 2010.

I've heard it said that children are the future. Does it not count for people like me? At what age do I go from being an innocent child to being a threat? Maybe it's at 17 for walking to my house with a hoodie on. Or maybe it's at 12 for playing with a toy gun. Or maybe it's even before I had a chance to defend myself in my mother's womb.[1]

—Sydney Hart, teenage Black Lives Matter organizer, 2020

Democracy's Child. Alison L. Gash and Daniel J. Tichenor, Oxford University Press.
© Oxford University Press 2022. DOI: 10.1093/oso/9780197581667.003.0004

Introduction

The open letter, smoldering with defiance and hopeful purpose, laid bare deep generational conflict. Authored by four young activists of the Dreamer movement, the op-ed in *Dissent* magazine stunned established leaders and allies of the immigrant rights community when it appeared in print and online on September 21, 2010.[2] It was, in fact, a declaration of political independence by young dissident Dreamers who only a few years earlier were being trained by experienced immigrant rights organizers to lobby on Capitol Hill. But now they bristled when older immigrant rights leaders "encouraged us to avoid implementing 'controversial' tactics" in pursuit of legal protection for roughly two million undocumented youth. Inspired by "the youth activists of Birmingham" and "just as the Student Nonviolent Coordinating Committee followed the advice of Ella Baker to create their own organization independent of older organizations," these Dreamers insisted on a break with their original political mentors. "We do not want immigrant rights 'advocates' speaking for us any longer," they proclaimed. "We demand the right to represent ourselves!"[3]

The rift centered on a major difference over strategy: whether to push for a stand-alone DREAM Act to provide a conditional path to legal permanent residency for undocumented youth, or to make it part of a larger Comprehensive Immigration Reform Act (CIRA). Seasoned immigrant rights advocates, along with their allies in the Obama administration and Congress, favored the comprehensive approach and urged young Dreamers to show restraint.[4] Yet by 2010, many Dreamers were restless after CIRA, like so many previous efforts at comprehensive immigration reform, went nowhere in Congress, having failed to marshal bipartisan support. Dreamers also disagreed with older immigrant rights advocates that they had a friend in the White House. Although President Obama publicly championed legalization for an estimated ten to twelve million undocumented immigrants residing in the United States, Dreamers noted that he made immigration reform a lower priority than other initiatives in his first term. Even worse, in their eyes, was the fact that his administration deported a record number of undocumented immigrants under the mistaken view that it would make enforcement-oriented Republicans more willing to compromise on legalization.[5] While old guard reformers favored more conciliatory, insider tactics to pressure their allies in the administration, young Dreamers openly assailed Obama, branding him the "Deporter-in-Chief." They also launched a number of protest actions in 2010, designed to disrupt the political status quo, from high-profile marches and hunger strikes to getting arrested for blocking traffic and staging sit-ins at congressional offices.[6] Although considered ill-advised by more august immigrant organizers, Dreamers made it clear that "we have decided to put our bodies on the line. Repeatedly, undocumented youth have risked the threat of physical violence, incarceration, and deportation by engaging in acts of non-violent direct action in order to push the immigrant rights movement forward."[7]

The relationship between young Dreamers and established immigrant rights reformers had been markedly different only a few years earlier. Before 2010, experienced organizers recruited and trained young undocumented immigrants for media appearances, legislative testimony, and other public events. They typically selected youth who exemplified all-American values and enormous promise, such as high school academic and sports stars, in order to highlight the most sympathetic faces of the undocumented population. In turn, during much of this period, Dreamers eagerly followed the scripts they were given. Over time, however, deference gave way to anger and frustration among young activists as comprehensive reform languished and experienced organizers preached patience.[8] "Should we wait until there are another 1.8 million undocumented youth with little chance at a successful future?" the authors of the combative *Dissent* letter asked their elders. "We say hell no!" By 2010, the Dreamers were adamant that they would lead rather than follow in their quest for legal rights and democratic inclusion. "We are tired of our third-class status, and we are tired of the social justice elite dictating what we can and cannot do, all the while speaking on our behalf and pretending they represent our interests," they declared. "Undocumented students have shown the country and the world that we are more than capable of leading a new freedom-rights movement in this decade."[9]

As we elaborate later in this chapter, the Dreamers, in fact, did draft and execute their own blueprints for political action in the years that followed. Their mobilization placed them on a collision course not only with nativists and immigration restriction groups but also with President Obama, who would ultimately partner with them in producing major policy innovation. The fervent insistence of these young Dreamers that they forge their own path in the quest for social justice captures well the desire and ability of young people to act independently in the political realm. It is precisely this capacity of young people to make their own free political choices—and to leave their own significant marks on the polity—that is the focus of this chapter on *the political agency of children*. The Dreamers' trajectory of engagement reflects one important form of independent political activism, namely, the *emergent agency* of young people who are initially sponsored by adults but later break off to advance their own tactics, strategies, and goals. In addition to exploring emergent agency in the pages that follow, we will also consider various ways children can serve as political pioneers and agenda setters and their ability to reverse prescribed political (and social) roles by taking on crucial responsibilities unmet by adults. Whenever children exercise political independence, their agency can be both stirring and unsettling.

At the heart of the tensions described in Chapters 2 and 3 lies a profound struggle to identify the "special" role that children play in society, with equally profound implications for state actors, public resources, and the rule of law. Young people's dependency licenses significant state action and control. But what if children require no special status? What happens when young people break free of the constraints, reject the protections and instead assert themselves as autonomous actors? In important ways, it is this possibility—youth independence—that has fueled more than a few child-centered policies. As we have stated in previous chapters, lurking below the surface of many protective pleas, and more plainly visible in age-dependent limitations, is a concern or fear that children will reject their special status and demand equal recognition under the law.

For the most part, young people have accepted their dependency, and the benefits and limitations that follow. Yet, throughout history young people have stood up and demanded to be heard, not to appease adult leaders but as agents of their own interests and ideals. These moments have driven much of the youth-focused policy struggles we see. The potential for young people to unite for change and lead their own movements troubles even the most progressive adults. At the same time, organized youth outrage has facilitated watershed political and policy breakthroughs. When young people declare independence, act on their own, and assume command, the political world becomes both disconcerted by their audacity and inspired by their courage.

Thus far, in Chapters 2 and 3, we have looked at the ways in which policy reforms are advanced *for children*, in protectionist frames, and *through children* as symbols, participants, and collateral to be leveraged. Both approaches hinge on paternalistic assumptions about youth dependency, regardless of their intentions, and are based on the notion that children require adult supervision. But there are multiple landmark policy debates that have been initiated and shaped *by young people*. These instances highlight the capacity for children to simultaneously confront the constraints of their presumed dependency while also leading the charge for youth-centered political and policy transformation. Partly because of their presumptive deficiencies, youth-led calls for substantive reform prompt public attention—and surprise— in ways that adult-led movements do not. Young leaders benefit from the low expectations that adults continue to harbor (despite an abundance of history suggesting that their doubts are misplaced). But youth advocacy also may evoke dread. Some adults, even those who share the same passions as young people, perceive young leaders and movements as rash, ill-considered, and a challenge to adult authority. This chapter features young people as leaders and instigators of significant political reform with a focus on the emergent tensions between adult reliance on youth submission and youth demands for control.

Emergent Agency: From Foot Soldiers to Independent Activists

For many Millennials and others who grew up with the *Harry Potter* books and movies, the notion that children can evolve from innocent protégés to dauntless leaders is decidedly familiar. Harry Potter entered the world as the ultimate symbol of innocence—completely unaware of the role he played in a violent battle between good and evil and shielded from his own gifts as a wizard. When he is finally apprised of his "origin story," after years of emotional abuse and physical deprivation in the Dursley home, Harry enrolls at Hogwarts School of Witchcraft and Wizardry where he is taken under the wing of its fabled headmaster, Albus Dumbledore. Yet even as he develops enduring friendships with Ronald Weasley and Hermione Granger, and demonstrates talent as a young wizard (and as something of a Quidditch prodigy), his adult mentors ultimately cannot protect him from the dark wizard Lord Voldemort and his craven Death Eaters.[10]

While most adults in their lives proved either inept or complicit in the face of existential threats, Harry, Ron, Hermione, and other students like Ginny Weasley, Neville Longbottom, and Luna Lovegood became more reliant on each other—and more skeptical of their teachers and other authority figures. These students, in defiance of the feckless Ministry of Magic and in preparation for battling Voldemort, form a secret militia mockingly called "Dumbledore's Army"—a shout out to the Ministry's paranoid fears of a Dumbledore-inspired student coup. Harry realizes that his best option is to go after Voldemort and his Death Eaters. He leaves the safety of Hogwarts with Hermione and Ron in tow—Hermione taking the extra step of erasing herself from her muggle parents' memory to protect them, a form of selfless magical emancipation. Here, students are positioned as stalwart warriors who lead the charge to defeat Voldemort and his followers, rejecting adult attempts to deceive them or to shield them from harm.[11]

We see related themes in Susan Collins's *The Hunger Games*. As we discussed in Chapter 3, the series centers on annual survival games that were designed to discourage a revolution staged by resource-starved sectors against the opulent capital, requiring teenage representatives of each sector to battle to the death to appease authoritarian rulers and entertainment-seeking publics. As such, the games are meant to leverage the welfare of children to punish and constrain the behaviors of adults. The books showcase the actions of a resourceful teenage girl, Katniss Everdeen, who exploits a loophole in the games and takes the place of her younger sister when her sister is called to serve. Once drafted, Katniss does the unthinkable and saves the life of her sector partner (and supposed paramour), Peeta Mellark. Katniss's actions challenge those who believe that they could exploit the power of young people without also awakening their potential for free will and rebellion. The brewing gossip over Katniss and Peeta's relationship becomes fodder for a government-led campaign to market the games. Ultimately, Katniss and Peeta harness their popularity to overthrow the order. *The Hunger Games* series serves as a warning to those who dare to conflate age with disposition. Rather than accepting the benefits that accompany subservience, Katniss and Peeta position themselves as formidable opponents in a battle of wills against a government bent on command and control.[12]

Chapter 3 focuses on the ways in which young people have been used to shoulder the burdens of the adult world. However, those who have served as symbols, warriors, or collateral have also become leaders, innovators, and catalysts for their own reforms. In the Progressive Era, for instance, children who were used as cheap and flexible labor—particularly for the nation's largest publishers—banded together to fight their exploitation. In the industrializing United States, children in urban centers who were not employed by factories or as "home-work" assistants spent most of their days outdoors, playing on the streets. Publishing giants Joseph Pulitzer and William Randolph Hearst quickly identified the potential for profit in using these children to sell newspapers in the nation's most populous urban centers and "contracted" their services to sell papers on the street. The young workers earned pennies on the dollar of adult wages, but they were eager to please and willing to be exploited—to a point. In 1899, as the (largely media-driven) Spanish-American war came to an end, newspaper sales took a nosedive. Pulitzer and Hearst analyzed their options and realized that they could expand their profits by inflating the wholesale prices of the newspapers they sold to their already cash-strapped newsboys. They figured that the newsboys were too young and too poor to revolt, so the publishing giants squeezed them for additional profits. The newsboys demanded that the wholesale price be reduced to the pre-war amount of 50 cents for 100 newspapers and that the publishers reimburse the newsboys for any leftover inventory.[13]

Pulitzer and Hearst refused, vastly underestimating the organizing capacity of the newsboys; they shouldn't have. Inspired by unionizing among adult factory workers, newsboy strikes had occurred with increasing regularity in the nation's urban centers.[14] On July 19, 1899, Manhattan's newsboys and newsgirls collectively walked out, refusing to return to work until wholesale prices were reduced. The young protestors "didn't expect any aid from the grown-up unions, but declared that they would win anyway without extraneous aid."[15] Incensed and inspired, the "newsies" amassed in droves, as far away as Boston, Pittsburgh, and Providence, Rhode Island,[16] to protest the publishing giants, yelling "scab!" at the few who dared to cross their picket lines.[17] The newsie labor supply quickly dried up, as did newspaper sales.[18] And when competing publishing houses noticed the increasing protests, they eagerly publicized the strikes—generating widespread support.[19] On July 24, 1899, 5,000 newsboys gathered in and around New York's Irving Hall for a mass meeting called by the nascent Newsboys' Union.[20] Although the newsies were unable to secure the price reduction that motivated their strike, they forced the publishing giants to honor their original agreement of allowing newsboys to return any unsold newspapers—a significant cost saver for the underpaid laborers.[21]

The initial Newsboy Union did not outlast the 1899 strike, but the possibility of unionizing took root. In 1901, Boston's newsboys formed the Newsboys' Protective Union, which expanded in 1908 to affiliate with the American Federation of Labor (AFL).[22] The Chicago Newsboys' Protective Association organized in 1902 to facilitate efforts to get better working conditions. The group later unionized in 1909, affiliating (as did the Boston branch) with the AFL, and went on strike in 1912, prompting Hearst men to assault newsboy protestors.[23] Eight years later, in 1920, 175 Boston newsgirls unionized to combat the low wages they were paid by the Hotel and Railroad News Company.[24] Once envisioned as pawns or ways to make easy profits, the newsies changed their own fate, securing their legacy as revolutionaries.

In Chapter 3, we witnessed Diane Nash's stoic resolve, as she and fellow Freedom Riders "signed [their] last wills and testaments," refusing orders from Attorney General Kennedy to back down in the face of murderous white protestors. This is one of many examples of the *emergent agency* of young people that iconized civil rights era activism—something, as we have seen, that Dreamer activists carefully referenced as they went their own way in 2010. Roughly fifty years before them, in 1959, a small group of African American college students from a handful of southern cities had launched a series of dramatic sit-ins at segregated lunch counters to directly challenge Jim Crow discrimination. Trained at church and college workshops funded by Martin Luther King Jr.'s SCLC, these young people learned the tactics of nonviolent civil disobedience. One year later, a grant of $800 from the SCLC had allowed 126 student delegates representing fifty-eight sit-in groups from twelve southern states and various northern colleges to gather. Significantly, however, when Martin Luther King Jr., Ella Baker, and other SCLC leaders had convened the conference of young people who formed SNCC, they agreed that the gathering "should be youth centered" and that adults would speak "only when asked to do so."[25] It was this conference that would lead to the formation of the SNCC, as an important new movement player. Although originally conceived by King and others as a potential "youth division" of the SCLC, the young people who gave the SNCC life—including John Lewis, Diane Nash, James Bevel, Angeline Butler, Stokely Carmichael, and Marion Barry—were determined to be independent and to develop their own strategies for attacking racial subjugation and terror in the United States. The young SNCC insurgents proudly became known as "the shock troops of the revolution."[26]

One of the most important and dangerous campaigns led by young SNCC activists, without the blessing of more established civil rights organizations like the SCLC and the NAACP, was its Mississippi voter registration project of 1962–1966. This struggle to register African American voters led to an epic clash at the 1964 Democratic National Convention between older party and movement leaders, on the one side, and younger SNCC activists and their Mississippi Freedom Democratic Party (MFDP), on the other. At the Atlantic City convention that President Lyndon Johnson hoped to orchestrate as a unanimous coronation of his candidacy, SNCC and MFDP activists challenged the seating of an all-white delegation that the regular, segregationist Mississippi Democratic Party had selected to represent the state at the national convention. President Johnson negotiated with more established civil rights leaders of the SCLC, like Martin Luther King Jr., to avoid conflict at the televised party convention. Yet the MFDP delegates had been trained during Freedom Summer by fiery young SNCC leaders, like Robert Moses, who preferred confrontation over compromise. To the chagrin of Johnson and other Democratic leaders, a prime-time national audience was riveted when MFDP vice chair Fannie Lou Hamer spoke compellingly about their cause at televised hearings of the Democratic Credentials Committee. Hamer poignantly expressed the view of the MFDP and SNCC activists that the delegate fight was part of a larger struggle for the basic right to register to vote—to "become first class citizens."[27]

At the same time as journalists noted that "Hamer's account of her struggle for the right to vote against stubborn and violent resistance of white supremacists brought tears to the eyes of credential committee members," the Johnson White House worried that the Freedom Party controversy would steal the spotlight and fracture the convention. After Hamer's moving testimony was broadcast, the White House received 417 telegrams—all but one in support of seating the Freedom Democrats.[28] Hamer and other MFDP insurgents found themselves surrounded by news reporters after the Credentials Committee hearing, and state delegations from outside the Deep South greeted the Mississippi insurgents warmly when they presented their case against the selected Mississippi delegation. On the Atlantic City boardwalk, MFDP and SNCC activists assembled an outdoor exhibit documenting voter suppression, racial violence including Ku Klux Klan bombings, and segregated housing and public facilities. But the centerpiece of the display featured a tribute to James Chaney, Andrew Goodman, and Michael Schwerner, three young SNCC voting rights activists whose murders only a few months before had shocked and outraged the nation.[29] The new celebrity and political traction of MFDP and SNCC activists led President Johnson, with the assistance of Senator Hubert Humphrey and labor leader Walter Reuther, to pursue compromise on the Mississippi situation.[30] Humphrey, who would be selected as Johnson's running mate in 1964, told the president that SNCC and the Freedom Party insurgents had made a powerful case for meaningful party reform; their protest, he said, was "an expression of the conscience of the Democratic party, as to the importance of the right to vote . . . by all peoples in this country."[31]

In the end, Humphrey and Reuther were instructed to seek agreement on a three-part bargain: (1) seating the all-white Mississippi delegation if it pledged support for the party's presidential ticket; (2) giving two voting seats to the MFDP and making the rest of the

MFDP delegates honored guests of the convention; and (3) pledging to require racially integrated state delegations from the 1968 convention onward. Older civil rights reformers and liberal party politicians saw this bargain as both pragmatic and a significant stride forward toward racial justice. Southern state delegations were threatening to walk out of the convention if the selected Mississippi delegation was turned away. Moreover, Johnson warned established civil rights leaders, including Reverend King, that an unruly convention would threaten an electoral landslide and, with it, the possibility of enacting other major civil rights reforms beyond the Civil Rights Act of 1964.[32] As Johnson explained, "We don't want to cut off our nose to spite our face. If they [MFDP protesters] give us four years, I'll guarantee the Freedom delegation somebody representing views like that will be seated four years from now."[33] While he clearly was seeking to avoid a major rupture at the 1964 national convention, Johnson was in fact proposing a fundamental reform of convention rules that would have significant long-term consequences for the Democratic Party. For generations, state parties had sole authority to establish delegate selection procedures. Johnson's proposed solution to the MFDP controversy would establish a centralizing principle that would give the national party power in the future to decide not only how many votes each state delegation got at the national convention, but also to enforce uniform rules on what kinds of persons could be selected for those voting delegations.[34]

Through determined activism in Mississippi under the most dangerous circumstances, young SNCC and MFDP insurgents had forced dramatic change in partisan and electoral rules and ultimately the future composition and character of the Democratic Party. This was not lost on the African American press, which saw the fundamental revisions in party rules that would be enforced at the 1968 Democratic Convention as an important accomplishment, and cheered the SNCC and MFDP reformers for winning "a big change." The *Chicago Daily Defender*, for instance, celebrated that "the Democratic National Committee served notice that the convention will not seat 'lily white' delegations." Future delegations would be admitted "only from states where voters will have the opportunity to participate fully in party affairs, and to cast their ballots regardless of race, color, creed or national origins.'"[35]

Not surprisingly, SNCC leaders and Freedom Party delegates were in anything but a celebratory mood when the delegate controversy was officially concluded. They saw clearly that the long-term gains were proffered in exchange for capitulation at the 1964 convention on seating the Freedom Party with full credentials. These young activists scorned King, Reuther, and other movement elders for allowing Johnson to largely dictate the terms of compromise. For SNCC's Robert Moses, the 1964 MFDP compromise was akin to the "white plantation boss making all the decisions for his Black sharecroppers."[36] Although SNCC occasionally invited King and other SCLC figures to help with their voter-organizing efforts in Mississippi, which began in 1961, this struggle was led and run by young SNCC staff working closely with local civil rights groups within the state. The Mississippi Freedom Democratic Party challenge at the Democratic Convention was itself the product of a larger campaign involving hundreds of Black and white student volunteers—organized and coordinated by SNCC—to register and educate Black voters at Freedom Schools across the state. Little wonder that SNCC activists and MFDP delegates bristled when older movement leaders sought to negotiate a deal in Atlantic City with liberal Democratic allies. The resolution engineered by Johnson, Reuther, Humphrey, King, and others had the effect of further distancing the younger reformers of SNCC and the Congress of Racial Equality (CORE) from more moderate and established forces in the movement. As SNCC's Cleveland Sellers described this transformation, "Never again were we lulled into believing our task was exposing injustices so that the 'good people' of America could eliminate them. We left Atlantic City with the knowledge that the movement had turned into something else. After Atlantic City, our struggle was not for civil rights, but for liberation."[37] Indeed, the divide that emerged between SNCC and SCLC leaders over the process and substance of resolving the MFDP challenge presaged a more decisive break between these two iconic civil rights organizations in 1966, as SNCC chairman Stokely Carmichael preached Black Power and questioned nonviolence while King argued that "effective political power for Negroes cannot come through separatism."[38]

Through their defiant Mississippi campaign for Black voter registration and party recognition, the young SNCC advocates reached beyond more august civil rights groups and generated extraordinary pressure on an enormously powerful president and the Democratic establishment. Despite the deep tensions and disillusionment that surfaced at the 1964 convention between younger and older movement leaders and between young reformers and Johnson, all of these figures formed an uneasy partnership in pressing major rules reform on the Democratic party and in championing the passage of the landmark Voting Rights Act of 1965.[39] The young people who founded the SNCC had participated in early 1960 sit-ins and were dedicated to nonviolent, direct action, and they built it as an independent youth-driven organization that generated its own projects and strategies. Through their emergent political agency, young SNCC activists played pivotal and distinctive roles as both leaders and foot soldiers, from the Freedom Rides of 1961 to the Birmingham Children's Crusade and March on Washington for Jobs and Freedom of 1963. Yet these young civil rights reformers demonstrated a new level of political independence and proficiency in 1964 with Freedom Summer and the formation of the Mississippi Freedom Democratic Party, efforts that relied heavily on the energy and talents of dynamic SNCC field secretaries and an interracial army of student volunteers.[40] Their independent activism helped fuel dramatic party and electoral reform and, ultimately, the enfranchisement of millions of African Americans.[41]

As we discussed at the start of this chapter, one can discern similar patterns of emergent agency in the conflicts that surfaced in the early twenty-first century between younger and older immigrant rights leaders and between the movement and President Barack Obama. During the early 2000s, a number of key immigrant rights organizations like the National Immigration Law Center (NILC) and Center for Community Change (CCC) worked closely with allies in Congress to author and advance the Development, Relief, and Education for Alien Minors Act (DREAM Act). This legislative proposal sought to extend legal status to young undocumented immigrants who had arrived in the United States as minors and who were succeeding in school and performing various forms of community service. Established immigrant rights groups recognized that undocumented youth—who became known as the Dreamers—were among the most sympathetic and appealing members of the more than ten million people living in the

United States without legal status. Indeed, the narrative that was care-fully developed about Dreamers was that they were typical American kids who shared core national values (countering nativist images of foreignness), that they were among the "best and brightest" who could bolster US economic and social life (rather than dreaded freeloaders), and that they were innocents who lacked legal status through "no fault of their own" (rather than culpable law-breakers).[42] To help under-score this narrative, seasoned immigrant rights organizers from NILC, CCC, and other groups carefully recruited and trained Dreamers who could be spotlighted as exceptional and deserving immigrants. These politically inexperienced young people were coached on public speaking and media relations, provided with talking points, and paired with seasoned advocates on lobbying days. As one established immi-grant rights lobbyist later candidly explained, in early DREAM Act efforts, hand-picked Dreamers arrived on Capitol Hill with "an immi-grant rights organizer next to them. It was very much like they were there to be shown—they didn't have agency."[43]

Once activated by the DREAM Act campaigns, many undocu-mented young people sought organizational vehicles to further their cause. Existing national, state, and local organizations favoring im-migrant rights were welcoming, but many Dreamers wanted to play more than an auxiliary role. "When we started, there was no space for us," recalls one young Dreamer. "It was like, 'Oh, you guys can come to our conference.'" Other Dreamers felt they were "being marginal-ized" in more established immigrant associations, and "always seen as a secondary or additional thing within organizations."[44] By the late 2000s, however, these young activists had developed dozens of inde-pendent organizations, especially on various college and university campuses across the country. Following the 2008 election, several of these groups came together to launch a national, Dreamer-led net-work, United We Dream (UWD), to help coordinate their efforts. Many Dreamer activists had, by the close of the decade, grown weary of following more established immigrant rights leaders and were in-creasingly resentful of being scripted. "This immigration movement was being led by politicians and allies and never undocumented people," one undocumented youth complained. "We were kind of fol-lowing what they were saying. Whenever a politician needed one of us, they would say, 'Hey, bring a student, we need him at this press conference.' There were many among us who felt like puppets, like we were being used."[45]

As this chapter's opening story recounts, Dreamer activists openly broke with their political mentors in 2010. In particular, they refused to follow the instructions of established organizers to exercise patience while comprehensive immigration reform (CIR) languished in Congress and the Obama administration detained and deported record numbers of undocumented persons. As one UWD leader put it, "We don't believe in burning any bridge. But we also know that our movement requires vision and leadership, and that leadership won't come from seniority or years of experience—it comes from inspiration."[46] Undocumented youth were also inspired by a more aggressive insurgency campaign. In particular, the UWD and other Dreamer groups focused on a series of direct actions to protest both state anti-immigrant legislation, like Arizona's SB 1070 "show-me-your-papers" law, and the Obama administration's enforcement policies. Regarding the latter, the Education Not Deportation (END) campaign rejected claims by Obama and Department of Homeland Security Secretary Janet Napolitano that until Congress passed reform legislation, they were obliged to enforce existing laws vigorously.[47]

In early 2010, four undocumented young people garnered extensive media attention through their 1,500 mile Trail of Dreams walk from Miami to Washington, DC. A few months later, Dreamers staged sit-ins at the offices of such US Senators as John McCain (R-AZ) and Kay Bailey Hutchison (R-TX), lawmakers who once supported DREAM legislation but reversed their stance under pressure from anti-immigrant groups in their base. At the same time, Dreamers challenged the narrative that they were especially deserving because their undocumented status was "no fault of their own." The problem with earlier portrayals of them as innocents, Dreamers argued after 2010, was that it vilified their undocumented parents and other elders as morally corrupt and undeserving. "We were brought here by our parents who are courageous and responsible and who would not let their children die and starve in another country," one activist proclaimed. "We no longer say 'through no fault of their own.'" Another demanded that politicians and reporters "stop blaming our parents for pursuing a

Figure 4.1 Obama and Dreamer Protestor, Chicago, 2014.

Source: Photo by Mandel Ngan. Getty Images. https://www.gettyimages.co.uk/detail/news-photo/protestor-holds-up-a-banner-as-a-guest-beside-her-reaches-news-photo/459582474?adppopup=true.

better life for us."[48] Dreamer organizations in the 2010s made clear that they favored legalization for their entire families and communities. Several key Dreamer leaders also came out as "queer, undocumented, and unafraid" while openly describing the burdens of dual exclusion and denigration as "illegals" and "faggots." In US society, both groups share the experience of hiding one's identity to avoid harm and stigmatization, and both groups understand what it means to "come out."[49]

As the direct protest actions by UWD leaders and other Dreamer activists expanded the following year, so too did media coverage and the attention of Democratic political officials in Washington. In April 2011, twenty-two Democratic senators—including prominent leaders like Harry Reid (NV) and Dick Durbin (IL)—signed a letter to President Obama urging administrative deportation relief for undocumented youth. By the spring of 2012, Valerie Jarrett, the president's senior advisor, and Cecilia Munoz, the domestic policy advisor and former senior vice president for the Office of Research,

Advocacy, and Legislation at the National Council of La Raza (NCLR)—the nation's largest Latino civil rights organization—held a meeting with UWD leaders. They did so to express strong support for their cause, but also to insist that President Obama had no legal authority to issue an order granting deportation protection. Seeking expert support, Dreamers reached out to leading immigration lawyers and legal scholars around the country who developed arguments explaining why the president was authorized to grant temporary relief.[50] They also continued to press their cause through protests assailing the president as Deporter-in-Chief and sought to unnerve the White House by entering discussions with Republican Senator Marco Rubio, who indicated that he was interested in reviving the DREAM Act in Congress. Immigration activists told the White House about these negotiations and made clear that the president's failure to preempt them with administrative action would have serious consequences for the 2012 election, especially in Florida, a crucial swing state, where Latino support would be critical to his re-election prospects.[51]

Officials in the Obama White House and leaders of the Dreamer movement predictably disagree on what specific developments tipped the scales, but the administration moved decisively in the spring of 2012 to use its unilateral executive powers to temporarily protect undocumented youth.[52] First, Secretary of Homeland Security Janet Napolitano, who hitherto had echoed the White House's demurrals, issued a memorandum that instructed the Immigration and Custom Enforcement (ICE) agency to exercise "prosecutorial discretion" to provide leniency for most undocumented immigrants who came to the United States prior to the age of sixteen. Then, following tense negotiations with immigration rights activists, Obama announced in June 2012 an executive initiative—Deferred Action for Childhood Arrivals (DACA)—that granted relief to an entire category of young immigrants, as many as 1.4 million people, who would otherwise have been subject to deportation.[53] Defying the reform blueprints of more established immigrant rights organizers, Dreamer activists had advanced an insurgent strategy that helped pressure the Obama administration to extend significant executive relief while Congress remained gridlocked.

Political Pioneers and Agenda Setters

SNCC and Dreamer activists followed a comparable path of evolving political agency in the 1960s and 2010s, starting as the recruits of established organizations before developing into independent-minded political actors successfully executing their own plans and strategies. But young people are, of course, fully capable of developing their own political acuity without first having worked with adults. In this section we focus on young people who launched their foray into politics as unconstrained activists, leaders, or movement-builders and shocked policy systems by making direct appeals to world leaders and disregarding age-related norms. Ten-year-old Samantha Smith wrote a letter to the Soviet leader Yuri Andropov urging him to pursue peace at the height of Cold War conflict in 1982.[54] In 2015, eight-year-old Mari Capeny wrote a letter to President Obama that inspired him to visit Flint and authorize $100 million in aid to address the city's water crisis.[55] In this section we examine young self-starters and trailblazers who launched their advocacy careers as solo-practitioners.

When the extraordinary creativity and drive of gifted children meet formal oppression, their collision can produce potent transgressive acts that challenge the prevailing social and political order. Not all of these acts need be overtly political ones; sometimes these transgressions can be influential artistic and literary contributions that indict the status quo. Consider Sister Juana Ines de la Cruz (originally named Juana Ramirez de Asbaje), the first published feminist in the Americas whose face currently adorns Mexico's two hundred peso bill. Born to a single Mexican mother in 1648, Ramirez was a prodigy who taught herself to read as a toddler. Denied access to formal schooling because she was a girl, she secretly took books from her grandfather's extensive library (also forbidden to girls) and hid in a nearby chapel to read. Intellectually voracious, Ramirez had taught herself basic math and Latin by the age of five. At eight, she was independently learning philosophy, Greek logic, and the Aztec language of Nahuatl. She soon started writing her own poetry and essays, and at age thirteen she was teaching other children in her town to read and write in Latin. Three years later, Ramirez's mother sent her to live with relatives in Mexico City, where she could continue her studies clandestinely, since she remained excluded from formal education. Privately she devised plans to disguise herself as a man to gain entrance to university classes. Her genius caught the attention of Mexico City's viceroy, who invited her to court as a lady-in-waiting; and when she was seventeen-years-old, he summoned forty noted scholars to test her on various scientific, literary, philosophical, and historical subjects. Ramirez famously wowed both the court and her inquisitors with her knowledge and intelligence.[56]

At the age of twenty, Ramirez determined that she had a "total disinclination to marriage" or any fixed occupation that "might curtail my freedom of study." Instead, she became a nun at the Convent of Santa Paula, where she taught schoolgirls and served as accountant and archivist. Thanks to the patronage of the city's viceroy, Sor Juana amassed in her own apartment an enormous private library and collection of scientific and musical instruments. In the years that followed, she emerged as a prolific and popular author of drama, poetry, and prose in Mexico and Spain. Yet with her renown came controversy, especially since her work attacked misogyny and criticized the hypocrisy of key church leaders. When she was forty-six, Sor Juana was condemned by the Bishop of Puebla and compelled to sell her library and collections to provide alms to help the poor. She died one year later nursing sister nuns during an epidemic. Yet her writings remained popular with Mexican and Spanish readers, and her work as the first published feminist of the New World gave her new prominence for contemporary audiences. Now a national icon of Mexico, Sor Juana provides a powerful story of a gifted girl with the courage to defy existing strictures to become a beacon for feminism and educational opportunity.[57]

A similar saga played out in nineteenth-century North Carolina, where the creative talent and rebellious spirit of another child challenged the odious slave system into which he was born, George Moses Horton, who disobeyed the slave codes to teach himself to read using spelling books, the Bible, and hymnals that he secretly procured. During tedious farm work on a tobacco plantation, which he loathed, Horton began composing poetry in his head. As a teenager, he sold poems along with plantation produce at the Chapel Hill farmers' market, soon being commissioned by University of North Carolina students to compose love poems for 25–50 cents each. While love poems won him a small profit, Horton preferred to focus his poetry on the weightier subjects of liberty and slavery:

> Oh, Heaven! and is there no relief
> This side the silent grave—
> To soothe the pain—to quell the grief
> And anguish of a slave?

> Come Liberty, thou cheerful sound,
> Roll through my ravished ears!
> Come, let my grief in joys be drowned,
> And drive away my fears . . . .

Horton's literary talents caught the attention of novelist Caroline Lee Hentz who helped him publish his first poetry collection, *The Hope of Liberty*, in 1829. Publicly protesting his slavery in poetry, Horton became the first Black person—let alone slave—to publish a book in the South. He continued to author and publish transgressive poetry in coming years, while in bondage, garnering the attention of key political leaders, abolitionists, and artists nationwide.[58]

Young trailblazers have also demonstrated the capacity to challenge the political status quo through bold direct action. Clara Lemlich, a young Ukrainian immigrant, did just that when she impatiently seized the spotlight at a mass rally of shirtwaist workers at New York's Cooper Union in November 1909. Lemlich got a job in the garment industry, as a child laborer, to help support her family soon after they arrived in New York. She and her coworkers endured grueling hours, low pay, and harsh treatment from their supervisors. Outraged by these conditions, Lemlich became active in the International Ladies Garment Workers' Union (ILGWU). Her fellow shirtwaist workers, nearly all women, admired her boldness in challenging the male leadership of their union and elected her to the executive council of the ILGWU's Local 25. She was soon leading shirtwaist makers in several local strikes.[59]

Lemlich gained broad notoriety, however, at the 1909 Cooper Union mass meeting of shirtwaist workers and their supporters. After listening for two hours to prominent US labor organizers and Lower East Side politicians give speeches, she grew angry that none of these leaders offered a clear call to action against low wages and inhumane working conditions. Convinced that these speakers were out of touch with women shirtwaist laborers, Lemlich demanded, from the floor of the Cooper Union, an opportunity to speak to the packed crowd. Her coworkers lifted her onto the platform, where she made a remarkable impromptu appeal to her fellow garment workers:

> I have listened to all the speakers and I have no further patience for talk. I am a working girl, one of those striking against intolerable conditions. I am tired of listening to speakers who talk in generalities. What we are here for is to decide whether to strike or not to strike. I make a motion that we go out on a general strike.

The crowd cheered enthusiastically and soon voted for a general strike that resulted in a massive walkout of 20,000 shirtwaist workers. Given her central role in catalyzing the mass strike that would become known as the Uprising, Lemlich became one of its key leaders and electrified fellow workers with fiery speeches at regular rallies. She also inspired striking garment workers with her courage when she refused to leave the picket lines even after her ribs had been broken by employer-hired thugs. The strike lasted nearly three months, ending only after almost every shop had agreed to a union contract. After serving as a beacon for shirtwaist worker rights, Lemlich was blacklisted by the industry for her labor insurgency and marginalized by the ILGWU's male leadership who resented her demands for activism. Lemlich responded by becoming a full-time advocate, first for women's suffrage and later consumer rights.[60]

When the moral character of young political pioneers is openly questioned, their contributions to meaningful reform can be actively suppressed by adults. This is precisely what happened when Claudette Colvin was arrested at the age of fifteen for refusing to give her seat to a white woman on a segregated bus in Birmingham, Alabama, in 1955. Colvin was a high school student at the time and a member of the NAACP Youth Council who had grown passionate about civil rights. On March 2, 1955, Colvin sat in the "colored section" of a bus on her way home from school but was ordered by the bus driver to vacate her seat for a white woman when all of the "white seats" in the front were filled. Police were summoned but Colvin refused to move; at the time she was thinking about a school paper she was writing about the US Black struggle. "History kept me stuck to my seat," she later explained. "I felt the hand of Harriet Tubman pushing down on one shoulder and Sojourner Truth pushing down on the other." Colvin was handcuffed, arrested, and forcibly removed from the bus, with witnesses reporting that she repeatedly yelled that her constitutional rights were being violated. After being bailed out of jail, Colvin's minister proclaimed that she had initiated a civil rights revolution in Birmingham. Yet for adults in the city's Black community, there was a problem: Colvin was pregnant, which made her a flawed beacon for the cause. "If the white press got ahold of that information, they would have a field day," the NAACP leadership concluded. "They'd call her a bad girl, and her case wouldn't have a chance." Their solution was to have Rosa Parks, the beloved secretary of the local NAACP, induce her own arrest by refusing to surrender her seat on a segregated seat nine months after Colvin had done so. This later incident made Parks a civil rights icon. Colvin's mother told her "to be quiet about what I did. She told me to let Rosa be the one: white people aren't going to bother Rosa, they like her." Colvin was one of five plaintiffs in a 1956 federal court case that successfully challenged bus segregation as unconstitutional. And even as her role in helping spark the Montgomery bus boycott in 1955 was unheralded by movement leaders, Colvin remained confident that "mine was the first cry for justice, and a loud one."[61]

Whereas Claudette Colvin's civil rights activism may be unfamiliar to many, the story of Malala Yousafzai is well known across the globe. Yousafzai was raised in Pakistan's Swat Valley, where she attended a girls' school founded by her father. Her life changed dramatically in 2008 when the Taliban took control of her town and removed many freedoms, including education for girls. After seeing dozens of her classmates leave school, Yousafzai at eleven-years-old gave a speech in Peshawar titled, "How dare the Taliban take away my basic right to education." She also blogged regularly for the BBC about Taliban threats to girls' schooling and continued to speak publicly about the fundamental right of girls and women to an education. The Taliban responded by issuing a death threat against her. In October 2012, when Yousafzai was fifteen, a gunman boarded a bus she was riding and shot her in the head. Critically wounded, she underwent months of emergency care, a medically induced coma, and numerous surgeries. Yousafzai's shooting produced a worldwide outpouring of support, and after five months of special care in Birmingham, England, she began attending school in the city. Only nine months after she was attacked, Yousafzai delivered a poignant speech at the United Nations on her sixteenth birthday in 2013, serving notice to the Taliban that "nothing changed in my life except this: weakness, fear and hopelessness died. Strength, power and courage were born." Then she underscored the importance of educational access for girls and the capacity for literacy to defeat terrorism. "The extremists were, and they are, afraid of books and pens," she declared. "The power of education frightens them. They are afraid of women. Let us pick up our books and pens. They are our most powerful weapons." In October 2014, Yousafzai became the youngest person to be awarded the Nobel Peace Prize for her activism. While studying philosophy and politics at the University of Oxford, Yousafzai continued to advocate for free, safe, quality education for the roughly 130 million girls denied schooling.[62]

Even the youngest of children can serve as role models and change agents. In direct defiance of "conventional wisdom," history is replete with examples of young children facing off against adult forces—and changing the world. Nicole Maines, née Wyatt, was two-years old when she first showed signs that she might be transgender, feeling uncomfortable and betrayed by her birth-assigned male anatomy. "When do I get to be a girl?" she had frequently asked. "When will my penis fall off?"[63] As conservative parents raising twin boys in a small Maine town, Wayne and Kelly Maines had few role models to consult about Wyatt's clear and growing insistence that she was female and were wrestling with their own discomfort about Wyatt's gender identity. On the few occasions when they had forced Wyatt to wear boy's clothes or to adopt other stereotypically male behaviors, Wyatt had been crushed and his parents heartbroken. So as Wyatt advanced through elementary school and wanted a girl's name to match her now long hair and "feminine" clothing, the Maines family followed her lead and went to court to change her name. As Wayne recalls of his young daughter:

even at that age, [she had an] extremely strong personality. If I would say to her, "You don't want to be a girl," she'd say, "Yes I do." I'm a

40-year-old guy having this debate with this little kid and I'm losing, you know?[64]

Wayne Maines was especially conflicted about Nicole's desires. But, whether inspired by Nicole's confidence and commitment or compelled by more visceral paternal instincts, Wayne publicly demanded justice for the child he now embraced as his daughter. When the judge presiding over Nicole's name change from Wyatt wondered aloud whether the Christian Civic League should be permitted to express their opposition—as was normal practice under the state's name change laws—Wayne Maines stood up, testified to his daughter's longstanding and unwavering belief about her gender identity, described her difficulties at school, and implored the court to protect her privacy. The judge acceded. Nicole had chosen her name, had inspired her parents to take action—and would now chart out her and her family's future.[65]

Children who identify as transgender encounter a range of medical, legal, and social challenges that exist throughout their efforts to affirm their gender identity. Nicole describes her transition as a long, gradual process that started at a very young age—but which brought her immediate relief. As she later explained:

> Between second and third grade I had gone from wearing longer hair to wearing girl's clothes all the time. I don't know if it was even just my father, but by everyone, but that is when I started feeling like I was being seen. Then in fifth grade was when I had fully transitioned. I was allowed to pierce my ears and I was allowed to wear skirts and dresses. That really felt like "I am seen."[66]

By late elementary school she had also started calling herself Nikki. With her family's support, Nicole explored additional protocols like hormone therapy or gender reassignment surgery. At the time, there were few physicians who worked with transgender individuals and even fewer who understood the implications for young people in transition. But after several attempts, the Maines family located a doctor and once again supported Nicole's decision to undergo first hormone therapy (the same treatments that are now barred in multiple states) and, later, gender reassignment surgery.

To be sure, there are medical challenges to transitioning, Some of the treatments can be physically and emotionally demanding. However, as we referenced in Chapter 2, the social and legal obstacles can be equally onerous. Accessibility to treatments has become increasingly scarce, contingent on state policy, physician availability, and financial means. Schools are frequently resistant to accommodating transgender students. Bathrooms, sports teams, locker rooms—each present hurdles for transgender students if schools, districts, or even state legislatures outlaw gender-affirming practices. Even if a school offers initial support for transgender students, through gender-affirming restroom or locker room policies, for instance, these decisions are often revisited when transphobic parents or students are informed of the policy. For instance, parents in Pittsburgh, Pennsylvania, convinced their school board to prohibit transgender students from using the bathroom associated with their gender identity—even though the students had already been using the bathrooms (with the school's support) without incident.[67] A court eventually overturned the school board policy, but the consequences of community backlash on students and their families can be traumatizing. Transgender students who encounter significant harassment and bullying are far more likely to be diagnosed with depression, to have urinary or kidney infections (from denied bathroom use), to suffer from drug abuse, and to attempt suicide.[68]

Nicole had encountered these kinds of confrontations at every stage of her childhood and her transition. But just as she had at a very young age, by steadfastly refusing to identify as a boy despite the insistence of many adults around her, Nicole Maines persisted. She refused to cave to bullies at her school (and their parents) who said that dressing as a girl was wrong. She refused to back down when her elementary school forced her to use the staff bathroom rather than the girls' bathroom after another student's grandparent complained. She eventually ended up suing the school and took her case all the way to the Maine Supreme Court. The court ruled in her favor, finding that the school and the district's actions violated the state's Human Rights Act and marking the first time that a state high court ruled in favor of transgender rights.[69] Nicole's actions inspired other young people facing similar restrictions and indignities to follow her lead and stand up against an increasingly hostile policy environment for transgender youth.

Schools and school-aged children are the frequent subjects of transgender advocacy and the most vulnerable targets of anti-trans assaults, propelling young people like Nicole into the epicenter of trans rights activism.[70] Even as elementary school students, these young heroes have taken the lead in first convincing their family and friends and then compelling administrators and courts that the transgender community deserves the same rights and dignities as individuals who are cis-gender. In the words of eleventh-grade, nonbinary-activist Eli Bundy, speaking out "feels like a necessity. I feel like I can't afford to not pay attention, because it's my life and the life of my friends on the line, and that feels like much too high of a cost not to be paying attention to, even though it definitely can be very painful."[71] These young activists are keystones in an arch of child-activists—both within the longer history of Queer rights and across a range of social justice communities.[72] Trailblazers like Jaycen "Jayce" Marcus, a Black transmale student at George Fox University in Oregon, navigated both racism and transphobia. The Christian university denied Marcus's request to be transferred from the women's dormitory to a men's residence hall.[73] Although Marcus had completely transitioned—as reflected in his birth certificate, driver's license, and social security card—university administrators refused to accept his gender, forcing him to either live with women or in off-campus housing.[74] Marcus sued the school, and although he lost his case he became an advocate for other "voices at George Fox and in the broader Christian community, [who] get silenced or ignored, including the voices of people of color, the LGBTQ community, and people with disabilities."[75] Young leaders who are targeted in these especially treacherous environments transform hostility into opportunities for advocacy and reform. By using their own voices and their own instincts, they become pioneers and beacons of hope.

"Oh the Times They Are a Changin' . . . "
(But Not So Fast)

Grambling State University student Vivian Stovall and her friends hadn't planned on participating in the protests outside of the

Democratic National Convention. But as they were driving back to school, during the summer of 1968, they decided to make an impromptu stop in Chicago. "We were talking while we were on our way there about the assassination of Robert Kennedy, the assassination of Martin Luther King [Jr.]. We talked about the Vietnam War," Stovall says. "We just felt nobody was listening to us at that time anyway, and we wanted to just have our say or at least be part of something."[76] Sometimes political moments or periods foment youth activism. We have mentioned the Progressive Era as one such period—when young newsies organized and protested wage reductions in cities across the country. The year 1968 would become another turning point for young people's movements worldwide. Students like Vivian Stovall, who protested in Chicago, joined the cries of young people in Germany who, in the spring of 1968, held protests to, among other things, press government officials, party leaders, and their parents to take responsibility for Nazi atrocities.[77] They were joined by Parisian "Mai '68" student activists who led month-long protests and riots in the Left Bank—momentarily bringing the iconic city to its knees.[78] In 1968, youth rage and protest had taken hold worldwide, leaving adults in awe, frustration, and fear of widespread and persistent insurrection.

Stovall and her friends joined a peaceful gathering outside of Chicago's International Amphitheater, where Hubert Humphrey stood ready to accept the Democratic nomination for the upcoming presidential election. But the protest—of at least 10,000 people, mostly young—quickly turned violent when police intervened under orders to "shoot to maim."[79] The protest had started as a counter-convention to call out government greed and middle-aged, white-male elitism in the Democratic Party. Lyndon Johnson's decision to forfeit a second full term infused an already restive generation of new voters with a taste of opportunity and a sense of urgency and ignited a hailstorm of controversy over who would fill the unexpected vacancy. As Johnson's vice president, Humphrey was the presumptive nominee among Democratic elites—and a shoo-in at the largely delegate-dependent Democratic Convention. However, the growing anti-war, racial justice wing of the Democratic Party, comprised largely of younger voters, voiced their disdain for Humphrey and the party's old guard in state primaries. Humphrey did not participate in any primaries (which at the time did not determine the allocation of delegate votes), leaving Eugene McCarthy and Robert Kennedy to rouse a new generation of young voters with largely anti-war, pro-equality campaigns. United by the tragedy of their fallen civil rights leaders, their outrage over the Vietnam War, and their disgust for what they perceived as a profoundly corrupt primary system, students amassed in Chicago demanding to be heard. Rennie Davis, one of the protest organizers, saw the convention-centered protests as both catalytic and cathartic. "Many of our people have already gone beyond the traditional electoral processes to achieve change," he explained in the days leading up to the convention. "We think that the energies released . . . are creating a new constituency for America. Many people are coming to Chicago with a sense of new urgency, and a new approach."[80] But they also understood the risks of attending and were ready to defend themselves.

Under Mayor Richard J. Daley, a legendary political boss who ruled the city with an iron hand, Chicago was still recovering from riots sparked by Dr. King's assassination in April; looters and arsonists had left the city scarred and the city's police force on edge and combat ready. Not only did Daley deny the many applications he received for permits to organize at Lincoln Park during the week of the convention, he amassed 12,000 police officers, 6,000 National Guard members, and 6,000 army troops and gave the order to "shoot to kill arsonists and shoot to maim looters."[81] The protest started small. Both the anticipation of violence and Daley's refusal to grant permits had initially chilled enthusiasm for attendance. Few wanted to break the law and provoke the police, and marching without a permit would mean just that. However, the gathering of protestors grew from an initial 600 to a massive crowd of 10,000 in solidarity against Humphrey Democrats and the continuing war in Vietnam. When the crowd defied an 11 p.m. curfew, police responded with nightsticks and tear gas, even against peaceful gatherings. Stovall recalls her brush with police violence. In Grant Park, she and her friends had joined other black, indigenous, and people of color (BIPOC) and white protestors to form a human chain before the police moved in with batons and gas cannisters.

Next thing we knew, we were being kicked, being pulled apart and some very racial statements being made. And then I looked up, and when I looked up that's when I got hit. I still have the scar . . . . I remember feeling that warm wet stuff on my face, and I was bleeding.[82]

Journalists watched the mayhem from across the street inside the Conrad Hilton, high above the park. Recalls Fred Turner, a CBS engineer who witnessed the attacks on the young demonstrators:

> Now they're moving in, the cops are moving and they are really belting these characters. They're grabbing them, sticks are flailing . . . Cops are just belting them; cops are just laying it on. There's piles of bodies on the street. There's no question about it. You can hear the screams, and there's a guy they're just dragging along the street and they don't care. I don't think . . . I don't know if he's alive or dead. Holy Jesus, look at him. Five of them are belting him, really, oh, this man will never get up.[83]

Videos of unprovoked violence by police officers against students and members of the media overwhelmed footage from the convention, forever linking Humphrey's nomination and the party convention with unbridled police brutality. In the months after the violence, Chicago lawyer Daniel Walker led a wide-ranging study of what happened during the week of the Democratic National Convention. Drawing on 20,000 pages of testimony from 3,437 eyewitnesses and participants, as well as 180 hours of film and over 12,000 still photographs, Walker's Chicago Study Team reported its findings to the National Commission on the Causes and Prevention of Violence. Walker's report begins by noting that multiple protestors provoked police with "obscene epithets" and hurled "rocks, sticks, bathroom titles, and even human feces at police."[84] Yet, Walker's research team concluded that the unrestrained police reaction was both "indiscriminate" and unjustified:

> The nature of the response was unrestrained and indiscriminate police violence on many occasions, particularly at night. That violence was made all the more shocking by the fact that it was often inflicted upon persons who had broken no law, disobeyed no order, made no threat. These included peaceful demonstrators, onlookers, and large

numbers of residents who were simply passing through, or happened to live in, the areas where confrontations were occurring.[85]

Televised footage of the convention violence opened a chasm between young and older voters in their reactions to the graphic scenes. As with Civil Rights protests, videos of police officers assaulting mostly young, unarmed protesters stained the reputation of Mayor Daley and his Chicago police force. The footage also cemented a generational divide that had been growing since the dawn of social unrest in the 1960s over civil rights, the Vietnam War, anti-war protests, political assassinations, and a counterculture generation gap. While many young people were fighting for peace and equality, older generations yearned for order. Eye-witness testimony and the Walker Report faulted Chicago law enforcement for the violence, but most of the public sided with the police, according to polls conducted shortly after the events. Especially vexed by public reactions were the journalists who were on location, covering the violence. Lew Koch had been on the street, reporting on the protests and capturing what he thought was a clear battle for good over evil—with police rage at the forefront. He quickly realized that many viewers saw the opposite. Where he saw excessive or unwarranted police violence against innocent and young protestors, viewers read the students as "aggressors" and the police as heroes. Explains Charles Kaiser, "The biggest impact was on the older generation because they were so completely freaked out by it, this spectacle of anarchy was really terrifying."[86] Public fear of youth uprising—even in the face of clear and documented police brutality—constrained some journalists from reporting what they saw. Hank DeZutter from the *Daily News* witnessed "[s]cores of Chicago police freely using clubs and spraying tear gas [to drive] hundreds of anti-war and anti-convention youth out of Lincoln Park and into nearby streets."[87] But he never published those observations. Instead, he felt pressured to report that "[t]housands of shouting, chanting hippie-clad youths ... clashed with police on Sunday night in a series of incidents [that] began in Lincoln Park."[88] His "reportage," he later confessed, and "the reportage of the newspapers, was pretty bad."[89]

Among those who lost the most in the protests were the old guard of the Democratic Party. Richard Nixon's agenda held new significance in light of the protests and the violence showcased from the convention, catalyzing voters to send the "law and order" Republican to the White House in a landslide election victory. "The spectacle of upper-middle-class white college students fighting with policemen in Chicago, [was] as useful to Richard Nixon's campaign as anything else that happened in the whole year," Charles Kaiser observes. "They contributed in a big way to this whole sense that everything is out of control and therefore the man who is preaching law and order becomes very attractive."[90] In the wake of the disastrous 1968 national convention, and fearing an expanding rift with younger, anti-war Democrats and supportive progressives, the Democratic National Committee in 1969 formed a Commission on Party Structure and Delegate Selection to rewrite the rules for delegate selection. The twenty-four-member body recommended and won adoption of open procedures and affirmative action in selecting delegates. These McGovern-Fraser reforms, named for commission chairs Senator George McGovern (SD) and Representative Donald Fraser (MN), established a near-universal system of state-level primaries and open caucuses for nominating presidential candidates and mandated greater representation of racial minorities, women, and young people among state delegations at national conventions.[91] Significantly, the contemporary US primary election system is largely the product of two youth-initiated insurgencies: the 1964 MFDP challenge propelled by SNCC organizing and the 1968 mobilization of young anti-war activists at the Chicago Democratic convention.

Of course, youth insurgencies are viable in a variety of partisan settings. During the 1960s, young people of all ideologies and partisan stripes used their voice to compel policy change. While millions of young people mobilized against the Vietnam War and fueled a counter-culture insurgency that rocked US social norms, a smaller group of committed conservative students launched the Young Americans for Freedom (YAF). This new group was devoted to promoting free market economics, conservative states' rights, a limited role for government, and firm support for US geo-political interests. Their effort began in the fall of 1960, when conservative icon William F. Buckley hosted ninety students at his Sharon, Connecticut, home. There, the young leaders mapped out principles and strategies for a new national conservative youth movement. Their planning culminated with the adoption of the Sharon Statement (SS), which asserted that political freedom is impossible without economic freedom, that communism is "the greatest single threat" to US interests, and that constitutional democracy and communism could not peacefully co-exist.[92] Putting their plan into action, YAF leaders organized the "rally for world liberation from communism" at Madison Square Garden on March 8, 1962. The event, hailed as "the birthday of the conservative movement," drew 18,500 mostly young conservatives and was headlined by Senator Barry Goldwater of Arizona.[93] That same year, Ronald Reagan, who had recently announced his switch to the Republican Party, joined the YAF National Advisory Board and served as honorary chairman for the next forty-two years. YAF activists played a large role in Goldwater's 1964 presidential campaign that helped spark a conservative resurgence in the United States, especially within the Republican party. In subsequent years, YAF focused its energies on lobbying and electing conservative candidates for office. Its most vigorous campaign efforts were devoted to elevating their beloved and long-time honorary chair Ronald Reagan to the highest office in the land. Their members eagerly volunteered for and formally endorsed Reagan's presidential campaigns in 1968, 1976, 1980, and 1984. Throughout its history, YAF groups promoted their conservative beliefs and causes on college campuses across the United States.[94]

"Okay, Boomer": When Children Are the Adults

Of course, yesterday's radicals often become today's traditionalists. The spirit of anarchy that ran rampant among 1960s youth activists dissipated as they shifted into middle age. The Boomers of the 1960s may have upended a political system, but today many young activists and radicals view aging members of this generation as sell-outs—a sentiment concretized in the two-word barb: "okay boomer." The quip, turned Internet sensation, is meant, in the minds of Millenials to be a light-hearted, yet targeted dismissal of "old-time" thinking. However, it now also represents a sometimes-hostile divide between older generations who crave respect and younger generations who blame them for the world's calamities.

While hardly unique to environmental policy, the "okay boomer" ethos has taken center stage in recent stand-offs between seasoned policy officials and younger environmental leaders. In New Zealand, for instance, twenty-five-year-old Member of Parliament Chloe Swarbrick shut down a heckling older colleague with "okay boomer" during a 2019 climate change speech, a call-to-arms she delivered in support of a climate crisis bill. The clip of the quip went viral, and Swarbrick received both push back and praise from fellow lawmakers and fellow Millennials across the world. In response she penned an op-ed explaining the term and its significance in the context of environmental policy and her time in Parliament. Swarbrick described her comment as an "off-the-cuff" remark in response to the steady stream of doubters she encountered as a young elected official. "More years on earth" she argues, "does not necessarily equate to wisdom."[95] Rather, wisdom, she continues,

> comes from consistently exposing oneself to new and novel situations, in turn developing greater understanding of the world, those in it and how to solve evolving problems. When you close yourself off to new ways of looking at things; when you become conservative in mind [and] shut down conversation and the potential for progress ... you become intrinsically less likely to hold the requisite open, critical and creative ability to tackle unprecedented, evolving sociopolitical challenges.[96]

As with many political leaders and activists of her generation, Swarbrick sees the term as encapsulating the "collective exhaustion of multiple generations set to inherit ever-amplifying problems in an ever-diminishing window of time."[97]

Perhaps no young person of her time has captured the "okay boomer" ethos more than Greta Thunberg, the teenage climate activist turned internet sensation, made famous for her early protests and more recently for her pithy responses to Donald Trump's Twitter tantrums. In reality, Greta was just a young girl, fighting for her generation's increasingly unattainable right to clean air and potable water. Although climate activism may be in her genes (she is related to Nobel Laureate Svante Arrhenius who won the Nobel Prize for Chemistry for his work on estimating the earth's greenhouse effect), Greta first became aware of climate change and its accompanying dangers at the age of eleven, and took the impending climate crisis to heart. She started with her parents, asking them to shrink their carbon footprint, and then moved on to her community. Her first foray into public life took the form of a written appeal; Greta entered an essay contest sponsored by a local newspaper and won. "I want to feel safe," she wrote. "How can I feel safe when I know we are in the greatest crisis in human history?"[98]

Greta's words resonated with several important environmental leaders—including the leader of the nonprofit Fossil Free Dalsland. Greta attended several of the group's brainstorming sessions, during which one participant raised the idea of student strikes. This made sense to Greta. She had been tracking the activism of student protestors from Marjorie Stoneman Douglas High School who—after surviving one of the deadliest school-based mass shootings in the world—channeled their rage into a targeted, directed, and multi-pronged effort to demand public action. As we discussed in Chapter 1, the Parkland students organized protests, stormed legislative sessions, and bombarded social media. Within a few short weeks of the deadly Valentine's Day massacre, survivors like David Hogg and X González had amassed millions of followers on Twitter. They had also impressed skeptics with their passionate yet disciplined messaging—captivating millions with their public speeches, moments of silence, and impassioned pleas to policymakers and journalists. Their efforts culminated in the largest student protest since the Boomer-led anti-war movement. On March 24, 2018, over one million students and allies joined the Marjorie Stoneman students in Washington, DC, and across the world to demand gun safety laws. These protests, and their continued advocacy efforts, made 2018 a landmark year for gun safety laws: twenty-five states and the District of Columbia passed stringent gun restriction laws.[99]

Greta studied these strategies (just as the Marjorie Stoneman students had been inspired by civil rights era student-led efforts), and, in 2018, after a devastatingly hot summer in Sweden, she decided to go on strike. Instead of attending school she stood outside of the Riksdag,

Sweden's Parliament, holding a sign reading "Skolstrejk för klimatet" (school strike for climate). She posted a selfie of her one-person protest on Instagram and Twitter, captioning the photograph in her signature unequivocal style: "We children don't usually do what you grown-ups tell us to do. We do as you do. And since you don't give a shit about my future. I don't give a shit either."[100] People listened—especially young people. Student leaders across Sweden shared photographs of Greta's strike, rapidly raising her social media profile and garnering her a following in the hundreds of thousands within a few days of her first post. Greta returned to school in September—after the Swedish general election—but continued to strike every Friday. By that time the idea of school strikes had found a global audience. On September 20 and 27, 2018, over four million students and allies across the world responded to Greta's call, staging massive school walkouts to call attention to the climate crisis. In September, Greta admonished world leaders at the United Nations climate change summit. "This is all wrong" she said through angry tears. "I shouldn't be standing here. I should be back in school on the other side of the ocean. Yet you all come to me for hope? How dare you! You have stolen my dreams and my childhood with your empty words."[101] The speech caught the attention of influencers like Elon Musk and, by December, Greta had inspired over 20,000 student leaders to initiate walkouts in over 270 cities worldwide.[102] Greta had not only become a leading voice for climate change, but a catalyst for transforming youth unrest into a global uprising.

Among those 20,000 student leaders were two young Americans whose introduction to environmental advocacy had, quite literally, arisen in the ashes and who would change the face of US climate policy. After a summer spent indoors in Seattle to avoid smoke-choked air from nearby forest fires, sixteen-year-old Jamie Margolin decided she had had enough. Moved to action by panic and the need to be a part of the global protest movement, Margolin co-founded Zero Hour, a youth-led nonprofit organization focused on training young people to be climate advocates. Seventeen-year-old Jonah Gottlieb's idea to form the National Children's Campaign, a youth-focused policy institute specializing in climate change, emerged soon after neighbors knocked on his door trying to escape fires in Petaluma, California. Certain that "no one was going to protect our future for us," Margolin, Gottleib, and the many other young people inspired to protest determined that they had two choices, wake the world up to the reality of climate change or face a dying future.[103] Motivated by little more than a longing to play their part as disaster ensued, young people across the country took a stand and joined the ranks of youth leaders around the world demanding climate action.

These young environmental leaders organized over email, on Slack, at protests, or at their own gatherings, devising strategies to bring the fight to their own communities. They presented at town meetings, organized clean-up efforts, created public awareness campaigns, and staged school sit-ins and walkouts. And they realized that adults were transfixed by the unexpected insurgency of young activists. "We had more power than we'd ever imagined in our wildest dreams," recalls a nine-year-old youth activist after she and her sister convinced town officials in Lexington, Massachusetts, to invest in solar power (and received a standing ovation.) "We weren't just helpless girls."[104]

Young activists made a difference, emerging as forceful voices and faces of the environmental movement. Other kids their age may have been anxious about preparing class presentations or studying for exams. But for young environmentalists like Zero Hour co-founder Nadia Nazar providing witness testimony to members of Congress or lecturing to audiences numbering in the tens of thousands is just part of the job. And they are undaunted by the prospects of facing off against adults. "Why do we have to clean up the mess that past generations, and your generation, has left us?" Nazar asked Congress.[105] Climate strikes, youth trainings, lawsuits, and partisan campaigns are all part of the toolbox for young activists. Zero Hour, for instance, holds training summits every year, encourages young people to open up chapters in their own cities, and facilitates a network of sister organizations. Their calls have been heard by politicians, lawyers, and activists worldwide. Bernie Sanders relied heavily on young climate change activists during his 2020 presidential campaign. Lawyers teamed with twenty-one youth litigants in Oregon to form Our Children's Trust, representing the voice of young people in climate change litigation.[106]

In important ways, these young activists are uniquely positioned to disrupt policy paralysis. They are exceptional because not many who are invited to speak to the UN would have the courage to take the world leaders to task—let alone a teenager. Because children often are downgraded by adult leaders who consider them either ill-equipped or disinterested in policy reform, the defiance of youth activists who surpass expectations makes them even more visible—and all the more capable of catalyzing fence sitters into action. Sympathetic adults feel both shamed and responsible when young people mobilize on problems that adults should have resolved. Greta's "how dare you" and X's "we call bs" are notable because they are blunt indictments of not only policy failures but of adult abdications. With these statements, children are taking adults to task, and some adults are humbled enough by youth activists to take action. Paul Kramer, for instance, sponsored a citizen-led initiative to regulate guns in Washington State precisely because of the Parkland students. "I was inspired by the response of the high school students from Parkland," he explained, "and the way that they responded following that shooting, speaking out. And it seemed to me that people were listening in new ways."[107]

Young activists also have the capacity to catalyze a massive, captive audience. Problems like climate change or gun violence, for instance, pay little attention to political or geographic borders and can create a shared destiny regardless of place, time zone, or language. So, fluency in digital activism makes young leaders in these policy realms all the more uniquely qualified to galvanize a global audience. Zero Hour and the Parkland Students made efficient use of social media platforms like Twitter and Instagram to spread news of their efforts and spark an international response. They tapped into a network of socially conscious and motivated student activists, seeking ways to take action when adult policymakers had failed to address critical problems. Their walkouts, protests, and strikes snowballed precisely because of their station in life—their proximity, as young people, to masses of unencumbered spirits willing to protest and waiting for the right cause.

Of course, they accomplish all of this—managing global networks, organizing media campaigns, leading political initiatives, preparing Congressional testimony, delivering lectures, instigating international protests, and navigating backlash—while studying for calculus,

taking the SATs and applying to colleges. Young leaders have to sand-
wich their activism between classes at school during the day or when
their homework is finished at night. They manage national campaigns
on the bus ride to school, sneaking away to the drama room closet, or
by pulling all-nighters. Or sometimes they just use class time. Jonah
Gottlieb created a website advertising a joint venture between the
National Children's Campaign and Zero Hour while "bored in history
class."[108]

However, youth-led activism comes as a cost. For one, an activist's
age—especially if young—can also provide a perfect target for
opponents who are intent on waging personal attacks instead of
making substantive appeals. As with denials of Kent State and Sandy
Hook, both youth environmentalists and the Parkland students have
been dismissed as either paid actors or pawns of the left by conservative activists and conspiracy theorists. And everything from Greta's
autism[109] to X's sexual orientation[110] has been fodder for opposition attacks. True to form, Donald Trump took to Twitter to denigrate Thunberg's activism by belittling her: "Greta must work on her
Anger Management problem, then go to a good old fashioned movie
with a friend!," he chided the then ninth-grade activist. "Chill Greta,
Chill!"[111] Tellingly, the Twitter slap was prompted by *Time* magazine
naming Thunberg its 2019 Person of the Year, a distinction coveted by
Trump. Students who organized local climate change walkouts risked
being castigated by their communities—and, in some cases, faced sus-
pension and verbal or physical attacks from parents, teachers, and
school administrators for using school time to demand reforms.[112]
Youth advocates also may face the challenge of adults growing weary
of or disinterested in youth mobilizations over time. Youth leaders
like Jamie Margolin understand that "[p]eople are getting tired of,
'Oh, kids are in the streets.'"[113] They try to stave off adult fatigue by
exploring new strategies and narratives and by building alliances
with advocates of all ages. By defying expectations—and challenging
adults to examine their own failures—young leaders are potent forces
for change. At the same time, by upending age-based hierarchies,
child activists face heavy scrutiny from patronizing adults and vicious backlash from critics who take offense at the audacity of their
commitment.

Unrequited and Recruited: Manufacturing
Youth Mobilization

Thus far we have focused on the more obvious expressions of youth agency: young people seizing the reins from adult advocates and leading the charge for policy reform. Yet, some of the most profound forms of youth political agency are expressed in their rejection of adult-designed campaigns. Consider, for example, the failed efforts of adult activists to recruit young people to the fight for fiscal responsibility. One of those key recruiters was the Concord Coalition, a political advocacy group begun in the 1990s by a bipartisan collection of prominent national officials to challenge federal deficit spending and a mounting national debt.[114] In the late 2000s, a Youth Advisory Board was established by the Concord Coalition to coordinate "field operations" for youth organizations impassioned about the fiscal future. As the Youth Advisory Board stated in 2010, "we are passing an enormous debt burden onto young people and future generations of Americans who had no choice in the decision to incur the debt and no ability to oppose it."[115] In the view of established budget hawks, the national debt is fundamentally a matter of intergenerational injustice, ripe for youth support and mobilization.[116]

In the same period, a handful of high school seniors at the elite Phillips Academy, a selective private high school in New England, formed another group dedicated to reducing federal spending and debt—Concerned Youth of America (CYA). CYA launched a media blitz "to give young people a voice" on government overspending, which drew plaudits from fiscal watchdogs in Washington, DC. Although CYA had a limited youth following, their leaders scored interviews on major cable news shows and were invited to testify before the National Commission on Fiscal Reform and Responsibility created by President Obama.[117] A variety of budget lobbies and think tanks also teamed in those years.to create a student advocacy group, Students Facing Up to the Nation's Finances. By 2013, lobbyists and corporations favoring budget austerity funded a new nonprofit focused on organizing young people to force the government to control spending and reduce entitlement programs, called The Can Kicks Back—a reference to the idea that Congress must stop "kicking the can" on debt reduction. Developing a significant social media presence, the new organization set up eighty chapters and recruited several thousand volunteers in its first year. However, its mobilization efforts soon stalled, leading wealthy sponsors to focus their efforts elsewhere.[118] For more than a decade, powerful budget hawks from the political and corporate worlds sought to energize young people in their fight against deficit spending and national debt, framing these challenges as irresponsible and unsustainable burdens on future generations. Yet their appeals ultimately failed to galvanize large-scale youth outrage and action. Sometimes adult designs to leverage young people to advance their political agendas flounder.

Around the same time that budget hawks struggled to win young people to their cause in the 2010s, the Koch Brothers funded the creation of a youth wing of their signature organization Americans for Prosperity. The new youth-focused organization, Generation Opportunity, developed a twenty-college campus campaign encouraging students to "opt out" of the Affordable Care Act.[119] So-called brand ambassadors marketed "opt out" at tailgate parties, wooing students to sign petitions with free Taco Bell, beer, and "opt out" beer koozies. According to the organization's twenty-nine-year old president, young people provided a quick fix to the challenge of defunding Obamacare. "We're happy to watch the law crumble under its own weight by young people making good decisions . . . This is a creepy law."[120] The organization later shifted to climate change, asking youth to oppose climate reform on the grounds that it promoted "overregulation and out-of-control spending." In the summer of 2008, however, Generation Opportunity was dissolved.

More recently, the conservative, Chicago-based Heartland Institute sought to manufacture youth converts to climate denial. Their slick media campaign featured a blond, eloquent German teenager Naomi Seibt, a Greta Thunberg look-alike, who gave speeches and recorded widely distributed videos for young people that promoted climate skepticism. Dubbed the "anti-Greta," Seibt is a self-described YouTube influencer who first gained notoriety for essays and online videos linked to the extreme right, anti-immigrant Alternative fur Deutschland (AfD) party. Clips of Seibt at a poetry slam contest organized by the AfD garnered a following and also caught the attention of the US-based Heartland Institute, which lobbies for tobacco and coal companies and adamantly opposed climate reform. Seibt was hired, on a monthly salary, by the Heartland Institute to star in a series of videos challenging "climate change alarmism." When Thunberg addressed a 2019 United Nations global warming summit in Madrid, Seibt delivered a keynote address at a rival conference organized by the Heartland Institute only a few miles away. More recently, Seibt has been a featured speaker at the Conservative Political Action Conference (CPAC), the largest annual gathering of US political conservatives.[121] Seibt deploys Thunberg's famous "How dare you?" line in speeches that proclaim that "climate change science really isn't science at all." As *The Washington Post's* Desmond Butler and Julliet Ellperin note, "If imitation is the highest form of flattery, Heartland's tactics amount to an acknowledgement that Greta has touched a nerve." But media analysts like Graham Brookie doubt Heartland's anti-Greta strategy will sway audiences beyond those of the far right. "The tactic is intended to create an equivalency in spokespeople and message. In this case it is a false equivalency between a message based in climate science that went viral organically, and a message based in climate skepticism trying to catch up using paid promotion."[122] Strikingly, once again, conservative political forces sought to bankroll manufactured youth messages and images to counter the activism of young people at the other end of the ideological spectrum.

In the nurturing of symbolically powerful youth spearheads, conservative agency can also be developed at the grassroots to produce new right-wing leaders. In 2001, soon after the September 11 terrorist attacks, a sixteen-year old Santa Monica High School student named Stephen Miller was angered that many of his peers refused to say the Pledge of Allegiance in classrooms. Miller was particularly outraged that his high school failed to enforce the California code requiring the pledge be recited. In response, Miller phoned into a radio show hosted by prominent conservative Larry Elder to complain. Elder found Miller to be "bright, funny, and passionate," and before long, Miller became a frequent and welcome caller on the syndicated radio show.[123] All told, Miller talked with an encouraging Elder on air as a high schooler sixty-nine times, providing the teenager with a prominent platform to hone and gain an audience for his white nationalist beliefs. Miller also launched a successful pressure campaign that brought right-wing activist and author David Horowitz to speak at his high school, despite resistance from school administrators and a mostly progressive student body. Growing up in California during a surge of anti-immigrant fervor, a time when Republican Governor Pete Wilson won elections by castigating undocumented residents, Miller lashed out against classmates of Mexican descent, telling them to speak English and go back to their home country. He also appeared at school board meetings to vigorously speak out against measures to advance racial equity. During this period, Miller was mentored by ultra-right giants like Steve Bannon and Andrew Breitbart. David Horowitz also had an enormous influence on the teenage Miller, tutoring him on white nationalist conceptions of immigrants, Muslims, economics, and national security.[124] Soon after graduating from college, Miller worked on Capitol Hill first as press secretary for Representative Michelle Bachmann and then Senator Jeff Sessions. Miller later crafted Trump's acceptance speech at the 2020 Republican National Convention and, at age thirty-one, became a senior adviser in the Trump White House.[125]

Uniquely Qualified for the Job: Skills and Locations of Change

Of course, political reform happens in a variety of spaces. In many ways, changing the hearts of a community is just as important as changing the minds of policy officials. High school juniors, Erika Alvarez, and Jeffrey Jin understood the power of community action. The students had known each other from March for Our Lives Houston, having developed their activist credentials amid massive national youth uprisings against gun violence.[126] By the time Black Lives Matter (BLM) protests exploded during the summer of 2020 to denounce the epidemic of police brutality in the Black community, each had become relatively seasoned movement organizers. So in early June 2020, when Alvarez had the idea to organize a protest against police brutality in her hometown of Katy, Texas, she knew exactly who to call. She reached out to Jin and the two began to hatch a plan for holding the town's first BLM protest, and to do so in four days' time.[127]

It would not be easy. By any measure, Katy was a typical small, conservative Texas town—more likely to resist or ignore a BLM protest than support it. Foyin Dosunmu, co-founder of Katy4Justice and co-facilitator of the protest, would later describe Katy, in an interview for Rolling Stone, as a "very conservative" town with "a lot of privilege."[128] Like many small towns, gentrification had sequestered an already small Black population (7 percent by Dosunmu's estimate) to largely racially segregated communities (Dosunmu's is the only Black family in her neighborhood). Nevertheless, when Jin reached out to Dosunmu for help with the protest, Dosunmu felt that the three of them could pull it off.

They were right. Although the students had initially reserved a small park to hold what they thought would be a few hundred supporters, they had to quickly pivot to a larger venue after setting up an Eventbrite page on Facebook to advertise the march. Within a day of posting the event, over a thousand people had responded.[129] As had climate change and gun control activists, the three students leaned heavily on their social media expertise to transform a modest community gathering into a large march attracting local media attention. After switching locations, the three high school students began fielding phone calls and tweets from volunteers, journalists, and speakers and working with Katy Police Chief Noe Diaz on strategies for crowd and opposition control.[130] For the Katy youth, what began as an idea to gather a few hundred supporters had, within only a few days, morphed into one of the largest marches in recent Katy history.

In many ways their success—and the success of the many youth leaders highlighted in this chapter—is not surprising. As previously discussed in this chapter and Chapter 3, adult activists and policy actors have long recognized the innate capacity of young people to instigate and catalyze action. The same qualities that make young activists attractive recruits can make them equally effective leaders. First, for young activists, age is an asset. Young people are always enthralling and often sympathetic voices and leaders in the public square. Even when some adults discount their motivations or capabilities, politically engaged children still command attention. It is precisely because many adults expect so little of young people that when they speak with clarity and resolve adults listen. Second, young people are generally more inclined to see injustices or take risks and less likely to accept compromise. The Katy youth understood that their protest might incite opposition, but they plowed ahead all the same. Even when opponents threatened to bring guns and other weapons to the march or attempted to intimidate the young leaders with threats of bodily harm (one woman promised to break Dosunmu's arms if she continued preparations) they persevered.[131] Alvarez, Dosunmu, and Jin dismissed these threats and focused on the groundswells of support: the volunteers as far away as Austin who called the students to offer themselves as medics and to provide water and other supplies;[132] and candidates and public officials who offered their voices as speakers. The outpouring of community support dwarfed these threats and energized the students.

Their capacity to both elicit empathy and take risks makes young leaders who are activating communities or inspiring world leaders better positioned to attract supporters. The Katy march, for instance, attracted an impressive slate of public officials who were willing to speak from the heart about racism and police violence. Local District Attorney Brian Middleton talked openly about his own experiences with racism on his road to professional success.[133] Hope Martin, then candidate for County Commissioner and an eight-year army veteran, explained how she managed and negotiated systemic racism as a Black woman in the military. She praised the young leaders as "the key to making a change in the world" and implored participants to "get rid of the stereotypes. We are humans. We are human beings. We want to be treated just like everyone else."[134] Chris Hollins, local county clerk, spoke of his father's ongoing internal conflicts as a Black man, police officer, and father as he prepared his son to navigate the world of anti-Black police violence.[135] And each of these prominent public officials or political candidates spoke alongside Katy students who issued their own painful indictments of systemic racism. Young speakers like high school student Sydney Hart, whose haunting questions launch this chapter, implored adult listeners to acknowledge the everyday specters of violence that young people of color face because of pervasive and systemic racist aggression.

By the end of the march, an estimated 3,000 participants had joined the students' call for action.[136] Three students, without the traditional trappings of means or experience, organized in four days what more formal organizations could not deliver with weeks or months of planning. It was *because of* rather than *in spite of* their youth that this small Texas town shed its apathy and united to protest policy brutality. The organizers' youth made Katy's protest more inviting and more impactful, especially to reticent Katy and nearby residents. No one expected high school students to take on a leadership position of this magnitude. Community members were both surprised by their initiative and motivated to support the young students, though joining the protest was as much about fighting anti-Black racism as it was about supporting the three local teenage heroes. One participant—a Black parent—grieving over George Floyd's murder and what it meant for her children—attended the event specifically because it had been organized by young people.

> A group of teenagers initiated this. They took it upon themselves to be the change this world needs. It devastated me when I had to tell my children what happened to George Floyd, and that as Black Americans, they will have to face racism in their lives. But being here at an event put on by kids—I grieve, but I grieve with hope.[137]

Youth is a powerful conduit for action. But young people also have relevant skills and resources that make them especially proficient at building community. Their mastery of social media, for instance, makes young people more adept than their adult counterparts at navigating digital networks that attract multitudes of participants. Just as climate change activists used the internet to inspire protests and attract supporters, the Katy students took to Facebook and other social media platforms to quickly disseminate their plan—reaching thousands of participants in a matter of hours. Even without money or connections, Dosunmu explained, "our generation [is] on the forefront of social media" which "gives you the ability to mobilize so fast . . . it was just so easy for us to pick up and start doing what we needed to do."[138] Young leaders see the value of community building and can harness the power of social media to focus and expand their efforts as needed. For instance, sixteen-year-old Stephanie Hu saw the Internet as a perfect platform for communicating with other Asian youth about escalating anti-Asian violence during the COVID-19 pandemic. When she realized that her online zine "Dear Asian Youth" had struck a chord with youth across the world, she used the space to catalyze a global network of community organizations. She helped students establish more than 160 chapters in seventeen countries in just over a year.[139] Recalls Hu, "it was supposed to be a platform where I could publish my own poetry relating to the Asian-American experience. It never was meant to be an organization, it kind of just spontaneously happened to build up into this."[140]

Anywhere that young people congregate, there is an opportunity for young people to advocate and organize. And any young person with a digital audience is capable of transforming the policy landscape. Platforms like Twitch, for instance, have provided young "influencers" with extraordinary fundraising power. For instance, the seventeen-year-old Twitch gamer and influencer who goes by "Ranboo" raised $100,000 for the Trevor Project—a group that provides support services to LGBTQIA+ youth—in just one hour while live-streaming a gameplay of Minecraft.[141] For young people ,there is no barrier between advocacy and entertainment. And neither is there a bright line separating seasoned activist from political novice. Anyone with a following—whether on TikTok, Instagram, Twitch, or Twitter—can be an advocate. And any subject—gameplays, unboxings, TikTok reviews, or even cat videos—can provide an opportunity for fundraising. Young activists are, therefore, changing the modalities and locations of political and civic engagement.

For similar reasons (and as intimated earlier), schools and students are especially potent sources of policy change. While young people may not always have a direct say in how policies are generated or implemented, the sheer volume and mass of their protest potential makes them attractive publicists, particularly when schools are populated with classrooms full of activists-in-waiting. For instance, the pro-life movement has its roots in US colleges and universities and owes its continuing relevance in part to the efforts of pro-life youth organizers, particularly to the youth-led anti-war movement of the 1970s. Even prior to the announcement of the Supreme Court's decision in *Roe v. Wade*—declaring a constitutional "right to choose"—a small but committed contingent of pro-life advocates had organized to combat abortions—legal or otherwise. But their tactics had produced little headway by the mid-1970s and young abortion opponents saw an opening for a different kind of political contestation. These youth leaders, trained as anti-war activists, saw echoes of the atrocities of Vietnam in the now increasing availability of abortion services after *Roe*. Young pro-lifers perceived abortion as a war on women—a culmination of women's ongoing exploitation.[142] Informed by a morality steeped in Roman Catholic values and inspired by Gandhi, King, and anti-war movement heroes, young pro-lifers sought to distinguish themselves from older pro-life stalwarts. Young activists replaced the tactics deployed by "angry, right-wing, uptight, conservative" pro-life stalwarts with sit-ins and compassionate interventions.[143] They borrowed from anti-war tactics in part because they understood pro-life activism as a logical extension of the anti-war movement. Tactics like sit-ins and protest circles provided a pathway for advocates to physically protect the fetus while emotionally connecting with mothers by "counsel[ing] and . . . offer[ing] loving support."[144] They perceived themselves as partners and heroes—saving women from making desperate decisions caused by enduring oppression. These young activists—mostly college educated—operated on feminist principles. Female youth leaders, particularly in the early days, commanded men to stay off the front lines: pregnant women didn't need "a bunch of men forcing their morality on women."[145]

Young pro-lifers used their connection to the anti-war movement to garner more attention from anti-war supporters, many of whom harbored deep apprehensions about abortion, eventually founding the Pro-Life Non-Violent Action Project in 1977. Originally headquartered at Harvard and then at Yale, they centered their efforts on helping "college educated liberals" establish their own groups and organize sit-ins and other protests at college campuses.[146] The National Youth Pro-Life Coalition, founded in 1972, similarly harnessed the energy of student activists in the anti-war and anti-nuclear movements in order to propel young people into action. Initially comprised of "60 young people from 23 different states," the group first organized around a shared commitment to opposing abortion.[147] Quickly they expanded their focus to safeguarding the "dignity of every human life."[148] They rejected the partisan and ideological assumptions that linked anti-war efforts with pro-choice values and pro-life activism with "pro-war, pro-capital punishment attitudes" and perceived young people as the best hope for bi-partisan action.[149] Student leaders recruited young pro-lifers by combing through editorials and comments in their college newspapers or newsletters. They met in dorm rooms to plan protests, present campus lectures, host movies, and publish newsletters. Most importantly, they trained new recruits in the art of non-violent, compassionate protest.[150]

These approaches quickly attracted middle-aged abortion opponents. Both the substantive appeal of pro-life messaging as well as the lure of uncharted student activism inspired middle-class abortion opponents to cut their activist teeth on youth-organized pro-life sit-ins. Ordinarily law-abiding pro-life supporters found a new sense of pride in their increasing entanglement with police officers. Ultimately, however, the protests grew too popular, and too unwieldy, to sustain their more intimate, compassion-driven goals. As sit-in crowds grew—attracting more and more supporters of all ages and backgrounds—the capacity for organizers to maintain control waned and the sit-ins became increasingly more aggressive.[151]

Youth remain a critical resource for pro-life advocates and, although colleges and universities are no longer the bastions of pro-life advocacy, college students still command significant attention and provide invaluable resources. Groups like Students for Life—founded at Georgetown in 1988[152]—are at the forefront of national youth advocacy and are widely perceived as pivotal organizers in attempts to mainstream the pro-life movement. The group's Rock for Life initiative, for instance, has highlighted the presence of college pro-lifers at mainstream music events. Concerts and other venues that have long been perceived as domains for pro-choice organizations are now welcoming student pro-life groups to publicize their programs.[153] These strategies help replenish the ranks of an aging pro-life movement hoping to capitalize on increasingly pro-life court decisions. Recent surveys indicate a widening chasm of support for pro-choice policies between 18–29 year-olds and those who are thirty or older. Whether because of decreasing levels of religiosity among younger generations or more gender uniformity about abortion, younger generations are steadily becoming more pro-choice.[154] Groups like Students for Life hope to energize an aging cause.

More recently, conservative free speech advocates counted on the protest potential of college students to condemn liberal attacks on hate speech. Alt-right shock jock Milo Yiannapoulos—whose outspoken rhetoric against Islam, feminism, immigrants, trans students, and other marginalized groups propelled him to right-wing fame—focused squarely on colleges (and liberal college students) as enemies of free speech. Radical conservatives, buoyed in part by the increased prominence of white supremacist groups in Trump's Republican base, denounced calls for more inclusive curricula and pedagogies and limits on race, gender, or sexuality-based hostilities as dangerous attacks on free speech, beliefs, and association. In the process, they sought to turn the tables on progressives. Conservatives deployed free speech rhetoric to lambast increasingly common pedagogical measures that would support marginalized students, by casting liberals as tyrants and conservatives as the innocent victims in a war on speech and religious values.

Yiannapoulos rose to fame during the ascendance of Trumpism in US politics, a Breitbart polemicist who was unabashedly gay, uncompromisingly racist, and always eager to sell his brand as "the internet supervillain" of the alt-right.[155] In 2017, he set his sights on antagonizing young progressives on elite college campuses, in particular University of California, Berkeley, to showcase what he perceived as the illiberal pathologies of political correctness. As the birthplace of the 1960s Free Speech Movement, Berkeley offered an ideal venue for Yiannapoulos's one-man free speech performance. He hoped that by formally targeting college campuses as settings for his racist and transphobic ranting he would be able to trigger liberal student outrage. Their anger, he hoped, would provide a potent expression of "the left's war on free speech."[156] After securing a speaking invitation from a small group of conservative Berkeley students, Yiannapoulos and his staff broadly publicized the event. Students of color, Queer students, and a variety of progressive allies mobilized against his appearance on campus, arguing that Yiannapoulos's racist, xenophobic, and anti-trans rhetoric would promote a hostile and unsafe educational environment. When protests, set off by Yiannapoulos, turned violent after "a group of 150 masked agitators came onto campus," Berkeley administrators made the decision to cancel his speaking engagement.[157] On cue, Yiannapoulos expressed outrage that his free speech was being censored by liberal thought police, and he blamed young "anti-fascists" for destroying property and the left-wing "communist tantrum" for incurring $600,000 in property damage and security.[158]

Once the match had been lit, Yiannapoulos had to do very little to nationalize his battle between free speech and political correctness. As a social media guru, he knew exactly how to trigger enough righteous indignation from free speech hawks to villainize the very students who were being targeted by his hateful and assaulting rhetoric. President Trump quickly tweeted a threat to withdraw federal funds from Berkeley—and any other university who tried to squelch conservative speech—as Yiannapoulos had requested. And, as planned, his book, *Dangerous*, quickly rose to second-place on the bestseller list. Moderate and liberal first amendment scholars described student protests on college campuses as the "single greatest threat facing free speech today."[159] Warned first amendment lawyer Floyd Abrams, these threats "come from a minority of students, who strenuously, and I think it is fair to say, contemptuously, disapprove of the views of speakers whose view of the world is different from theirs and who seek to prevent those views from being heard."[160] In this light, students were cast as bullies and aggressors robbing speakers and college administrators of their speech rights and also as privileged "snowflakes" who were thin-skinned and too easily "triggered." All it took were a few carefully phrased tweets and some edited video clips of masked college-aged vigilantes and Yiannapoulos's alt-right free speech movement had developed a life of its own. Yiannapoulos and other alt-right speakers had counted on student agency and outrage in their college tours. They choreographed the perfect catalyst to compel a predictable student response and used that response to justify extraordinary limitations on hate speech regulations.

Conclusion

In liberal democracies like the United States, governing children often has inspired fervent struggles between parents, state officials, and other adults over disparate interests and ideals—including but not limited to conflicts over how to best promote the welfare of young people. Democratic politics has also regularly featured efforts to leverage children for a variety of political agendas. In both cases, the dependency, manipulability, and limited capacities of children are assumed. Yet as this chapter documents and analyzes, young people over time have exercised significant political agency. Indeed, youth leadership and engagement in political life long have played important and distinctive roles in fueling democratic change. What emerges is a complicated pattern of adults both discounting the capabilities of young people and responding to the power of their political activism when they defy expectations. Young activists, however, are well aware of the transformative possibilities of their political agency. As Dreamers observed while launching a protest offensive in 2010, young people are often at the fore of profound democratic change:

> From the anti-apartheid movement in South Africa to the freedom movements in the 1960s and to the Chinese student rebellions in Tiananmen Square, youth have always been at the forefront of successful movements and radical social changes. Unfortunately, it seems we have not learned from this rich heritage of youth speaking truth to power.[161]

Despite numerous historical and contemporary examples of children engaging in and leading campaigns for political reform, adults regularly lament "low levels of youth political engagement" and treat child activism in movements as anomalous to the presumed rule of youth apathy. Due to myopic self-interest, so the argument goes, young people generally disconnect from public affairs. Prominent experts of political behavior, for instance, warn that a growing digital divide has "induced young people into a self-indulgent social-media haze."[162] According to these analysts, a steady diet of video stimulation coupled with a shrinking exposure to civic duty has rendered an entire generation (and those to come) disinterested in government or democracy. Yet this chapter tells a different story. Rather than being pushed into action, the young leaders, role models, and risk-takers featured here instigated change despite encountering formidable barriers and daunting risks. And they often waged these battles against not only those who are ideologically or politically opposed to their calls for reform, but also sometimes against organizations who are substantively aligned but strategically resistant. And they do so using the very technologies and platforms that adults dimiss as irrelevant. In this way, child advocates may be fighting along multiple fronts. When child activists succeed, they produce not only substantive reforms but also transform their own normative communities. It is for this reason that sometimes the most tumultuous and productive moments of political transformation occur when children are leading the way.

Youth advocacy, though, often comes at a hefty cost. For one, it is typically born out of tragedy. Civil rights activists were inspired to mobilize in response to violent white terror and systematic oppression. Dreamers took action after their families were torn apart by record numbers of arrests and deportations. Mass shooting at Marjory Stoneman High School propelled the Parkland activists into action. Fires and other disasters brought on by climate change have inspired young people to march, protest, and organize. These young people are driven by fear and anxiety, by a compulsion to tackle disaster, through taking command. Thunberg, Hu, and Margolin, for example, channeled their profound distress and bouts of depression into a global strategy. This takes a toll. While other kids fret about grades, athletic performance, or the prom, young activists worry about gun violence, racial oppression, or the perilous degradation of the planet. It is an all too real reminder of the world that they have inherited, the failure of adults to protect them, and their perception that they have to address these unbearable crises on their own.

5

Centering Children
in Democratic Politics

We will not be turned around or interrupted by intimida-
tion because we know our inaction and inertia will be the
inheritance of the next generation, become the future.
Our blunders become their burdens.
But one thing is certain.
If we merge mercy with might and might with right then love
becomes our legacy and change our children's birthright.
                    —Amanda Gorman, "The Hill We Climb"

When we embarked on this project, we set out to make visible the significant and varied roles that young people play in democratic politics on a regular basis. Despite key work on political socialization,
identity formation, social policy, and education, children generally
are neglected in most political science research and analysis, as we
discussed in Chapter 1. "For a very long time," Simone Abendschon
aptly observed recently, "there was a consensus in democratic theory
and social sciences that children and politics do not go well together."[1]
What we have theorized and presented in these pages is directly at
odds with this deeply flawed "consensus" that sidelines, brackets, or
altogether ignores minors in political life. The issues discussed in this
book—such as education, social welfare, labor, civil rights, immigration, climate, criminal justice—are bedrock policy arenas that center
children in distinctive and important ways. Children are subjects, to
be sure. But they are also important catalysts and advocates in the political and policymaking processes. Their continued erasure from politics renders our understandings of democratic politics incomplete and
propagates the misperception that young people are not (and have not
been) critical political actors. It is not just that children and politics so

Democracy's Child. Alison L. Gash and Daniel J. Tichenor, Oxford University Press.
© Oxford University Press 2022. DOI: 10.1093/oso/9780197581667.003.0005

often "go together," but that each profoundly shapes the other. Their relationship is mutually reinforcing, a reflection of the ways young people are influenced by their political environs, as well as the kinds of politics that children inspire and create. By now, you know well that our strategy for building a more capacious understanding of this crucial relationship is to offer a framework that illuminates how the control, leveraging, and agency of young people in politics fuels persistent struggle and occasional democratic transformation.

Our focus on the politics of control in Chapter 2, exploring when, how, and why children are governed, highlights their status as incomplete, dependent, citizens-in-waiting in need of protection. Paternalistic laws, policies, and practices consistently ignite fierce political conflict and debate over what are the best interests of children, and they often boil down to battles over *who* is invested with the authority to determine and ensure those interests—parents or the state? While an extensive set of programs and regulations have emerged over time to protect young people, we also have learned that child welfare is more than occasionally subservient to adult interests and can be vulnerable to adult tyrannies, hard and soft. As frequent subjects and targets of collective control, children carry the burden of being receptacles for policy investments—even ones they do not need. Their failures and achievements are monitored, assessed, and archived in order to legitimize or denounce policies and programs. Children's spaces and interactions are among the most highly regulated—speech, dress, where they congregate, how they interact. Each are ripe for state control. Sometimes in the name of their own best interest, or sometimes because they are simply expected to submit to adult authority, children's actions are scrutinized, their freedoms constrained, and their voices silenced. We also illuminate the often contingent and inconsistent character of how children are governed over time. State actors and other adult authorities are, in one moment, too quick to usurp parental control under the guise of child welfare and in another equally willing to completely abdicate responsibilities to care for other children. Sometimes this control over parents and children shelters and confines children—inhibiting their ability to express themselves, advocate for their needs, make informed decisions. And sometimes this control divests children of critical support, too quickly thrusting them into the role of adult or leaving their livelihood to fate.

Of course, children figure into the political process as more than dependents, subjects, or policy targets. Politicians, movements, interest groups, and other actors recognize the broader power that young people hold in democratic politics. As we explain in Chapter 3, children are politically useful. They can be employed as symbols of political inspiration or as tools of political manipulation, used to curry sympathy or stoke fear in the electorate. Children's images, voices, and examples can shift entire tides of public opinion—even affecting issues and decisions that may be only marginally relevant to their needs. Rival political actors look to children, to their hypothetical fates and their real experiences, to their vulnerabilities, their promise and their potential for destruction, as provocative marketing tools. Whether as poster children for AIDS or as cautionary tales for immigration restrictions, we see opposing political camps elevating some young people as sympathetic innocents and demonizing others as menacing threats. Young people also are politically useful as recruits or activist armies for both progressive and conservative causes. As discussed in Chapter 3, for instance, civil rights leaders wrestled with the moral dilemmas of deploying young people in a struggle against white supremacy that was fraught with danger. Yet they ultimately deployed children on the front lines of protest, where their vulnerability and outsized sacrifice captivated public audiences and cornered politicians. Children also are leveraged by those whose principal goal is to ostracize or punish their parents. The story of marriage equality provides a striking example of invoking children to marginalize and deny rights to their parents. Same-sex marriage opponents repeatedly advanced their agenda by showcasing the purported struggles of hypothetical children raised by lesbian or gay parents, claims that often were knocked down by the real children of same-sex parents. Policies promoting family separation at the border illustrate the will and capacity of officials to politically exploit children as bargaining chips. These efforts traded on parental love for their children in order to discourage immigrant families from crossing the border. The message was clear: enter the country and we will lock up your children. Whether as powerful symbols, recruits, or collateral, young people offer significant opportunities for political leverage to those willing to seize them.

Once mobilized, we know that young people are neither incapacitated by their age nor readily subservient to their older political leaders and mentors. As we elucidate in Chapter 4, the emergent agency of the young SNCC civil rights activists and more contemporary undocumented Dreamers challenged the tactics and approaches of their movement elders and uniquely contributed to dramatic political action and policy reform in the process. We also chronicle numerous instances— during landmark political crises and struggles—where young people from Claudette Colvin to Nicole Maines have taken bold, independent action to affirm their self-worth and to realize their visions of inclusive democracy. Still other young people spotlighted in these pages— including anti-war protestors, gun control and school safety advocates, and youth climate activists—stepped forward as political pioneers and agenda-setters. In challenging US involvement in Vietnam, lax gun laws, and policy inertia on climate reform, young people as agents of political change have demonstrated a capacity to reverse prescribed political (and social) roles by assuming crucial responsibilities (including existential crises) unmet by adults. Little wonder that the political agency of children can be both energizing and unsettling to the larger demos.

It is our hope that this book opens up space for more attention to childhood or age as a concrete difference, one that combines with gender, race, class, immigration status, or sexual orientation to produce systems of advantage and disadvantage. Our analysis showcases the ways in which children are valued unevenly, because of stereotypes, presumptions, and biases, and are therefore subjected to inequitable treatments and benefits. The politicized origins and development of "childhood," we have shown, is impossible to adequately understand except by studying how age combines with patriarchy, racial supremacy, heterosexism, economic privilege, ableism, and other forms of hierarchy and oppression to structure children's lives and futures. The past and present of US public education is indelibly defined by the intersection of age with gender, racial, ethnic, religious, and class differences. From Black slave children and imported London street kids to young workers like Reuben Dagenhart, Clara Lemlich, and Dozier's real-life Nickel Boys, the epic struggle over child labor in US political development reflects overlapping systems of exploitation and subjugation. When read through the lens of race, ethnicity, sexuality, gender identity, or other locations of exclusion, age provides a powerful weapon for disenfranchisement and repression. The murder of seventeen-year-old Trayvon Martin at the hands of George Zimmerman is a continual reminder of the dangers that "Black teenagers in hoodies" face when simply walking in their neighborhood or grabbing a snack at the corner store. The pages of this book are full of evidence and stories that highlight the ways in which age, when combined with race, gender, class, or sexuality, amplifies silos of privilege and precarity. Black and Brown children, for instance, are more likely to be on the losing end of legal and policy debates—prematurely promoted to adulthood in the criminal justice system, denied critical welfare or social service supports, cast aside and penalized at school. The Covid-19 pandemic has inflicted costs and harms on nearly all children, but it has imposed inequitable burdens on children from low-income households and those in racial and ethnic minority groups.

The cases and evidence presented in this book also reveal the ways in which political debates frequently and deliberately place young people at odds with each other over categories of difference, rendering their interests and safety as mutually exclusive rather than mutually reinforcing. Anti-LGBTQ activists, as we have shown, frame LGBTQIA+-inclusive curricular innovations, LGBTQIA+-reflective library acquisitions, and GSAs as threatening to heterosexual students by pressuring them into same-sex relationships. Like Anita Bryant and Jerry Falwell decades before, conservative officials and activists have mobilized against bathroom and sports access for transgender students in the name of guarding the safety of cis-students or protecting cis-female student athletes from unfair competition. We also have chronicled the persistent use by nativists over time of "our children" versus "their children" narratives in political struggles over immigration and refugee policy. During the 1920s and 1930s, national policymakers drew on eugenicist research to argue that the best interests of US-born children demanded the exclusion of "new immigrant" families and later Jewish refugee children seeking to escape the Holocaust. Far from confined to the past, nativists today claim that the children of undocumented immigrants steal public health and education dollars from "our children," and that the "anchor babies" of undocumented parents are undeserving of the citizenship benefits enjoyed by other US-born children. Thinking about age or childhood as a concrete difference sheds new light on the intersections of categorically based exclusions that are centuries old—providing new frontiers for evaluation and investment.

We have only scratched the surface of three issues in this book that strike us as very promising for future research and analysis of children and democratic politics. First, we wonder how our conceptual frameworks—the politics of control (paternalism, subjugation, membership, and abandonment), the politics of leveraging young people as symbols, recruits, and bargaining chips, and the politics of youth agency—play out in contexts beyond our primary focus of the US polity. Although we discuss several young political icons and youth movements in other countries, we draw almost exclusively from research and cases from historical and contemporary US politics. It would be valuable to study the political control, leveraging, and agency of young people in comparative and cross-national perspectives.

Second, our framework also raises important questions about the trajectory of youth activism as technology expands opportunities for young people to reach large audiences as voices for change. One question concerns legal doctrines on student speech, which suggest a liminal space for youth autonomy. School provides an exception to the rule of free speech. At school, students are restricted from engaging in a wide variety of speech. Yet increasingly the line between school space and private space is blurring—especially as technology becomes a more salient presence in education. If state regulation of student speech expands into spaces that had once been reserved as private, how will this change student opportunity to promote policy reform? If students can no longer take to Twitter, Instagram, or some other media platform, where can their views be voiced? And how will the hamstringing of youth voices change reform efforts?

Third, our analysis highlights potential recurrent patterns or cycles of control, leverage, and agency of young people in politics—especially evident in struggles for reform—that merit further investigation. Putting our substantive chapters together, one can discern movement between core categories as young people travel through different phases—first as subjects or dependents impacted by state intervention or inaction (control), then as symbols or activist armies (leverage), and finally as leaders and instigators (agency). We saw this play out in the context of the "long" civil rights movement, as Black children in the post–Second World War United States were subjected to horrific violence, subjugation, and marginalization at the hands of a white supremacist system. Their oppression, suffering, *and murder* served as powerful symbols and substance for massive nonviolent protest, anti-segregation litigation, and shifting public opinion. Young people themselves became important and stirring foot soldiers in the fight against Jim Crow, drawing widespread sympathy as they faced down fire hoses, German Shepherds, and baton-wielding local police defending Southern racism. Yet over time, SNCC activists and other young protesters grew weary of following directions from older civil rights leaders and took charge of their own advocacy efforts—launching freedom rides, voter registration drives, and Black Power campaigns despite cautions and resistance from civil rights elders. The quest for democratic inclusion by Dreamers reflects a similar trajectory. Undocumented children who have spent most of their lives in the United States live in the shadows of US social and political life, facing uncertain futures under a broken immigration system. Treated as unwanted, liminal subjects by the federal government in the early 2000s, Dreamers were barred by the state from a variety of public benefits programs, denied key educational, economic, and professional opportunities, and always remained vulnerable to deportation or family separation. As we saw in Chapter 4, immigrant rights advocates trained and deployed model Dreamers as compelling and sympathetic symbols of the urgent need for comprehensive reform. By 2010, however, Dreamers had broken away from their political mentors and pursued confrontational tactics that ultimately influenced a president and secured major policy change two years later. It would be useful in future research to study in greater depth the movement of young people across categories of control, leverage, and agency, exploring patterns and dynamics that surfaced in the civil rights and Dreamer movements.

Figure 5.1 *Climate Strike*, Eugene, Oregon, September 20, 2019.
Source: Photo by Andy Nelson. AP Images. http://www.apimages.com/
metadata/Index/Climate-Strike/714fbc8f5df54b10ba0a8fec6c652
ca4/99/0.

In November 2021, former President Obama drew cheers and applause in a packed auditorium at the Glasgow Climate Change Conference when he declared "the most important energy in this movement [for climate reform] is coming from young people." Obama then took pains to underscore that the youth climate movement transcended any single figure. "The world is filled with Gretas," he said. "They're not just working for their own countries, they are forming a movement across borders to make the older generation that got us into this mess see that we all have an obligation to dig ourselves out." At the same time, Obama also quickly acknowledged that many young people are either too busy or alienated from politics to engage in the struggle for climate reform. "Some of the young people watching or listening may be thinking, 'I don't have time to organize 200,000 people or propose a constitutional amendment, I've got a math exam next week,'" Obama said. "I get that, I promise you. Unlike Greta, I was not on the cover *Time* magazine when I was sixteen-years-old. And if I was skipping school, it had nothing to do with climate change," he told a giggling audience. But then the battle-worn former president advised young people on what he deemed an unavoidable truth: "I recognize that a lot of young people may be cynical about politics, but the cold hard fact is that we will not have more ambitious climate plans coming out of governments unless governments feel some pressure. Don't think that you can ignore politics. You don't have to be happy about it, but you can't ignore it. You can't be too pure for it. It's part of the process that's going to deliver all of us."

Of course, Obama's call for youth voting was directed at those eighteen years of age and older. It also foregrounds the pivotal issue of when young people ought to be extended the fundamental right to vote. From protest marches to school strikes, child activists often vote with their feet precisely because they have very little recourse for making demands of their elected officials. Whereas adults can make their preferences known at the ballot box, young people under the age of eighteen in the United States cannot cast votes to hold elected officials accountable or to register a verdict on competing political and policy agendas. The underlying rationale for denying voting rights to minors, as we discussed earlier, is that they are citizens in waiting who are presumably too immature to be informed, reasonable, and independent participants in democratic elections. One of the imperatives for liberal democratic societies, as philosophers, educators, and politicians have underscored for centuries, is to nurture and develop in children the capacities for vibrant social, economic, and political membership in adulthood. Yet this logic hinges on the premise that young people under a prescribed age lack some or all of the necessary abilities and qualities to participate in the electoral process, while those above that age magically possess all (or most) of them. If more than an insignificant number of minors have the intellectual capacity, knowledge, and emotional maturity to make reasonable electoral choices, then eighteen years looms as an arbitrary line of demarcation for political enfranchisement. While eighteen is the most common minimum voting age across the globe, sixteen-year-olds can vote in a small number of countries including Argentina, Austria, Brazil, Nicaragua, Scotland, and Wales.

Youth voting rights advocates in the United States reject classic arguments that anyone under the age of eighteen lacks the core capacities needed for voting in democratic elections. "We work, we pay taxes, we care for family members, we can drive, we can do so many other things," said Adam Shyer—one of many high school students who have been lobbying the District of Columbia City Council since 2017 to lower the voting age to sixteen. "Adding voting onto that isn't going to be that big of a responsibility. We can handle it."[2] If reformers succeed, the District of Columbia would be the first legislative body in the nation to reduce the voting age in federal elections to sixteen. The efforts of district youth voting advocates are among the most prominent in a rapidly expanding number of cities and states to consider lowering the minimum voting age. Takoma Park, Maryland, became the first jurisdiction to lower the voting age to sixteen for local elections and several other cities in Maryland have followed suit. Over ten states allow seventeen-year-olds to vote in presidential primaries so long as they are eighteen when they cast ballots in the general election. But there are many who oppose this trend. As a Takoma Park city counselor remarked in opposition, "the vast, vast majority of 16- and 17-year-olds simply lack common sense."[3] Added John Caldara from the Denver Independence Institute, a group that actively opposes these efforts, "I find it entertaining; so we're going to put out warnings not to eat Tide pods, but we're also going to let them vote."[4] By contrast, child and adolescent development experts Daniel Hart and James Youniss propose that enabling sixteen- and seventeen-year-olds to vote in municipal elections would be a valuable way for youth to develop long-term engagement with democratic citizenship during a crucial period of identity formation.[5]

If history is our guide, this most recent push to lower the voting age—in part fueled by student outrage over gun violence, racial injustice, and the climate crisis described earlier—is likely to pick up steam. This youth-focused voting rights movement is both rhetorically and structurally similar to the movement to lower the voting age to eighteen, which culminated in the ratification of the Twenty-Sixth Amendment in 1971. While young people propelled the country into a new era of reform politics, they had little recourse at the polls. Traditionally, only those twenty-one or older could vote. Section 2 of the Fourteenth Amendment protects the right to vote for "the male inhabitants of [each] state, being twenty-one years of age, and citizens of the United States." It is no surprise, then, that protest politics emerged as the most direct and accessible mechanism for young people to express their growing dissatisfaction with the trajectory of democracy in the United States. Public officials in support of these youth-led efforts responded. In 1968, a few months before the Chicago convention, the Senate held hearings to extend voting rights to those eighteen and older. Senator Birch Bayh, a Democrat from Indiana, described his support for decreasing the voting age as "right[ing] an injustice that . . . was being heaped on young people . . . where you had young people that were old enough to die in Vietnam but not old enough to vote for their members of Congress that sent them there."

Others held more utilitarian motives for lowering the voting age. Upon the passage of a 1970 federal statute allowing eighteen-year-olds to vote, for instance, Vice President Agnew expressed hope that, with the youth vote in hand, "there will be less need [for them] to sound off in the streets."[6] Just as they do now, however, naysayers argued, as voting policy analyst Thomas H. Neale summarizes, that young people "lack the maturity and experience that the exercise of the right to vote demands in a free society."[7] Yet despite this resistance to youth enfranchisement, Georgia, Kentucky, Alaska, and Hawaii had already enfranchised those between eighteen and twenty-one with little negative affect on voting outcomes. Whether motivated by the continuing reliance on young people to populate the ranks in Vietnam or a shift in public sentiment brought on by ongoing exposure to youth leaders, Congress in 1970 lowered the voting age to eighteen for all elections—first through an expansion of the Voting Rights Act and then, in response to a Court ruling excluding state and local elections, by quickly crafting and ratifying the Twenty-Sixth Amendment.

Few sizeable and significant groups in democratic societies are legitimately denied basic freedoms or adequate political representation and power on a regular basis. Yet this is exactly the circumstance in which more than 22 percent of Americans (74.2 million of them in 2021) routinely find themselves as a matter of course, with little to no controversy over their diminished status. Indeed, equal membership is out of the question for this population. We are referring, of course, to any person under the age of eighteen. As clarified by the political philosophers discussed at the outset of this book, these decidedly undemocratic arrangements are theoretically acceptable because the diminished political status of children is understood to be impermanent. As future citizens, children will gain all of the democratic rights enjoyed by others upon their inevitable passage to adulthood. Until then, the argument goes, their political marginalization is justified. "No one seriously contends that children should be full members of the demos that governs the state," writes the legendary political scientist Robert Dahl.[8] There is, clearly, an obvious problem with Dahl's summary exclusion of children from the demos laid out in these pages: it presumes neat, clear boundaries where the lines are always blurred. Moreover, as we have shown, children are profoundly engaged in political life long before official adulthood. Indeed, many teenagers may be more civically informed, ethical, and reasonable than many fully enfranchised adults. How do we know precisely when young people ought to gain voting rights and other features of full citizenship? If young people are as much *citizens-in-training* as they are citizens-in-waiting, what aspects of democratic membership and self-realization should they be able to exercise before the age of majority? The answers are not as cut and dried as many adults, including brilliant political scholars like Dahl, would like to think.

As we have chronicled throughout this book, childhood itself is a politically labile and contested concept. Age of consent laws, driving privileges, and criminal sentencing are just a few familiar examples of policies and practices based on inconsistent and contested conceptions of adulthood. Within a single policy domain, we see significant variation among states and other jurisdictions regarding the "age of majority." Across policy domains different logics are applied to usher in or shutter the potential for young people to exert their autonomy. Those who reject or dismiss youth engagement in democratic politics characterize young people as anywhere from indecisive to impetuous, selfish, and lazy. However, negative portrayals of young people as Tide-ball-inhaling lemmings or video-game-addicted parasites crumble against the real stories of SNCC activists, Dreamers, pre-teen transjustice pioneers, middle school environmentalists, or high school March for Our Lives and BLM trailblazers. Assertions that young people's insights are irrelevant to policy debates ring even more hollow against recent and substantial conservative investments in college-based student body elections and student-led campus groups—especially when those same leaders and organizations attempt to curtail young people's political agency when that agency benefits young liberals. These stories reveal an inescapable truth, that age operates more as a foil or as pretext than as an objective and consistently applied standard. Young people can drive, seek employment, lead campaigns as minors, but are deemed too young to vote. They can become parents themselves, responsible for their children's welfare, but yet are unable to sign a rental agreement or make other decisions on their own behalf. They are frequent victims of mass shootings—and are expected to navigate that possibility at all levels of their schooling—and yet they are regularly shut out of any discussion on gun reform. They are deployed to the front line of the most hostile political campaigns—deliberately subjected to physical and emotional assaults—but are barred from having or exerting agency in the political world or over their own health and bodily autonomy. On the whole, young people are often saddled with a heavy load of responsibilities and challenges, but often are marginalized from having autonomy over how to carry these burdens—largely because of their supposed indifference, innocence, or insolence. Age may be a facile legal or policy proxy, but the assertions used to scaffold age-based restrictions frequently bear little resemblance to the facts on the ground.

Our project places children at the heart of US politics, not only as targets of regulation but also as formidable political actors. Centering them in political science theory and research, we believe, advances the study of democratic politics and public policy in important ways. In the critical space that minors often occupy between being political dependents and becoming full citizens, they assert themselves as consequential stakeholders, catalysts, and agents of political reform. Our continued sidestepping of children—even as they occupy primary rather than ancillary roles in the reshaping of US policy and governance—distorts our knowledge of both the motivations and the levers of power in our country's most significant political struggles and transformations. So much of the work of politics, policy, and governance is either about young people, framed around young people, or led by young people—and yet they are frequently rendered as irrelevant to or incapable of political decisions. This study demonstrates that young people are crucial voices in democratic political conflicts and settlements—and that it is time for us to listen.

Notes

Chapter 1

1. Jack Beresford, "Fight Breaks out after School Board Votes in Favor of Mask Mandate," *Newsweek*, September 8, 2021, https://www.newsweek.com/fight-breaks-out-pleasant-hill-school-board-mask-mandate-missouri-1626957.

2. Ryan Mills, "Fights Break Out, Doctor Shoved as Florida School Board Addresses Mask Mandate," National Review, September 1, 2021, https://www.yahoo.com/video/fights-break-doctor-shoved-florida-212015893.html.

3. Regular School Board Meeting, Eastern Carver County Schools, Meeting Livestream, September 27, 2021, 41:21, https://vimeo.com/604410023.

4. Anya Kamenetz, "School Boards Are Asking for Federal Help as They Face Threats and Violence," *NPR.org*, September 30, 2021.

5. Stephen Groves, "Tears, Politics, and Money: School Boards Become Battle Zones," *AP News*, July 10, 2021; Stephen Sawchuk, "Why School Boards Are Now Hot Spots for Nasty Politics," *Education Week*, July 29, 2021; and Campbell Robertson, "While Politics Consume School Board Meetings, a Very Different Crisis Festers," *The New York Times*, December 1, 2021.

6. Nicole Gaudiano, "An Important School Board Group is Unraveling," *Business Insider*, December 6, 2021.

7. Margaret Talbot, "The Increasingly Wild World of School-Board Meetings," *The New Yorker*, October 8, 2021.

8. Ibid.

9. Nina Agrawal, "The Coronavirus Could Cause a Child Abuse Epidemic," *The New York Times*, April 7, 2020; and Emily Brindley, "Vulnerable Children at Greater Risk," *The Hartford Courant*, March 29, 2020.

10. Erica Green, "'Pacing and Praying': Juvenile Youths Seek Release as Virus Spreads," *The New York Times*, April 14, 2020; Tyler Kingkade, "'I'm Scared for My Child': Coronavirus Hits Louisiana Juvenile Detention Centers," *NBC News*, April 13, 2020; and Robin McDowell and Margie Mason, "Juvenile Detention Centers May Become a Coronavirus Hotbed," *Time*, April 1, 2020.

11. John Bowden, "New Jersey Parents Charged with Child Endangerment," *The Hill*, March 31, 2020.

12. Megan Twohey, "New Battle for Those on Coronavirus Front Lines: Child Custody," *The New York Times*, April 7, 2020; and Matt Villano, "Navigating Child Custody in the Time of Coronavirus," *CNN.com*, April 9, 2020.

13. Kelly Tyko, "Can Kids Go to the Store?" *USA Today*, April 4, 2020; Billy Kobin, "Kentucky County Enacts Juvenile Curfew Amid Coronavirus Pandemic," *Louisville Courier Journal*, March 20, 2020; Kellen Quigley, "City of Salamanca Imposes 10pm Curfew for Youth," *Olean Times Herald*, April 13, 2020; Caren Lissner, "Westfield Implements Youth Curfew," *Patch.com*, March 16, 2020; Matt Kawahara, "San Francisco Closes Playgrounds amid Coronavirus," *San Francisco Chronicle*, March 23, 2020; and Anne Barnard and Nate Schweber, "Cooped-Up Children Lose Refuge," *The New York Times*, April 15, 2020.

14. Gary Fineout, Alexandra Glorioso, and Ben Schreckinger, "Will Spring Breakers Become Super Spreaders?," Politico, March 21, 2020; Christopher Brito, "Spring Breakers in Miami Say Coronavirus Pandemic Won't Stop Them from Partying," *CBS News*, March 25, 2020; and Patricia Mazzei and Frances Robles, "The Costly Toll of Not Shutting Down Spring Break Earlier," *The New York Times*, April 11, 2020.

15. Kate Dempsey, "'Overwhelmed' CT Teen Reflects on Working in a Grocery During Coronavirus," *The Stamford Advocate*, April 22, 2020.

16. Lauren Lee, "Pre-med Student Created a Network of Shopping Angels," *CNN.com*, March 30, 2020.

17. Ciara Nugent, "Governments Are Considering How to Ease Coronavirus Lockdowns," *Time*, April 9, 2020.

18. Jessica Bennett, "These Teen Girls Are Fighting for a More Just Future," *The New York Times*, June 26, 2020.

19. "Maryland Teenager Describes Police Attack on Protesters in D.C," *The Washington Post*, June 5, 2020.

20. Samantha Schmidt, "Teens Have Been Gassed and Hit with Rubber Bullets at Protests. They Keep Coming Back," *The Washington Post*, June 6, 2020.

21. Marian Wright Edelman, "Protect Children Not Guns!," *Child Watch Column*, Children's Defense Fund, September 27, 2019.

22. Barack Obama, "Speech at Sandy Hook Prayer Vigil," *NPR.org*, December 16, 2012. https://www.npr.org/2012/12/16/167412995/transcript-presid ent-obama-at-sandy-hook-prayer-vigil, accessed April 14, 2021.

23. Carol Leonnig, Beth Reinhard, and Tom Hamburge, "Newtown Massacre Divided NRA Leaders," *Hartford Courant*, July 5, 2019.

24. Vivian Yee and Alan Blinder, "National School Walkout: Thousands Protest against Violence Across the U.S.," *The New York Times*, March 14, 2018.

25. Charlotte Alter, "The School Shooting Generation Has Had Enough," *Time*, March 22, 2018.

26. "How Student Survivors of the Florida School Shooting Are Using Social Media to Demand Change," *New Statesman America*, February 21, 2018.

27. Emily Witt, "How the Survivors of Parkland Began the Never Again Movement," *The New Yorker*, February 19, 2018; " 'Prayers Won't Fix This': Florida Student Blasts Trump Shooting Response," *CTV News*, February 15, 2018.

28. Alter, "The School Shooting Generation Has Had Enough."

29. Clarissa Hamlin, " 'Look like I'm Dead': Black Florida Shooting Survivor on the Quick Decision that Saved her Life," *NewsOne*, February 28, 2018.

30. Kennedy Bell, "Parkland Survivor Turned Racial Equality Activist Is Fighting on Two Fronts," *ABC News*, June 17, 2020. https://abcnews. go.com/Politics/parkland-survivor-turned-racial-equality-activist-fight ing-fronts/story?id=71215736, accessed June 4, 2021.

31. Ibid.

32. Dakin Andone, "11-year-old Speaks Up for Black Girls Whose Stories Don't Make the Front Page," *CNN*, March 24, 2018.

33. Julie Turkewitz, Matt Stevens, and Jason Bailey, "Emma Gonzalez Leads a Student Outcry on Guns," *The New York Times*, February 18, 2018.

34. Alan Blinder, Jess Bidgood, and Vivian Wang, "In Gun Control Marches, Kids Led but Adults Provided Key Resources," *The New York Times*, March 25, 2018.

35. Ben Crandall, "March for Our Lives: Boomers Have Been There, Marched That," *South Florida Sun Sentinel*, March 18, 2018.

36. Turkewitz, Stevens, and Bailey, "Emma Gonzalez Leads a Student Outcry on Guns."

37. Witt, "How the Survivors of Parkland Began the Never Again Movement."

38. Mark Berman and David Weigel, "NRA Goes on the Offensive after Parkland Shooting," *The Washington Post*, February 22, 2018.

39. Blinder, Bidgood, and Wang, "In Gun Control Marches, Kids Led but Adults Provided Key Resources."

40. Jonah Engel Bromwich, "Parkland Students Find Themselves Targets of Lies and Personal Attacks," *The New York Times,* March 27, 2019.

41. Matt Stevens, " 'Skinhead Lesbian' Tweet about Parkland Student Ends Maine Republican's Candidacy," *The New York Times*, March 18, 2018.

42. Samantha Schmidt, "Rep. King's Campaign Ties Parkland's Emma Gonzalez to 'Communist' Cuba," *The Washington Post*, March 26, 2018.

43. Jonah Bromwich, "Parkland Students Find Themselves Targets of Lies and Personal Attacks," *The New York Times*, March 27, 2018.

44. Ibid.

45. Rachel Sklar, "Harry Potter Inspired the Parkland Generation," *CNN*, March 26, 2018; and Lisa Miller, "Teens Already Know How to Overthrown the Government," *The New York Times*, March 16, 2018.

46. Alter, "The School Shooting Generation Has Had Enough."

47. Ben Shapiro, "Students' Anti-Gun Views," *National Review*, February 20, 2018.

48. Obama, "Speech at Sandy Hook Prayer Vigil."

49. Emma Marris, "Why Young Climate Activists Have Captured the World's Attention," *Nature*, September 18, 2019.

50. Quoted in Grace Abbott, *The Child and the State*, Volume 1 (Chicago: University of Chicago Press, 1938), p.277.

51. Mary Harris Jones, *The Autobiography of Mother Jones* (Chicago: Charles H. Kerr Publishing Company, 1996), p.126.

52. *Congressional Record*, May 31, 1924, p.10001.

53. The quote is from the American Bar Association President Clarence Martin, see William Trattner, *Crusade for the Children* (Chicago: Quadrangle, 1970), p.199.

54. William Graham Sumner, *The Challenge of Facts: And Other Essays* (New Haven: Yale University Press, 1914), pp.18–19.

55. Judy Gillespie's analysis of "newsies" is inspired by a similar motivation to reintroduce planning theorists to the relevance of children in public policy. As she states "Yet with few exceptions the *adult-centric* bias in social and political theory has been largely ignored and even replicated in theories of difference." Judy Gillespie, "Being and Becoming: Writing Children into Planning Theory," *Planning Theory* 12(1) 64–80, 67.

56. See, for example, Ronald Dworkin, "Paternalism," *The Monist* 1 (1972), pp.64–84; Amy Guttman, "Children, Paternalism, and Education," *Philosophy and Public Affairs* 4 (1980) pp.338–358; Laura Martha Purdy, *In Their Best Interest?: The Case against Equal Rights for Children* (Ithaca, NY: Cornell University Press, 1992); Elizabeth Cohen, *Semi-citizenship in Democratic Politics* (New York: Cambridge University Press, 2009); Howard Cohen, *Equal Rights for Children* (Totowa, NJ: Rowman and Littlefield, 1980); Susan Limber and Brian Wilcox, "Application of the U.N. Convention on the Rights of the Child to the United States," *The American Psychologist* 51 (1996) 12, pp.1246–1250; Theodore Stein, *Child Welfare*

and the Law (New York: Longman, 1991); P. Ariès, *Centuries of Childhood: A Social History of Family Life* (New York: Vintage Books, 1962); Samantha Brennan, "Children's Choices or Children's Interests: Which do their Rights Protect?," in David Archard and Colin Macleod, eds., *The Moral and Political Status of Children: New Essays* (Oxford: Oxford University Press, 2002), pp.53–69; Harry Brighouse, "What Rights (if any) Do Children Have?," in Archard and Macleod, eds., *The Moral and Political Status of Children: New Essays*, pp.31–52; U. Bronfenbrenner, C. Condry, John, and Russell Sage Foundation. *Two Worlds of Childhood: U.S. and U.S.S.R.* (New York: Russell Sage Foundation, 1970); K. Capshaw, *Civil Rights Childhood: Picturing Liberation in African American Photobooks* (Minneapolis: University of Minnesota Press, 2014); A. Carter and R. Teten, "Assessing Changing Views of the President: Revisiting Greenstein's Children and Politics," *Presidential Studies Quarterly* 32 (2002) 3, pp.453–462; Theresa Chmara, "Do Minors Have First Amendment Rights in Schools?," *Knowledge Quest* 44 (2015) 1, pp.8–13; Hillary Rodham Clinton, "Do Children Have Any Natural Rights? A Look at Rights and Claims in Legal, Moral, and Educational Discourse," in Michael D.A. Freeman, ed. *Children's Rights: A Comparative Perspective*, Vol. 1 (Farnham, United Kingdon: Ashgate Publishing 2004); C. Cohen, *Democracy Remixed (Transgressing Boundaries)* (Oxford; New York: Oxford University Press, 2010); C. Cohen, "Millennials and the Myth of the Post-Racial Society: Black Youth, Intra-generational Divisions and the Continuing Racial Divide in American Politics." *Daedalus* 140 (2011) 2, pp.197–205; Howard Cohen, *Equal Rights for Children* (Totowa, NJ: Rowman & Littlefield, 1980); J. Coleman, "Rights and Interests: Raising the Next Generation," *American Sociological Review* 60 (1995) 5, pp.782–783. R. Coles, "Glen H. Elder, Jr.: Children of the Great Depression (Book Review)," *Social Forces* 54 (1975) 1, p.300; R. Coles, "Children and Political Authority," T.B. Davie Memorial lecture, University of Cape Town, 1974; R. Coles, The Political Life of Children, 1st edition (Boston: Atlantic Monthly Press, 1986); Gerald Dworkin, "Paternalism," *The Monist* 56 (1972) 1, pp.64–84; D. Easton, J. Dennis, and S. Easton, *Children in the Political System: Origins of Political Legitimacy* (Chicago: University of Chicago Press, 1969); G. Elder, John Modell, and Ross D. Parke, *Children in Time and Place: Developmental and Historical Insights. Cambridge Studies in Social and Emotional Development* (Cambridge; New York: Cambridge University Press, 1993; Philip Fetzer and Lawrence Houlgate, "Are Juveniles Still 'persons' under the United States Constitution?"

International Journal of Children's Rights 5 (1997) 3, pp.319–339; Michael Freeman, "The Future of Children's Rights," *Children and Society* 14 (2000) 4, pp.277–293; Michael D.A. Freeman, ed. *Children's Rights: A Comparative Perspective*, Vol. 1 (Farnham, UK: Ashgate Publishing, 2004); M. Goodman, *Race Awareness in Young Children*. New, revised edition (New York: Collier Books, 1964).; F. Greenstein, "The Benevolent Leader: Children's Images of Political Authority," *The American Political Science Review* 54 (1960) 4, pp.934–943; F. Greenstein, "Sex-Related Political Differences in Childhood," *The Journal of Politics* 23 (1961) 2, pp.353–371; Beatrice Gross and Ronald Gross, eds., *The Children's Rights Movement: Overcoming the Oppression of Young People*, 1st edition (Garden City, NY: Anchor Books, 1977); F. Greenstein, *Children and Politics*. Revised edition, Yale Studies in Political Science 13 (New Haven, CT: Yale University Press, 1969); F. Greenstein, "A Note on the Ambiguity of 'Political Socialization': Definitions, Criticisms, and Strategies of Inquiry," *The Journal of Politics* 32 (1970) 4, pp.969–978; F. Greenstein, "The Benevolent Leader Revisited: Children's Images of Political Leaders in Three Democracies," *The American Political Science Review* 69 (1975) 4, pp.1371–1398; Matthew Grenby, "Politicizing the Nursery: British Children's Literature and the French Revolution," *The Lion and the Unicorn* 27 (2003) 1, pp.1–26; Amy Gutman, "Children, Paternalism, and Education: A Liberal Argument," *Philosophy & Public Affairs* 9 (1980) 4, pp.338–58; T. Hacsi, *Children as Pawns: The Politics of Educational Reform* (Cambridge, MA: Harvard University Press, 2003); Harris, John, "The Political Status of Children," in Graham, K., ed., *Contemporary Political Philosophy: Radical Studies* (New York: Cambridge University Press, 1982), 35–58; J. Hochschild, Vesla M. Weaver, and Traci R. Burch, *Creating a New Racial Order: How Immigration, Multiracialism, Genomics, and the Young Can Remake Race in America* (Princeton, NJ: Princeton University Press, 2012); J. Lawless and Richard Logan Fox, *Running from Office: Why Young Americans Are Turned Off to Politics* (Oxford; New York: Oxford University Press, 2015); N. Lesko, "Denaturalizing Adolescence: The Politics of Contemporary Representations," *Youth and Society* 28 (1996) 2, p.139; John Locke, *Second Treatise on Government* (Indianapolis, IN: Hackett, 1980 [1690]); Joan Mahoney, "'We the Children'? How the Concept of 'Rights' Has Evolved and What It Means for Children and Society," *Update on Law-Related Education* 15, (1991) 2: 13–38: G. Markowitz and David Rosner, *Children, Race, and Power: Kenneth and Mamie Clark's Northside Center* (Charlottesville: University Press of

Virginia, 1996); Daniela Marzana, Elena Marta, and Maura Pozzi, "Social Action in Young Adults: Voluntary and Political Engagement," *Journal of Adolescence* 35 (2012) 3, pp.497–507; J. Marten, *Children in Colonial America*. Children and Youth in America (New York: NYU Press, 2006); F. Martin, *The Politics of Children's Rights* (Cork, Ireland: Cork University Press, 2000). J.S. Mill, *On Liberty. Utilitarianism and On Liberty*. 2nd edition. Edited by Mary Warnock (Blackwell Publishing, Oxford 2003 [1869]); N. Nie, Jane Junn, and Kenneth Stehlik-Barry, *Education and Democratic Citizenship in America* (Chicago: University of Chicago Press, 1996); R. Niemi and Jane Junn, *Civic Education: What Makes Students Learn* (New Haven, CT: Yale University Press, 1998); D. Oswell, *The Agency of Children from Family to Global Human Rights* (Cambridge: Cambridge University Press, 2012); Laura Martha Purdy, *In Their Best Interest?: The Case against Equal Rights for Children* (Ithaca: Cornell University Press, 1992); Michael J. Sandel, *Liberalism and the Limits of Justice* (Cambridge, UK; New York: Cambridge University Press, 1982); Tamar Schapiro, "What Is a Child?," *Ethics* 109 (1999) 4, pp.715–738; Ian Shapiro, *Democratic Justice*. Yale ISPS Series (New Haven, CT: Yale University Press, 1999); Theodore J. Stein, *Child Welfare and the Law* (New York: Longman, 1991); John Tobin, "Courts and the Construction of Childhood: A New Way of Thinking," in Michael D.A. Freeman, ed., *Law and Childhood Studies: Current Legal Issues* (New York, NY: Oxford University Press, 2012); Judith Torney-Purta and Joann Amadeo, "Participatory Niches for Emergent Citizenship in Early Adolescence: An International Perspective," *The Annals of the American Academy of Political and Social Science* 633 (2011), pp.180–200; Geraldine Van Beuren, "Multigenerational Citizenship: The Importance of Recognizing Children as National and International Citizens," *The Annals of the American Academy of Political and Social Science* 633 (2011), pp.30–51; Geraldine Van Beuren, "The 'Quiet' Revolution: Children's Rights in International Law," in Mary John, ed., *Children in Charge: The Child's Right to a Fair Hearing*. Children in Charge Series 1 (London; Bristol, PA: J. Kingsley, 1996), pp.27–37; Mark Walsh, "On Students' Rights, an 'Originalist' Stands Firm," *Education Week* 31 (2011) 8, p.1; E. Washington, "Politicizing Black Children," *The Black Scholar* 4 (1973) 8/9, pp. 2–7; and B. Woodhouse, *Hidden in Plain Sight: The Tragedy of Children's Rights from Ben Franklin to Lionel Tate* (Princeton, NJ: Princeton University Press, 2008).

57. See Daniel Hart and Robert Atkins. "American Sixteen- and Seventeen-Year-Olds Are Ready to Vote," *The Annals of the American Academy of*

Political and Social Science 633 (2011), pp.201–222; and John Harris, "The Political Status of Children," in K. Graham, ed., *Contemporary Political Philosophy: Radical Studies* (Cambridge University Press, 1982).

58. See, John Caldwell Holt, *Escape from Childhood: The Needs and Rights of Children* (New York, NY: Random House, 1975); and Mary John, ed., *Children in Charge: The Child's Right to a Fair Hearing.* Children in Charge Series 1 (London; Bristol, PA: J. Kingsley, 1996).

59. See Nancy E. Walker et al., *Children's Rights in the United States: In Search of a National Policy* (Thousand Oaks, CA: Sage Publications, 1999); Elizabeth Bartholet. "Ratification by the United States of the Convention on the Rights of the Child: Pros and Cons from a Child's Rights Perspective." *The Annals of the American Academy of Political and Social Science* 633 (2011), pp.80–101; Michael D.A. Freeman, *Law and Childhood Studies: Current Legal Issues*; Michael D.A. Freeman and Philip E. Veerman, eds., *The Ideologies of Children's Rights*, Vol. 23 (Norwell, MA: Martinus Nijhoff Publishers, 1992); and Andrew Rehfield, "The Child as Democratic Citizen," *The Annals of the American Academy of Political and Social Science* 633 (2011), pp.141–166.

60. Jan Mason and Toby Fattore. *Children Taken Seriously: In Theory, Policy and Practice.* Children in Charge Series 12 (London; Philadelphia: Jessica Kingsley Publishers, 2005); and Richard Evans Farson, *Birthrights: A Bill of Rights for Children* (New York, NY: Macmillan Publishing, 1974).

61. David Archard and Colin Macleod, eds., *The Moral and Political Status of Children: New Essays* (Oxford: Oxford University Press, 2002); David Archard, *Children, Family, and the State* (New York, NY: Routledge, 2003); Archard, David. "Do Parents Own Their Children?" *The International Journal of Children's Rights* 1 (1993) 3, pp.293–301

62. Cohen 2009

63. Shapiro 1999.

64. For instance, Torney-Purta and Amadeo establish the term "emergent participatory citizenship" to describe the evolving, yet unspecified, ways in which children's political socialization matters. Scholars call for institutions and educators to be more intentional about acknowledging the importance of childhood as a precedent for adulthood (and the responsibilities that follow). They highlight the ways in which children need to be given opportunities to practice citizenship by consenting to the spaces they occupy and the limitations they face (Liebel; Scarre) and the consequent importance of institutional flexibility (Van Beuren). Of particular importance to the subject of political socialization is the literature on education and pedagogy (Eckstein; Hacsi; Nie; Niemi; Mahoney).

65. Fred I. Greenstein, *Children and Politics* (New Haven, CT: Yale University Press, 1965).

66. Richard Niemi, *The Politics of Future Citizens* (New York: Jossey-Bass, 1974); and Robert Coles, *The Political Life of Children* (New York: Atlantic Monthly Press, 1986).

67. See, for example, Cedric Cullingford, *Children and Society: Children's Attitudes to Politics and Power* (London: Cassell, 1992); David Sears and Christia Brown, "Childhood and Adult Political Development," in Leonie Huddy, David Sears, and Jack Levy, eds., *Oxford Handbook on Political Psychology* (New York: Oxford University Press, 2003), pp.69–97; Virginia Sapiro, "Not Your Parents' Political Socialization," *Annual Review of Political Science* 7 (2004), pp.1–23; Simone Abendshon, ed., *Growing into Politics* (Colchester, UK: ECPR Press, 2013); Jan van Deth, Simone Abendshon, and Meike Vollmar, "Children and Politics: An Empirical Reassessment of Early Political Socialization, *Political Psychology* 32 (2011–2012) 1, pp.147–73; Martyn Barrett and Dimitra Pachi, *Youth Civic and Political Engagement* (New York: Routledge, 2019); Catherine Broom, ed., *Youth Civic Engagement in a Globalized World* (New York: Palgrave, 2016); Xenia Chryssochoou and Martyn Barrett, eds., *Political and Civic Engagement in Youth* (Göttingen, Germany: Hogrefe Publishing, 2018); and Sandi Kawecka Nenga and Jessica Taft, *The Civic-Political Lives of Children and Youth* (New York: Emerald Group Publishing, 2012).

68. Lawless and Fox, *Running from Office*.

69. Kimberlé Crenshaw, "Mapping the Margins: Intersectionality, Identity Politics, and Violence against Women of Color," *Stanford Law Review* 43 (1991) 6, pp.1241–1299; Ange-Marie Hancock, "When Multiplication Doesn't Equal Quick Addition: Examining Intersectionality as a Research Paradigm," *Perspectives on Politics* 5 (2007) 1, pp.63–79; Kathy Davis, "Intersectionality as Buzzword: A Sociology of Science Perspective on What Makes a Feminist Theory Successful," *Feminist Theory* 9 (2008) 1, pp.67–85; and Olena Hankivsky and Julia S. Jordan-Zachery, eds., *The Palgrave Handbook of Intersectionality in Public Policy* (Cham, Switzerland: Springer Nature: Palgrave Macmillan, 2019).

70. Sophie Bjork-James, "White Sexual Politics: The Patriarchal Family in White Nationalism and the Religious Right," *Transforming Anthropology* 28, 1, pp.58–63.

71. Lesbian, gay, bisexual, transgender, queer or questioning, intersex, asexual/agender/allies. The concept of Queer, according to refers to "anything that exists outside of the dominant narrative. Queer means that you are one of those letters [LGBT], but you could be all of those letters and not

knowing is OK." The plus sign refers to any individual who doesn't identify with one of the letters but considers themselves to be part of the Queer community. "What Does LGBTQIA+ Stand For?" June 24, 2020, Yahoo. com/video/does-LGBTQIA-stand141600051.html.

72. David Smith, "How Did Republicans Turn Critical Race Theory into a Winning Electoral Issue?," *The Guardian*, November 3, 2021.

73. Cathy Cohen, *Democracy Remixed: Black Youth and the Future of American Politics* (New York: Oxford University Press, 2012).

74. Amy Lerman and Vesla Weaver, *Arresting Citizenship: The Democratic Consequences of American Crime Control* (Chicago: University of Chicago Press, 2014), pp.1–2.

75. Erin Kerrison, Jennifer Cobbina, and Kimberly Bender, "'Your Pants Won't Save You:' Why Black Youth Challenge Race-Based Police Surveillance and the Demands of Black Respectability Politics," *Race and Justice*, 2018.

76. Alison Gash, Daniel Tichenor, Angelia Chavez, and Malori Musselman, "Framing Kids: Children, Immigration Reform, and Same-Sex Marriage," *Politics, Groups, and Identities* (November 2018), pp.44–70.

77. Jacob Soboroff, *Separated: Inside an American Tragedy* (New York: Custom House, 2020).

78. See, for example, Clayborne Carson, *In Struggle: SNCC and the Black Awakening of the 1960s* (Cambridge, MA: Harvard University Press, 1995).

79. Walter J. Nicholls, *The DREAMers: How the Undocumented Youth Transformed the Immigration Debate* (Pal Alto, CA: Stanford University Press, 2013); and Sidney Milkis and Daniel Tichenor, *Rivalry and Reform* (Chicago: University of Chicago Press, 2019), pp.293–305.

80. Bennett, "These Teen Girls Are Fighting for a More Just Future."

81. Harry Hendrick, *Children, Childhood, and English Society, 1880–1990* (Cambridge: Cambridge University Press, 1997), pp.3–4.

Chapter 2

1. Robert Bremner, *Children and Youth in America* (New York: Cambridge University Press, 1970), Volume 1, pp.7–8.

2. Ibid; and Mary Ann Mason, *From Father's Property to Children's Rights: The History of Child Custody in the United States* (New York: Columbia University Press, 1994), pp.1–2.

3. Ibid., pp.5–12; and R.W. Beales, "The Child in Seventeenth-Century America," in Joseph Hawes and H. Ray Hiner, eds., *American Childhood:*

A Research Guide and Historical Handbook (Westport, CT: Greenwood, 1985), pp.15–57.

4. Karin Calvert, *Children in the House: The Material Culture of Early Childhood, 1600–1900* (Boston, MA: Northeastern University Press, 1992).

5. Mason, *From Father's Property to Children's Rights*, p.2.

6. Bremner, *Children and Youth in America*, Volume 1, pp.7–8.

7. Phillipe Aries, *Centuries of Childhood: A Social History of Family Life* (New York: Vintage, 1962).

8. Lloyd deMause, *The History of Childhood* (New York: The Psychohistory Press, 1974), p.1.

9. Aries, *Centuries of Childhood*.

10. Lawrence Stone, *The Family, Sex, and Marriage in England, 1500–1800* (New York: Harper and Row, 1977); Jack Goody, *The Development of the Family and Marriage in Europe* (New York: Cambridge University Press, 1983); Barbara Hanawalt, *The Ties that Bound: Peasant Families in Medieval England* (Oxford: Oxford University Press, 1986); John Boswell, *The Kindness of Strangers: The Abandonment of Children in Western Europe from Antiquity to the Renaissance* (New York: Pantheon Books, 1988); Jacques Gelis, *The History of Childbirth* (Boston: Northeastern University Press, 1991); Barbara Hanawalt, *Growing Up in Medieval London: The Experience of Childhood in History* (New York: Oxford University Press, 1993); Daniele Alexandre-Bidon and Didier Lett, *Children in the Middle Ages: Fifth to Fifteenth Centuries*. Translated by Jody Gladding (Notre Dame, IN: University of Notre Dame Press, 1999); Sally Crawford, *Childhood in Anglo-Saxon England* (Gloucestershire, UK: Sutton, 1999); Joanne Derevenski, ed., *Children and Material Culture* (London: Routledge, 2000); Jack Goody, *The European Family: An Historico-Anthropological Essay* (Oxford: Basil Blackwell, 2000); Colin Heywood, *A History of Childhood: Children and Childhood in the West from Medieval to Modern Times* (Cambridge: Polity, 2001); Hugh Cunningham, *Children and Childhood in Western Society since 1500*, 2nd edition (New York: Longman, 2005); Margaret King, "Concepts of Childhood: What We Know and Where We Might Go," *Renaissance Quarterly* (2007), pp.371–407; Anthony Fletcher, *Growing Up in England: The Experience of Childhood 1600–1914* (New Haven, CT: Yale University Press, 2008); Paula Fuss, ed., *The Routledge History of Childhood in the Western World* (London: Routledge, 2013).

11. Nicholas Orme, *Medieval Children* (New Haven, CT: Yale University Press, 2001); Joanne Ferraro, "Childhood in Medieval and Early Modern Times," in Paul Fass, ed., *The Routledge History of Childhood in the Western*

World (London: Routledge, 2013), pp.61–77; Adrienne Gavin, *The Child in British Literature: Literary Constructions of Childhood, Medieval to Contemporary* (Basingstoke, UK: Palgrave Macmillan, 2012).

12. See, for example, Stone, *The Family, Sex, and Marriage in England, 1500–1800*; and Linda Pollack, *A Lasting Relationship: Parents and Children over Three Centuries* (London: University Press of New England, 1990).

13. Paula Fuss, "Is There a Story in the History of Childhood?" in Fuss, ed., *The Routledge History of Childhood in the Western World*, p.4.

14. Ibid, pp.4–6; and Ferraro, "Childhood in Medieval and Early Modern Times," pp.61–77.

15. Keith Bradley, *Slavery and Society at Rome* (Cambridge: Cambridge University Press, 1994); Keith Bradley and Paul Cartledge, eds., *The Cambridge World History of Slavery* (Cambridge: Cambridge University Press, 2011); Paul Lovejoy, "The Children of Slavery: The Transatlantic Phase," *Slavery & Abolition* 27 (August 2006), pp.197–217; Wilma King, *Stolen Childhood: Slave Youth in Nineteenth-Century America*, 2nd edition (Bloomington: Indiana University Press, 2011); Benjamin Nicholas Lawrence, *Amistad's Orphans: An Atlantic Story of Children, Slavery, and Smuggling* (New Haven, CT: Yale University Press, 2014).

16. Fuss, "Is There a Story in the History of Childhood?"; Ferraro, "Childhood in Medieval and Early Modern Times"; and Fuss, ed., *The Routledge History of Childhood in the Western World*.

17. Jean-Jacques Rousseau, *Emile, ou de l'éducation*. Edited by Michel Launay (Paris, France: GarnierFlammarion, 1966), p.32.

18. Larry Wolfe, "Childhood and the Enlightenment: The Complications of Innocence," in Fuss, ed., *The Routledge History of Childhood in the Western World*, pp.78–99.

19. Ibid.

20. Lester G. Crocker, *Jean-Jacques Rousseau—the Quest 1712–1758* (New York: Macmillan, 1974); and Leo Damrosch, *Jean-Jacques Rousseau: Restless Genius* (New York: Houghton Mifflin, 2005).

21. Mason, *From Father's Property to Children's Rights*, pp.2–47; John Demos, *A Little Commonwealth: Family Life in Plymouth Colony* (New York, 1970); and R.W. Beales, "The Child in Seventeenth-Century America," in Joseph Hawes and N. Ray Hiner, eds., *American Childhood* (Westport, CT: 1985), pp.15–57.

22. "An Awful Disaster: Burning of the Granite Woolen Mill at Fall River," *The New York Herald*, September 20, 1874; Marc Munroe Dion, "Mill Fire Sparked Workers' Rights Battle," *The Herald News*, April 14, 2009;

William Moniz, "Learning from Mistakes of the Past," *South Coast Today*, April 23, 2009; Mart Blewett, "Manhood and the Market: The Politics of Gender and Class among Textile Workers of Fall River, Massachusetts, 1870–1880," in Ava Baron, ed., *Work Engendered: Toward a New History of American Labor* (Ithaca, NY: Cornell University Press, 1991), pp.92–107; Marjorie E. Wood, "Emancipating the Child laborer: Children, Freedom, and the Moral Boundaries of the Market in the United States, 1853–1938" (Ph.D. diss., University of Chicago, 2011), pp.114–116; "History of Child Labor in the United States," *Monthly Labor Review*, January, 2007.

23. Steven Sugarman and David Kirp, "Rethinking Collective Responsibility for Children," *Law and Contemporary Problems* (Summer 1975), p.145.

24. Hugh Hindman, ed., *The World of Child Labor: An Historical and Regional Survey* (London: M.E. Sharpe, 2009); Monica McCoy and Stefanie Keen, *Child Abuse and Neglect*, 2nd edition (New York: Psychology Press, 2013); Lisa Aronson Fontes, *Child Abuse and Culture* (Guilford Press, 2008); Neil Howard, *Child Trafficking, Youth Labor Mobility, and the Politics of Protection* (London: Palgrave Macmillan, 2016); Michael Bourdillan, Deborah Levison, William Myers, and Ben White, *Rights and Wrongs of Children's Work* (New Brunswick, NJ: Rutgers University Press, 2010); Sarbajit Chaudhuri and Jayanta Kumar Dwibedi, *The Economics of Child Labor in the Era of Globalization* (London: Routledge, 2016); Anaclaudia Fassa, David Parker, and Thomas Scanlon, *Child Labour: A Public Health Perspective* (Oxford: Oxford University Press, 2010); Christine Watkins, *Child Labor and Sweatshops*, 2nd edition (New York: Greenhaven Press, 2010); Virginia Kendall and T. Markus Funk, *Child Exploitation and Trafficking* (Lanham, MD: Rowman and Littlefield, 2016).

25. Stuart Hart, "From Property to Person Status: Historical Perspective on Children's Rights," *American Psychologist* 46 (1991), pp.53–59.

26: Emily Baughan, "'Every Citizen of Empire Implored to Save the Children!' Empire, Internationalism and the Save the Children Fund in Inter-war Britain." *Historical Research* 86 (2013) 231, pp.116–137; Joelle Droux, "Life during Wartime: The Save the Children International Union and the Dilemmas of Warfare Relief, 1919–1947," in Johannes Paulmann, ed., *Dilemmas of Humanitarian Aid in the Twentieth Century* (New York: Oxford University Press, 2016), pp.185–206; Dominique Marshall, "International Child Saving," in Paula Fass, ed., *The Routledge History of Childhood in the Western World* (London: Routledge, 2015), pp. 469–490.

27. Elizabeth Clapp, *Mothers of All Children: Women Reformers and the Rise of Juvenile Courts in the Progressive Era* (State College, PA: Penn State University Press, 1998); John Fliter, *Child Labor in America: The Epic Struggle to Protect Children* (Lawrence: University Press of Kansas, 2018); Katharine Briar Lawson, Mary McCarthy, and Nancy Dickinson, eds., *The Children's Bureau: Shaping a Century of Child Welfare Practices, Programs, and Policies* (New York: NASW Press, 2013); John Rury, *Education and Social Change* (New York: Routledge, 2019).

28. Amy Gutmann, "Children, Paternalism, and Education: A Liberal Argument," *Philosophy and Public Affairs* (Summer 1980), p.341.

29. Elizabeth Cohen, "Neither Seen Nor Heard: Children's Citizenship in Contemporary Democracies," *Citizenship Studies* (May 2005), pp.221–223; see also, Cohen, *Semi-Citizenship in Democratic Politics* (New York: Cambridge University Press, 2009).

30. James Schmidt, "Children and the State," in Fuss, ed., *The Routledge History of Childhood in the Western World*, pp.174–175.

31. Susan Ferris, "The Trump Administration Knew that Migrant Children Would Suffer from Family Separations," *The Texas Tribune*, December 16, 2019; Eliza Collins and Alan Gomez, "Top HHS Official Warned Trump Administration against Separating Immigrant Families," *USA Today*, July 31, 2018.

32. For a provocative view of Horace Mann's thought, see Bob Pepperman Taylor, *Horace Mann's Troubling Legacy: The Education of Democratic Citizens* (Lawrence: University Press of Kansas, 2010).

33. Zhe Li, "Poverty among Americans Aged 65 and Older," *Congressional Research Service Report R45791*, July 1, 2019; Margaret Weir, Anna Orloff, and Theda Skocpol, eds., *The Politics of Social Policy in the United States* (Princeton, NJ: Princeton University Press, 1988); Andrea Louise Campbell, *How Policies Make Citizens: Senior Political Activism and the American Welfare State* (Princeton, NJ: Princeton University Press, 2005); Katherine Magnuson and Elizabeth Votruba Drzal, "Enduring Influences of Childhood Poverty," in Maria Cancian and Sheldon Danziger, eds., *Changing Poverty, Changing Policies* (New York: Russell Sage, 2009); and Monica Miller Smith, *Families and Children Living in Poverty* (New York: Congella Academic Publishing, 2020).

34. Dex McCluskey, "Paterno, Spanier Ousted in Penn State in Child Sex-Abuse Case," *Bloomberg News*, November 9, 2011; Jeffrey Toobin, "Former Penn State President Graham Spanier Speaks," *The New Yorker*, August 21, 2012; "The Penn State Scandal, Piece by Piece," *Pittsburgh Post-Gazette*,

July 12, 2019; Scott Jaschik, "Spanier Conviction Renews Debate on Penn State Post-Sandusky," *Inside Higher Education*, March 27, 2017.

35. Christine Hauser, "Ex-Michigan State Athlete's Lawsuit Says Larry Nassar Drugged and Raped Her on Camera," *The New York Times*, September 18, 2019; David Jesse, "Michigan State to Pay Record \$4.5 Million Fine in Larry Nassar Sexual Assault Scandal," *Detroit Free Press*, September 5, 2019.

36. Jen Kirby, Emily Stewart, and Tara Golshan, "Jim Jordan and the Ohio State Sexual Abuse Controversy," *Vox*, July 20, 2018; and Jessica Wehrman, Laura Bischoff, and Jennifer Smola, "Congressman Jim Jordan Knew About Sex Abuse at OSU," *Dayton Daily News*, July 3, 2018.

37. Matt Carroll, Kevin Cullen, Thomas Farragher, Stephen Kurkjian, Michael Paulson, Sacha Pfeiffer, Michael Rezendes, and Walter V. Robinson, *Betrayal: The Crisis in the Catholic Church* (Boston: Back Bay Books, 2008); and Michael D'Antonio, *Mortal Sins: Sex, Crime, and the Era of Catholic Scandal* (New York: Thomas Dunne Books, 2013).

38. Gerald Dworkin, "Paternalism," *The Monist* 56 (1972), pp.64–84; Gerald Dworkin, "Moral Paternalism," *Law and Philosophy* 24 (2005) 3, pp.305–319.

39. Nelson Mandela, "Foreword," in Etienne Krug, Linda Dahlberg, James Mercy, Anthony Zwi, and Rafael Lazano, eds., *World Report on Violence and Health* (Geneva: World Health Organization, 2002), p.xi.

40. Charles Dickens, *Oliver Twist: The Parish Boy's Progress* (Minneapolis, MN: Lerner Publishing Group, 2015).

41. Charles Strouse, *Annie* (New York: Hal Leonard, 1982).

42. J.K. Rowling, *Harry Potter and the Sorcerer's Stone* (London: Scholastic, 1999).

43. John Locke, *The Second Treatise of Government* (Indianapolis, IN: Hackett, 1980), sect.170, p.88.

44. Ibid.

45. John Stuart Mill, *On Liberty*, p.76.

46. William Golding, *Lord of the Flies* (New York: Penguin, 2006), p.200.

47. Mill, *On Liberty*, p.76.

48. Velma LaPoint, Lillian Holloman, and Sylvan Alleyne, "The Role of Dress Codes, Uniforms in Urban Schools," *NASSP Bulletin*, October 1, 1992, pp.20–26; Kneia DeCosta, "Dress Code Blues," *The Journal of Negro Education* (Winter, 2006), pp.49–59; Kira Barrett, "When School Dress Codes Discriminate," *NEA Today*, July 24, 2018.

49. William Trattner, *Crusade for the Children: A History of the National Child Labor Committee and Child Labor Reform in America* (New York: Quadrangle Books, 1970).

50. Brown v. Board of Education of Topeka, 347 U.S. 48.

51. Martha Minow, *Making All the Difference: Inclusion, Exclusion, and American Law* (Ithaca, NY: Cornell University Press, 1990), pp.284–285.

52. Elizabeth Cohen, "Neither Seen Nor Heard: Children's Citizenship in Contemporary Democracies," *Citizenship Studies* (May 2005), pp.221–240.

53. Amy Mullin, "Children, Paternalism, and the Development of Authority," *Ethical Theory and Moral Practice* (June 2014), pp.413–426.

54. Susan Tifflin, *In Whose Best Interest? Child Welfare Reform in the Progressive Era* (Westport, CT: Greenwood Press, 1982), pp.229–247; Minow, *Making All the Difference*, pp.247–251; Lela Costin, *Two Sisters for Social Justice* (Urbana: University of Illinois Press, 1983).

55. Ibid; and Jan Wilson, *The Women's Joint Congressional Committee and the Politics of Maternalism* (Urbana: University of Illinois Press, 2007), pp.129–137.

56. Wilson, *The Women's Joint Congressional Committee and the Politics of Maternalism*, p.136.

57. Tifflin, *In Whose Best Interest? Child Welfare Reform in the Progressive Era*, pp.229–247; Minow, *Making All the Difference*, pp.247–251; and Wilson, *The Women's Joint Congressional Committee and the Politics of Maternalism*, p.136.

58. Strouse, *Annie*.

59. Gerald Dworkin, "Paternalism," *The Monist* 56 (1972) 1, pp.64–84.

60. Mullin, "Children, Paternalism, and the Development of Authority," p.421.

61. Sam Brinton, "I Was Tortured in Gay Conversion Therapy," *The New York Times*, January 24, 2018.

62. Alison Gash, "What's the Backlash against Gender-neutral Bathrooms all About?" *The Conversation*, April 4, 2016.

63. See Katelyn Burns, "The Rise of Anti-Trans Radical Feminists, Explained," *Vox*, September 5, 2019, https://www.vox.com/identities/2019/9/5/20840101/terfs-radical-feminists-gender-critical.

64. Doha Madani, "J.K. Rowling Accused of Transphobia for Mocking 'People Who Menstruate' Headline," *NBC News*, June 7, 2020.

65. While the science behind testosterone levels and athletic performance demonstrates that testosterone-induced performance advantages decrease the longer (and the earlier) that testosterone blockers are provided, the legal and moral arguments remain fraught. Among the most salient arguments advanced by transgender athlete advocates is the fact that testosterone is an unreasonable focus of regulators who study athletic performance—and is wrongly used as the primary justification for promoting sex-segregated sports. While athletes may excel because of a

range of physiological differences, some of which may produce significant advantages, the primary focus is on testosterone—and specifically levels of testosterone among female athletes. See e.g., Dr. Rachel McKinnon and Dr. Aryn Conrad, "Including Trans Women Athletes in Competitive Sport: Analyzing the Science, Law and Principles and Policies of Fairness in Competition," in *Philosophical Topics: Gendered Oppression and Its Intersections* (Fayetteville, AR: University of Arkansas Press, 2018).

66. A recent study found that young trans patients on puberty blockers or hormone therapies were 73% less likely to have considered suicide during a twelve-month follow-up. Diana M. Tordoff et al, "Mental Health Outcomes in Transgender and Nonbinary Youths Receiving Gender - Affirming Care," JAMA Network Open, February 25, 2022, https://jama network.com/journals/jamanetworkopen/articlepdf/2789423/tordoff_20 22_oi_220056_1645136284.51531.pdf

67. Thomas Hobbes, *Leviathan* (Berkeley, CA: Mint Editions, 2020 [1651]), p.257.

68. David Gauthier, *The Logic of Leviathan* (Oxford: Clarendon Press, 1963), p.118.

69. Leviathan, p.257.

70. Sir William Blackstone, *The Commentaries of Sir William Blackstone, Knight, on the Laws and Constitution of England* (New York: American Bar Association, 2009), pp.62–64.

71. Mason, *From Father's Property to Children's Rights*, p.6.

72. Allen Pusey, "June 3, 1918: Child Labor Law Declared Unconstitutional," *ABA Journal*, June 1, 2015; John Blake, "Supreme Court a Force of Change?: Not So Far," *CNN.com*, June 27, 2015.

73. Samuel Gompers, "Let's Save Our Children," *The American Federationist*, October, 1917, p.860; Erwin Chemerinsky, *The Case Against the Supreme Court* (New York, Penguin: 2014), p.91.

74. Hammar v. Dagenhart 247 U.S. 251 (1918).

75. Ibid.

76. Allen Pusey, "Child Labor Law Declared Unconstitutional," *ABA Journal*, June 1, 2015.

77. "What Little Rueben Got," *The Textile Worker* (April 1923), p.483; Jyotsna Sreenivasan, *Poverty and the Government in America* (Santa Barbara, CA: ABC-Clio, 2009), pp.145–148; "The Supreme Court and the Children," *Social Science Review* (March, 1941), pp.116–119.

78. Fliter, *Child Labor in America*; Chaim Rosenberg, *Child Labor in America: A History* (New York: McFarland, 2013); and Hugh Hindman, *Child Labor: An American History* (New York; Routledge, 2016).

79. Sarah Donovan and Jon Shimabukuru, *The Fair Labor Standards Act (FLSA) Child Labor Provisions*, Congressional Research Services, June 29, 2016.

80. Article 32, Convention on the Rights of the Child, United Nations General Assembly, Resolution 44/25, November 20, 1989.

81. International Labour Organization, C182: Worst Forms of Child Labour Convention, 1989.

82. International Labor Organization, *Global Estimates of Child Labour* (Geneva, Switzerland: International Labor Organization, 2017), p.5.

83. Jeffrey Shulman, *The Constitutional Parent: Rights, Responsibilities, and the Enfranchisement of the Child* (New Haven, CT: Yale University Press, 2014), pp.135–137.

84. Caban v. Mohammed 441 U.S. 380 (1979).

85. Lehr v. Robertson 463 U.S. 238 (1983).

86. Schulman, *The Constitutional Parent*, p.13.

87. Ibid.

88. Bellotti v. Baird, 443 U.S. 622 (1979).

89. Abbey Marr, "Judicial Bypass Procedures," *Advocates for Youth* (June 2015).

90. Shelly Burtt, "Religious Parents, Secular Schools," *The Review of Politics* 56 (Winter 1994), pp.51–70; Amy Gutmann, "Civic Education and Social Diversity," *Ethics* 105 (April 1995), pp.557–579; Amy Gutmann, *Democratic Education* (Princeton, NJ: Princeton University Press, 1999); Stephen Macedo, *Diversity and Distrust* (Cambridge, MA: Harvard University Press, 200); William Galston, *Liberal Purposes: Goods, Virtues and Diversity in the Liberal State* (New York: Cambridge University Press, 1991); William Galston, *Liberal Pluralism: The Implications of Value Pluralism for Political Theory* (New York: Cambridge University Press, 2002); Mark Vopat, "Justice, Religion, and the Education of Children," *Public Affairs Quarterly* 23 (July 2009), pp.203–229; and Tim Fowler, "The Limits of Civic Education: The Divergent Implications of Political and Comprehensive Liberalism," *Theory and Research in Education* 9 (2011) 1, pp.87–100.

91. Ibid.

92. Shawn Frances Peters, *The Yoder Case: Religious Freedom, Education, and Parental Rights* (Lawrence: University Press of Kansas, 2003); William Fischel, "Do Amish One-Room Schools Make the Grade?" *University of Chicago Law Review* 79 (Winter 2012), pp.107–129.

93. Wisconsin v. Yoder, 406 U.S. 205 (1972).

94. Eamon Callan, "Galston's Dilemmas and Wisconsin v. Yoder," *Theory and Research in Education* 4 (2006) 3, pp.262.

95. Galston, *Liberal Purposes: Goods, Virtues and Diversity in the Liberal State*; and Galston, *Liberal Pluralism: The Implications of Value Pluralism for Political Theory.*

96. Gutmann, *Democratic Education*, 30.

97. Wisconsin v. Yoder 406 U.S. 205 (1972): 241.

98. Thomas Larson, "Child No More," *San Diego Reader*, July 22, 2015.

99. Ibid.

100. Bruce Hafen and Jonathon Hafen, "Abandoning Children to their Autonomy: The United Nations Convention on the Rights of the Child," *Harvard International Law Journal* (1996) 37, pp.449, 454.

101. Ibid., 451 (quoting Lee Teitelbaum, Forward: The Meanings of Rights of Children, 10. New Mexico Law Review (1980), pp.235, 238).

102. Tinker v. Des Moines, 393 U.S. 503, 1969.

103. Minersville School District v. Gobitis, 310 U.S. 586, 1940.

104. West Virginia State Board of Education v. Barnette, 319 U.S. 624, 1943.

105. Ibid.

106. Engel v. Vitale, 370 U.S. 421, 1962; Abington v. Schempp, 374 U.S. 203, 1963.

107. Wallace v. Jaffree, 472 U.S. 38, 1985.

108. Goss v. Lopez, 419 U.S. 565, 1975.

109. In re Gault 387 U.S. 1, 1967.

110. Ibid.

111. In re. Roger S. Crim. No. 19558. Supreme Court of California. July 18, 1977.

112. Ibid.

113. Jodi Picoult, *My Sister's Keeper* (New York: Atria Books, 2004), p.21.

114. In re EG, 549 N.E.2d 322, 1989. The case is of such doctrinal importance that the Illinois Supreme Court takes up the state's appeal—even after E.G. turns eighteen rendering the specific facts moot. The court upholds the rights of "mature minors" to exercise medical autonomy and reject treatment. Of particular interest to the court was whether the largely arbitrary age of eighteen that was articulate in Illinois statutes regarding medical consent created an "impenetrable barrier that magically precludes a minor from possessing and exercising certain rights normally associated with adulthood."

115. Lauren Cox, Emily Friedman, and Jason Ryan, "Man Who Survived Without Chemo: 'I'd Still Fight,'" *ABC News*, May 22, 2009. https://abcnews.go.com/US/story?id=7661834&page=1on, accessed April 20, 2021.

116. Judy Mann, "Illegal Abortion's Deadly Price," *The Washington Post*, August 3, 1990. https://www.washingtonpost.com/archive/local/1990/08/03/ille gal-abortions-deadly-price/bd016dad-2c53-4b3d-9b99-274b054c0c9b/.

117. Planned Parenthood v. Danforth, 428 U.S. 52 (1976).

118. Planned Parenthood v. Casey, 505 U.S. 833 (1992).

119. Barbara Brotman, "How Young Women in Illinois Get Abortions without Parental Notification," *Chicago Tribune*, October 9, 2015.

120. Jenny Kutner, "The War on Women is a War on Teenage Girls: How Judicial Bypass Laws Shame Pregnant Minors and Threaten Personal Safety," *Salon*, October 9, 2014.

121. Molly Redden, "This is How Judges Humiliate Pregnant Teens Who Want Abortions," *Mother Jones*, September/October 2014.

122. Jen Christensen, "Judge Gives Grandparents Custody of Ohio Transgender Teen," *CNN*, February 16, 2018. https://www.cnn.com/2018/02/16/health/ohio-transgender-teen-hearing-judge-decision/index.html.

123. Katie Mettler, "Why a Minn. Mom is Suing her Transgender Teen and the Clinic that Gave her Hormones," *The Washington Post*, November 18, 2016.

124. Aviva Katz, Sally A. Webb, and Committee on Bioethics, "Informed Consent in Decision-Making in Pediatric Practice," *Pediatrics*, August 2016, 138(2)

125. Hazelwood School District v. Kuhlmeier, 484 U.S. 260, 1988.

126. "Wild in the Streets," *Variety*, December 31, 1967.

127. J. Hoberman, "Are You Over 35? 'Wild in the Streets' Should Scare You," *The New York Times*, September 20, 2016.

128. Alexander Keyssar, *The Right to Vote: The Contested History of Democracy in the United States* (New York: Basic Books, 2000), pp.235–236.

129. Quoted in Sylvia Engdahl, *Amendment XXVI: Lowering the Voting Age* (New York: Greenhaven, 2010), p.18.

130. "Teen Rejected by Polygamous Family Finds New Life," *Arizona Daily Sun*, March 13, 2005. https://azdailysun.com/teen-rejected-by-polygam ous-family-finds-new-life/article_cb40e87e-3f9f-5dcd-8c71-0dc6943a4 881.html, accessed April 20, 2021.

131. David Kelly, "Lost to the Only Life They Knew," *Los Angeles Times*, June 13, 2005. https://www.latimes.com/archives/la-xpm-2005-jun-13-na-los tboys13-story.html, accessed April 20, 2021.

132. "Hundreds of 'Lost Boys' Expelled by Polygamist Community," *ABC News*, October 25, 2007.

133. Brooke Adams, "The So-Called Lost Boy wants the FLDS leader to approve a reunion," *The Salt Lake Tribune*, December 23, 2006. https://archive.sltrib.com/story.php?ref=/ci_4891049, accessed April 20, 2021.

134. Kimberly Sevcik, "The Lost Boys of Colorado City," *Salon*, July 6, 2006. https://www.salon.com/2006/07/06/lost_boys_4/, accessed April 20, 2021.

135. Wartluft v. Milton Hershey Sch. & Sch. Tr., United States District Court for the Middle District of Pennsylvania, March 18, 2020.

136. Ibid.

137. Ibid.

138. "Implied emancipation" can be satisfied when the minor's lifestyle reflects that of an emancipated minor. They earn their own money, pay their own rent, are responsible for their own education. In this case a parent can argue that their parenting is no longer required.

139. Ireland v. Ireland, 855 P.2d 40 (Idaho 1993).

140. S. Elise Kert, "Should Emancipation be for Adolescents or for Parents?" *Journal of Contemporary Legal Issues* 16 (Fall 2003), pp.307–310..

141. Tia Wallach, "Statutory Emancipation in California: Privilege or Poverty," *Journal of Contemporary Legal Issues* (1999), pp.669–673.

142. Carol Sanger and Eleanor Willemsen, "Minor Changes: Emancipating Children in Modern Times," *University of Michigan Journal of Law Reform* 25 (1992) 239, pp.239–355.

143. Amy Lehrman and Velsa Weaver, *Arresting Citizenship: The Democratic Consequences of American Crime Control* (Chicago: University of Chicago Press, 2014); Bruce Western and Becky Pettit, "Incarceration and Social Inequality," *Daedalus* 139 (2010) 3, pp.8–19; Michael Tonry, *Punishing Race: A Continuing American Dilemma* (New York: Oxford University Press, 2010); W.D. Bales and A.R. Piquero, "Racial/Ethnic Differentials in Sentencing to Incarceration," *Justice Quarterly* 29 (2012) 5, pp.1–32; D.M. Bishop, and M.J. Leiber, "The Role of Race and Ethnicity in Juvenile Justice Processing," in B.C. Feld and D.M. Bishop, eds., *The Oxford Handbook of Juvenile Crime and Juvenile Justice* (New York: Oxford University Press, 2012), pp.445–484.

144. Barry Feld and Donna Bishop, eds., *The Oxford History of Juvenile Crime and Juvenile Justice* (New York: Oxford University Press: 2012); Arnold Binder, G. Gilbert Geis, and Dickson Bruce, *Juvenile Delinquency: Historical, Cultural, and Legal Perspectives* (Cincinnati, OH: Anderson, 1997).

145. Tera Eva Agyepong, *The Criminalization of Black Children* (Chapel Hill: University of North Carolina Press, 2018), pp.2–6 and 133–137. On

the "new Jim Crow" and more generally race and criminal justice in US political development, see Michelle Alexander, *The New Jim Crow: Mass Incarceration in the Age of Colorblindness* (New York: New Press, 2010); Marie Gottschalk, *The Prison and the Gallows: The Politics of Mass Incarceration in America* (Cambridge: Cambridge University Press, 2006); Lisa Miller, *The Perils of Federalism: Race, Poverty, and the Politics of Crime Control* (New York: Oxford University Press, 2008); and Naomi Murakawa, *The First Civil Right: How Liberals Built Prison America* (Princeton, NJ: Princeton University Press, 2014). Agyepong's quote on children as "super-predators" is on p.156; see also John DiIulio, "The Coming of the Super-Predators," *The Weekly Standard*, November 27, 1995; and Anne Gearan and Abby Phillip, "Clinton Regrets 1996 Remark on 'Super-Predators' after Encounter with Activist," *The Washington Post*, February 25, 2016.

146. Alaska, Delaware, Florida, Hawaii, Idaho, Maine, Maryland, Michigan, Pennsylvania, Rhode Island, South Carolina, Tennessee, West Virginia. https://eji.org/news/13-states-lack-minimum-age-for-trying-kids-as-adults/.

147. Nina Totenberg, "The Supreme Court Rejects Restrictions on Life without Parole for Juveniles," *National Public Radio*, April 22, 2021; Adam Liptak, "Supreme Court Rejects Limits on Life Terms for Youths," *The New York Times*, April 22, 2021.

148. Miller v. Alabama 567 U.S. 460 (2012); Daniel Savage, "Supreme Court Rules Mandatory Juvenile Life without Parole Cruel and Unusual," *The Los Angeles Times*, June 26, 2012.

149. Totenberg, "The Supreme Court Rejects Restrictions on Life Without Parole for Juveniles"; Liptak, "Supreme Court Rejects Limits on Life Terms for Youths."

150. Daniel Tichenor, *Dividing Lines: The Politics of Immigration Control in America* (Princeton, NJ: Princeton University Press, 2002).

151. Most Jewish immigrants were viewed by immigration policymakers in the early twentieth century as *racially* inferior, Ibid.

152. CJLG v. Jefferson B. Sessions, 880 F. 3d 1122, 2018.

153. Astrid Galvan, "Kids as Young as 1 in Court, Awaiting Reunion with Family," *Associated Press*, July 8, 2018.

154. "US Centers Force Migrant Children to Take Drugs: Lawsuit," *NBC News*, June 21, 2018.

155. John Gramlich, "How Border Apprehensions, ICE Arrests, and Deportations Have Changed Under Trump," *PEW Research Fact Tank*, March 22, 2020.

156. Randy Capps et al., *Implications of Immigration Enforcement Activities for the Well-Being of Children in Immigrant Families* (Washington, DC: Urban Institute, September, 2015).

157. Teresa Wiltz, "If Parents Get Deported, Who Gets Their Children?" *Stateline*, October 25, 2018.

158. Jeree Michele Thomas and Mel Wilson, "'The Color of Youth Transferred to the Adult Criminal Justice System: Policy and Practice Recommendations," National Association of Social Workers, 2018.

159. Ibid.

Chapter 3

1. Christine Harold and Kevin Michael DeLuca, "Behold the Corpse: Violent Images and the Case of Emmett Till," *Rhetoric and Public Affairs* 8 (2005) 2, pp.263–286.

2. Elliott Gorn, "Why Emmett Till Still Matters," *Chicago Tribune*, July 20, 2018.

3. Aric Jenkins, "Jeff Sessions: Parents and Children Illegally Crossing the Border Will Be Separated," *Time*, May 7, 2018.

4. Jenkins, "Jeff Sessions," and Blair Guild, "Jeff Sessions Argues It's Necessary to Separate Children from Parents When Detained at Border," *CBS News*, June 10, 2018.

5. Philip Bump, "Here Are the Administration Officials Who Have Said that Family Separation is Meant as a Deterrent," *The Washington Post*, June 19, 2018.

6. Tal Kopan, "ICE Official Stands By Comparing Detention Centers to Summer Camp," *CNN*, September 18, 2018; and Camilo Montoya-Galvez, "Report Details Scope of Family Separation Policy," *CBS News*, July 12, 2019.

7. Jasmine Aguilera, "Ticking Time Bomb," *Time*, July 2, 2019.

8. "Law Professor Describes Poor Conditions Where Migrant Children Are Held," *NPR News*, June 23, 2019.

9. Ibid.; and Amanda Marcotte, "Why Are Republicans Grasping for Excuses on Family Separation," *Salon*, June 19, 2018.

10. Ronald Reagan, "The Morality Gap at Berkeley," speech at Cow Palace, May 12, 1966, in Ronald Reagan, *The Creative Society* (New York: The Devin Adair Publishing Company, 1968), 125–129; Jeff Kahn, "Ronald

Reagan Launched His Political Career by Using the Berkeley Campus as a Target," *UC Berkeley News*, May 4, 2004.

11. John Anderson, "Former Governor Shaped Politics of Alabama, Nation," *The Huntsville Times*, September 14, 1988, p.A8.

12. Alison Gash, Daniel Tichenor, Angelita Chavez, and Malori Mussleman, "Framing Kids: Children, Immigration Reform and Same-Sex Marriage," *Politics, Groups and Identities* (November 2018), 44–70. See also Robin Bernstein, *Racial Innocence: Performing American Childhood from Slavery to Civil Rights* (New York, NY: New York University Press, 2011)

13. Daniel Tichenor, *Dividing Lines: The Politics of Immigration Control* (Princeton, NJ: Princeton University Press, 2002).

14. C.K. McFarland, "Crusade for Child Laborers: 'Mother' Jones and the March of the Mill Children," *Pennsylvania History* 38 (July 1971) 3, pp.283–296; and Simon Cordery, *Mother Jones: Raising Cain and Consciousness* (Albuquerque: University of New Mexico Press, 2010).

15. Glenn Eskew, *But for Birmingham: The Local and National Movements in the Civil Rights Struggle* (Chapel Hill: University of North Carolina Press, 1997); and Diane McWhorter, *Carry Me Home: Birmingham, Alabama, The Climactic Battle of the Civil Rights Revolution* (New York: Simon & Schuster, 2001).

16. Arthur Delaney, "Marcelas Owens, 11-Year-Old Whose Mother Died Without Health Insurance: 'Get The Health Care Bill Passed,'" *Huffington Post*, May 12, 2010.

17. Ibid.; and Jennifer Wing, "The Obamacare Kid Grows Up," *KNKX News*, September 29, 2018.

18. Sidney Milkis, "Theodore Roosevelt: Family Life," *The Miller Center*, https://millercenter.org/president/roosevelt/family-life.

19. Josephine Livingstone, "America's 'Poster Child' Syndrome," *The New Republic*, June 20, 2018.

20. Kathleen Burge, "Girl in Famous Vietnam Photo Talks About Forgiveness," *The Boston Globe*, August 18, 2014; "The Girl in the Picture," *CBS Sunday Morning*, October 25, 2015; and "Girl, 9, Survives Napalm Burns," *The New York Times*, June 12, 1972.

21. "Nixon, the A-Bomb, and Napalm," *CBS News*, February 28, 2002.

22. Patricia McCormick, "The Girl in the Kent State Photo," *The Washington Post Magazine*, April 19, 2021; John Johnson, "That Picture Hijacked My Life," *Newser*, April 24, 2021, https://www.newser.com/story/305156/that-picture-hijacked-my-life.html; and "Kneeling with Death Haunted A Life," *The Associated Press*, May 6, 1990;

23. Vanessa Romo, "Sandy Hook Victim's Father Wins Defamation Suit," *National Public Radio*, June 18, 2019.

24. Ibid.

25. Alexander Nemerov, *Soulmaker: The Times of Lewis Hine* (Princeton, NJ: Princeton University Press, 2016); Robert Macieski, *Picturing Class* (Amherst: University of Massachusetts Press, 2015); Lewis W. Hine, *America at Work* (Paris: Taschen, 2018); Russell Freedman, *Kids at Work: Lewis Hine and the Crusade against Child Labor* (New York: Clarion Books, 1998); Alona Pardo, *The Politics of Seeing* (New York: Prestel, 2018); and Linda Gordon, *Dorothea Lange: A Life Beyond Limits* (New York: W.W. Norton, 2010).

26. Dominic Pondsford, "Agency Photographer Who Pictured Aylan Kurdi Wanted to 'Express the Scream of His Silent Body,'" *Press Gazette*, September 4, 2015.

27. Simeon Wright and Herb Boyd, *Simeon's Story: An Eyewitness Account of the Kidnapping of Emmett Till* (Chicago Review Press, 2010).

28. Interviews with Simeon Wright (Till's cousin) and Mamie Till-Mobley (Till's mother), in Talis Shelbourne, "Emmet Till: The Untold Story," *The Western Courier*, February 22, 2016.

29. Christopher Metress, "Let the World See," Oxford University Press Blog, September 26, 2017, https://blog.oup.com/2017/09/emmett-till-funeral-history/.

30. Alison Carrick, "Emmett Till and 'Eyes on the Prize,'" Washington University in St. Louis Blog.

31. Emmet's original resting place had been desecrated over the years, especially after Emmet's body had been exhumed as part of a new investigation, and interred in a new casket. Vandals discarded the old casket in a shed where it remained, deteriorating, despite promises by the cemetery that they would preserve it in a memorial to Emmett and his mother. Simeon Wright, a friend who had been with Emmett at the general store, recalls hearing about the casket through a radio interview. "A radio personality called me about six in the morning asking me questions about it. They were on top of what was going on at the cemetery. I told him what was supposed to happen to the casket. He kept asking me questions and I said 'Wait a minute, let me go out there and check and see. I don't know what's going on. Let me go out to cemetery and get some answers, find out what's going on out there.' That's when I saw the casket sitting in the shed deteriorating. The last time my cousin saw the casket it was inside of the building, preserved. We don't know who moved it out into the shed, but I got a chance to see it,

it was just horrible the way they had discarded it like that without even notifying us. They could have called the family, but they didn't." Abby Callard, "Emmett Till's Casket Goes to the Smithsonian," *Smithsonian Magazine*, November 2009. https://www.smithsonianmag.com/arts-cult ure/emmett-tills-casket-goes-to-the-smithsonian-144696940/#vYL4w dDxxdvU3Y6S.99.

32. Alison Gash, *Below the Radar: How Silence Can Save Civil Rights* (New York: Oxford University Press, 2016).

33. Michael Tackett, "Mourners Hail Ryan White," *The Chicago Tribune*, April 12, 1990.

34. Pat Buchanan, White House communications director in the Reagan administration, quoted in "History of the Anti-Gay Movement Since 1977," Southern Poverty Law Center. www.splcenter.org, accessed October 7, 2019.

35. Robert Scheer, "Early Indifference to AIDS is Blamed for its Spread," *LA Times*, November 29, 1986.

36. Joshua Green, "The Heroic Story of How Congress First Confronted AIDS," *Atlantic*, June 8, 2011.

37. Liz Meszaros, "On This Day in Medical History: Ryan White Succumbs to AIDS-related Pneumonia," *MDLinx*, April 4, 2018.

38. UPI, "Boy with AIDS Returns to School, *The Chicago Tribune*, April 11, 1986.

39. Meszaros, "On This Day in Medical History."

40. "The "Miracle" of Ryan White," *Time*, April 23, 1990.

41. Mark Carl Rom, "Gays and AIDS," in Wald Rimmerman and Wilcox, eds., *The Politics of Gay Rights* (Chicago: University of Chicago Press, 2000), pp.217–248.

42. Thomas Sheridan, "How a Dying Ryan White United Washington on the AIDS Crisis," *The Daily Beast*, June 29, 2019.

43. Tim Murphy, "The Program that Keeps Half a Million People with HIV Alive and Well Turns 30 This Month," *The Body*, August 10, 2020.

44. Amin Ghaziani, *The Dividends of Dissent: How Conflict and Culture Work in Lesbian and Gay Marches in Washington* (University of Chicago Press, 2008).

45. Gillian Frank, "'The Civil Rights of Parents': Race and Conservative Politics in Anita Bryant's Campaign against Gay Rights in 1970s Florida," *The Journal of the History of Sexuality* January 22 (2013) 1, pp.126–160.

46. Alison Gash, Daniel Tichenor, Angelita Chavez, and Malori Musselman, "Framing Kids: Children, Immigration Reform and Same-Sex Marriage," *Politics Groups and Identities* (2018).

47. Gash, *Below the Radar.*
48. Prepared Statement of Gary Bauer, "The Defense of Marriage Act: Hearing before the Committee on the Judiciary," United States Senate, July 11, 1996.
49. William M. Welch, "Californians Go To 'War' over Prop 8's Gay Marriage Ban," *USA Today*, October 29, 2008.
50. Laurie Goodstein, "In California, an 'Armageddon' for Same-sex Marriage Foes," *The New York Times*, October 27, 2008.
51. Chris Cillizza and Sean Sullivan, "How Proposition 8 Passed in California—and Why It Wouldn't Today," *The Washington Post*, March 26, 2013. https://www.washingtonpost.com/news/the-fix/wp/2013/03/26/how-proposition-8-passed-in-california-and-why-it-wouldnt-today/, accessed April 21, 2021.
52. Gash, *Below the Radar.*
53. Representative Charles Canady, Defense of Marriage Act; Congressional Record Vol. 142, No. 102 (House of Representatives—July 11, 1996)
54. Report filed by Representative Charles Canady to accompany HR 3396, House of Representatives, July 9, 1996.
55. Gash, *Below the Radar.*
56. Dennis Prager, Prepared Statement, Defense of Marriage Act: Hearing before the Subcommittee on the Constitution of the Committee on the Judiciary, House of Representatives, One Hundred Fourth Congress, Second Session, on H.R. 3396, May 15, 1996
57. Canady, Defense of Marriage Act.
58. Prager, Prepared Statement, Defense of Marriage Act.
59. Rummel v. Kitzhaber, Memorandum in Support of Motion for Summary Judgement, February 18, 2014.
60. Bryan Fischer, "Purposes of Marriage: Companionship, Sex and Children—Gay Marriage Strikes Out," *RenewAmerica*, March 21, 2013.
61. Geiger v. Kitzhaber, Plaintiffs Amended Memorandum in Support of Summary Judgment, Case 6.13 cv-02256-MC Document 33, February 18, 2014.
62. Florida Family Policy Council President John Stemberger, quoted in Jeremy Leaming, "Marriage Maneuver," *Church and State Magazine*, November 2007.
63. Voters Pamphlet, Vol. 1, Measure 36 Arguments, p.86.
64. James Dobson "Marriage Under Fire," re-printed in Voter Pamphlet for Measure 23.
65. Igor Volsky, "Concerned Women for America's Crouse Grows Agitated when Host Contradicts Gay Adoption Claim," *Think Progress*, August 29, 2011.

66. Gash, *Below the Radar*.

67. Supreme Court Oral Arguments, Dennis Hollingsworth, et al v. Kristina Perry et al., No. 12-14, March 26, 2013, p.19.

68. DeBoer v. Snyder, District Court Case No. 2:12-cv-10285.

69. Rebecca Nelson and National Journal, "The 21-Year old Becoming a Major Player in Conservative Politics," *Atlantic*, March 2015.

70. Turning Point USA Homepage. www.tpusa.com.

71. Professor Watchlist Homepage. www.professorwatchlist.org.

72. Marissa Wenzke, "This Controversial Website is Targeting "Radical" Left Wing Academics," *Mashable*, December 2, 2016.

73. Alex Chan, "3 Local Professors Are on a Website List of Those Who 'Advance Leftists Propaganda,'" *Daily Pilot*, December 13, 2016.

74. Christopher Mele, "Professor Watchlist is Seen as Threat to Academic Freedom, *The New York Times*, November 28, 2016.

75. Valerie Strauss, "'The Sort of Company We Wish to Keep': More than 1,500 Academics Ask to Join Controversial 'Professor Watchlist,'" *The Washington Post*, December 14, 2016.

76. Turning Point USA homepage, www.tpusa.com.

77. Joseph Guinto, "Trump's Man on Campus, *Politico*, April 6, 2018.

78. Ibid.

79. Matt O'Connor, "SSFC approves Muslim Student Association budget after contentious debate," *The Badger Herald*, October 16, 2017.

80. Guinto, "Trump's Man on Campus."

81. Isaac Stanley-Becker, "Pro-Trump Youth Group Enlists Teens in Secretive Campaign Likened to a 'Troll Farm,'" *The Washington Post*, September 15, 2020.

82. Alliance Defending Freedom website, www.adflegal.org.

83. Rebecca Beatrice Brooks, "Child Soldiers in the Civil War," *Civil War Saga*, December 16, 2011; and Candice Ranson, *Children of the Civil War* (New York: Lerner Publishing Group, 1998).

84. Tom Emery, "'Drummer Boy of Shiloh' Tale Quaint, But Questionable," *Dispatch-Argus*, August 31, 2013.

85. Laura June Davis, "The Drummer Boy of Shiloh," *The Civil War Monitor*, April 6, 2012.

86. Goren Blazeski, "The Little Drummer Boy," *Vintage News*, May 11, 2017.

87. Ray Bradbury, "The Drummer Boy of Shiloh," *Saturday Evening Post*, April 30, 1960.

88. Kathryn Harrison, *Joan of Arc: A Life Transformed* (New York: Anchor, 2015); Helen Castor, *Joan of Arc: A History* (New York: Harper Perennial, 2016); and Regine Pernoud, *Joan of Arc: By Herself and Her Witnesses* (New York: Scarborough House, 1990).

89. Shiamin Kwa and Wilt Idema, *Mulan: Five Versions of a Classic Chinese Legend, with Related Texts* (New York: Hackett, 2010); and Wei Jiang and Cheng an Jiang, *Legend of Mu Lan: A Heroine of Ancient China* (New York: Victory Press, 1997).

90. "Lost Innocence—Little Fighters: Children of the Resistance," CBC Radio, October 10, 2014 (rebroadcast).

91. Ibid.; see also Lore Cowan, *Children of the Resistance* (New York: Meredith Press, 1969); Richard Hanser, *A Noble Treason: The Revolt of the Munich Students against Hitler* (New York: Ignatius Press, 2012); and Mark Bles, *Child at War* (New York, Mercury House, 1991).

92. See Smith v. Allwright, 321 U.S. 649 (1944); Brown v. Board of Education, 347 U.S. 483 (1954); see also Richard Kluger, *Simple Justice* (New York: Vintage Books, 2004); James Patterson, *Brown v. Board of Education: A Civil Rights Milestone and Its Troubled Legacy* (New York: Oxford University Press); Michael Klarman, *From Jim Crow to Civil Rights: The Supreme Court and the Struggle for Racial Equality* (New York: Oxford University Press, 2006); Michael Klarman, *Brown v. Board of Education and the Civil Rights Movement* (New York: Oxford University Press, 2007); and Gerald Rosenberg, *The Hollow Hope: Can Courts Bring About Social Change* (Chicago: University of Chicago Press, 2008).

93. Daisy Bates, *The Long Shadow of Little Rock* (Fayetteville, AR: University of Arkansas Press, 2007); Melba Pattillo Beals, *Warriors Don't Cry: A Searing Memoir of the Battle to Integrate Little Rock's Central High* (New York: Simon Pulse, 2007); Karen Anderson, *Little Rock: Race and Resistance at Central High School* (Princeton, NJ: Princeton University Press, 2013); and Elizabeth Huckaby, *Crisis at Central High, Little Rock, 1957–58* (Baton Rouge, LA: Louisiana State University Press, 1980.

94. Julie Ray, "Reflections on the 'Trouble' in Arkansas," *Gallup Brain,* February 25, 2003.

95. Ibid.

96. Quoted in Michael Klarman, *Unfinished Business: Racial Equality in American History* (New York: Oxford University Press, 2007), p.162.

97. "The Problem We All Live With," Norman Rockwell, 1963. Oil on canvas, 36" x 58." Illustration for "Look," January 14, 1964. Norman Rockwell Museum Collection.

98. Ruby Bridges, *Through My Eyes* (New York: Scholastic, 1999); Robert Coles, *The Spiritual Life of Children* (New York: Mariner, 1991); and Lynn Okura, "Ruby Bridges on the Powerful Lesson She Learned from Her First-Grade Teacher," *Huffington Post*, December 6, 2017.

99. Robert Coles, *The Political Lives of Children* (New York: Atlantic Monthly Press, 2000); and Paul Wilkes, "Robert Coles: Doctor of Crisis," *The New York Times*, March 26, 1978.

100. David Swick, "Robert Coles and the Moral Life," *Lion's Roar*, January 1, 2006.

101. Paul Galloway, "A Child's Faith Led the Way," *The Chicago Tribune*, September 22, 1985.

102. Martin Luther King, Jr., *Letter From Birmingham Jail*, April 16, 1963.

103. David Garrow, *Birmingham, Alabama, 1956–1963: The Black Struggle for Civil Rights* (New York: Carlson Publishing, 1989), pp.165–66.

104. David Garrow, *Bearing the Cross: Martin Luther King, Jr., and the Southern Christian Leadership Conference* (New York: William Morrow and Company, 1986), p.246.

105. Bass, S. Jonathan, *Blessed Are the Peacemakers: Martin Luther King, Jr., Eight White Religious Leaders, and the "Letter from Birmingham Jail"* (Baton Rouge, LA: Louisiana State University, 2001), p.105; and McWhorter, *Carry Me Home*, p.307.

106. For an exceptional account of the Nashville campaign, see David Halberstam, *The Children* (New York: Fawcett Books, 1999).

107. Clayborne Carson, *In Struggle: SNCC and the Black Awakening of the 1960s* (Cambridge, MA: Harvard University Press, 1995).

108. Cynthia Levinson, *We've Got A Job: The 1963 Birmingham Children's March* (Atlanta, GA: Peachtree Publishers, 2015), pp.61–66.

109. Taylor Branch, *Pillar of Fire* (New York: Simon and Schuster, 1999), p.75.

110. Ibid., pp.75–76; and McWhorter, *Carry Me Home*.

111. Lottie Joiner, "How the Children of Birmingham Changed the Civil-Rights Movement," *The Daily Beast*, July 11, 2017.

112. Branch, *Pillar of Fire*, p.77.

113. Martin Luther King, Jr., Address Delivered at Mass Meeting, May 6, 1963.

114. Taylor Branch, *Pillar of Fire*, pp.75–78.

115. Ibid.

116. Joiner, "How the Children of Birmingham Changed the Civil-Rights Movement."

117. Relman Morin, "Court Reveals Birmingham Story," *Montgomery Advertiser*, May 9, 1963.

118. Anne Moody, *Coming of Age in Mississippi* (New York: Random House, 1978), p. 132.

119. Stephen J. Whitfield, *A Death in the Delta: The Story of Emmett Till* (New York: The Free Press, 1988), p.46.

120. Ellen Levine, *Freedom's Children: Young Civil Rights Activists Tell Their Own Stories* (New York: Penguin Group, 1993), p.viii.

121. Philip Roth, *American Pastoral* (New York: Vintage, 1998).

122. Nik Heynen (2009) "Bending the Bars of Empire from Every Ghetto for Survival: The Black Panther Party's Radical Antihunger Politics of Social Reproduction and Scale," Annals of the Association of American Geographers, 99:2, 406–422, DOI: 10.1080/00045600802683767.

123. Ibid.

124. Ward Churchill and Jim Vander Wall, *The COINTELPRO Papers* (Boston: South End Press, 1990), pp.144–145.

125. Franzisca Meister, *Racism and Resistance: How the Black Panthers Challenged White Supremacy* (New York: Columbia University Press, 2017) p.114.

126. Ibid.

127. Erin Blakemore, "How the Black Panthers' Breakfast Program Both Inspired and Threatened the Government," History Channel, August 30, 2018.

128. Utah State Rep. Grant Protzman, quoted in "In Utah, School Clubs Banned to Stop Gay Meeting," *The Philadelphia Inquirer*, February 23, 1996.

129. Judy Mann, "Where Homophobia Does the Most Harm," *The Washington Post*, March 1, 2000.

130. Shanelle Matthews and Malkia Cyril, "We Say Black Lives Matter. The FBI Says That Makes Us a Security Threat," *The Washington Post*, October 19, 2017.

131. Abby Jackson, "Americans Look to Columbine to Better Understand School Shootings—But Myths about the Shooters Have Persisted for Years," *Business Insider*, April 20, 2019.

132. Office of Juvenile Justice and Delinquency Prevention. https://www.ojjdp.gov/ojstatbb/crime/ucr.asp?table_in=1.

133. Annika Neklason, "The Columbine Blueprint," *Atlantic*, April 19, 2019.

134. James Shultz et al, "Fatal School Shootings and the Epidemiological Context of Firearm Mortality in the United States," *Disaster Health*, 1 (April–December 2013) 2, pp.84–101.

135. Chelsea Parsons and Anne Johnson, "Young Guns: How Gun Violence is Devastating the Millennial Generation," Center for American Progress, February 2014.

136. Katharine A. Fowler et al, "Childhood Firearm Injuries in the United States," *Pediatrics*, June 2017.

137. "U.S. Gun Violence Epidemic is Killing More Children, More Often," Children's Defense Fund, *The State of America's Children*, 2020 Report,

https://www.childrensdefense.org/policy/resources/soac-2020-gun-violence/.

138. Petula Dvorak, "The Nation Is Focused on Students and Gun Violence. But Kids in Urban Schools Want to Know, Where's Everybody Been?" *The Washington Post*, March 12, 2018.

139. Wanda Parham-Payne, "The Role of the Media in the Disparate Response to Gun Violence in America," *Journal of Black Studies* 45 (2014) 8, pp.752–68, p.757.

140. Michel Martin and Emma Bowman, "Why Nearly all Mass Shooters are Men," NPR, March 27, 2021.

141. Scott Duxbury, Laura Frizzell, and Sade Lindsay, "Mental Illness, the Media and the Moral Politics of Mass Violence: The Role of Race in Mass Shootings Coverage," *Journal of Research in Crime and Delinquency* 55 (July 2018), 766–797.

142. Sung-Yeon Park, Kyle J. Holody, and Xiaoqun Zhang, "Race in Media Coverage of School Shootings: A Parallel Application of Framing Theory and Attribute Agenda Setting." Journalism & Mass Communication Quarterly 89 (2012) 3, pp.475–494.

143. Ibid.

144. Kevin Simpson and Jason Blevins, "Klebold Came from Jewish Background," *Denver Post*, April 24, 1999.

145. Cynthia Willis-Chun, "Strategic Rhetoric in News Coverage of the Columbine and Virginia Tech Massacres," in Michael G. Lacy and Kent A. Ono, eds., Critical Rhetorics of Race (New York University Press, 2011), p. 51.

146. Joan Fallon, "Study of Untouchables Can Help End Human Rights Abuses," *Physorg*, February 9, 2010.

147. *Reports of the Immigration Commission: The Children of Immigrants in Schools*. Volume 13 (Washington, DC: Governing Printing Office, 1911), pp.77–79.

148. *Reports of the Immigration Commission: Abstracts of Reports*. Volume 1 (Washington, D.C.: Governing Printing Office, 1911), pp.23–47.

149. Daniel Tichenor, *Dividing Lines: The Politics of Immigration Control in America* (Princeton, NJ: Princeton University Press, 2002), pp.130–138; see also Katherine Benton-Cohen, *Inventing the Immigration Problem: The Dillingham Commission and Its Legacy* (Cambridge, MA: Cambridge University Press, 2018) .

150. Tichenor, *Dividing Lines*, pp.151–175.

151. Leo Chavez, *The Latino Threat: Constructing Immigrants, Citizens, and the Nation* (Stanford, CA: Stanford University Press, 2008).

152. Tichenor, *Dividing Lines*, chapter 8.
153. Julia Preston, "Citizenship from Birth is Challenged on the Right," *The New York Times*, August 6, 2010; and Alexandra Villarreal, "'Anchor Babies': The 'Ludicrous' Myth that Treats People as Pawns," *The Guardian*, March 16, 2020.
154. "A Timeline of Steve King's Racist Remarks and Divisive Actions," *The New York Times*, January 15, 2019; and Linh Ta, "Steve King Has a History of Controversial Remarks," *The Des Moines Register*, November 1, 2018.
155. D. Amari Jackson, "Murder, Forced Labor and the Forgotten Black Boys of Florida's Dozier School for Boys, *The Atlanta Black Star*, May 9, 2017.
156. Greg Allen, "Florida's Dozier School for Boys: A True Horror Story," *NPR.org*, October 15, 2012; John Eligon, "27 More Graves Found at a Notorious Florida Boys School," *The New York Times*, April 12, 2019; Roger Dean Kiser, *The White House Boys: An American Tragedy* (New York: Health Communications, 2009); and Elizabeth Murray, *The Dozier School for Boys* (New York: Twenty-First Century Books, 2019).
157. Colson Whitehead, *The Nickel Boys* (New York: Doubleday, 2019).
158. Suzanne Collins, *The Hunger Games* (New York: Scholastic Press, 2008).
159. Barry Strauss, "The Classical Roots of the Hunger Games," *The Wall Street Journal*, November 13, 2014; and "Suzanne Collins Talks about 'The Hunger Games,'" *The New York Times*, October 18, 2018.
160. Jamie Bouie, "The Most Discriminatory Law in the Land," *Slate*, June 17, 2014; and Teresa Wiltz, "Growing Number of States Repeal Family Welfare Caps," *Stateline*, July 13, 2016.
161. Ibid.; Sanford Schram, Joe Soss, and Richard Fording, *Race and the Politics of Welfare Reform* (Ann Arbor: University of Michigan Press, 2003); Sharon Hays, *Flat Broke with Children* (New York: Oxford University Press, 2004); and Felicia Kornbluth and Gwendolyn Mink, *Ensuring Poverty* (Philadelphia: University of Pennsylvania Press, 2018).
162. Testimony of Ron Haskins, *The Economic and Societal Costs of Poverty*, Hearing before the Committee on Ways and Means, U.S. House of Representatives, January 24, 2007, Serial No. 110-2 (Washington, DC: U.S. Government Printing Office, 2010), pp.41–49; Harry J. Holzer et al, *The Economic Costs of Poverty in the United States: Subsequent Effects of Children Growing Up Poor* (Washington, DC: Center for American Progress, January 2007); Arloc Sherman and Danilo Trisi, "Deep Poverty Worsened in Welfare Law's First Decade," Report of the Center on Budget and Policy Priorities, July 23, 2013; Stephen Freedman et al., *National Evaluation of Welfare-to-Work Strategies Evaluating Alternative*

Welfare-to-Work Approaches: Two-Year Impacts for Eleven Programs, U.S. Department of Health and Human Services, June 2000; and H. Luke Shaefer and Kathryn Edin, "Rising Extreme Poverty in the United States and the Response of Federal Means-Tested Transfer Programs," National Poverty Center Working Paper Series #13-06, May 2013.

163. Teresa Wiltz "Family Welfare Caps Lose Favor in Most States," *Stateline,* May 3, 2019; and "Lift the Cap on Kids in Massachusetts," *Children's HealthWatch,* January 25, 2017.

164. "California Deposes Its 'Welfare Queen,' *The New York Times,* July 23, 2016; Teresa Wiltz, "Growing Number of States Repeal Family Welfare Caps," *Stateline,* July 13, 2016.

165. Ibid.

166. Bouie, "The Most Discriminatory Law in the Land"; Wiltz, "Growing Number of States Repeal Family Welfare Caps"; Wiltz, "Family Welfare Caps Lose Favor in More States,"; and Kalena Thomhave, "Battle Over TANF Family Cap Intensifies," *Spotlight,* October 3, 2018.

167. Joe Soss, Richard Fording, and Sanford Schram, *Disciplining the Poor* (Chicago: University of Chicago Press, 2011).

168. Alison Gash, Daniel Tichenor, Angelia Chavez, and Malori Musselman, "Framing Kids: Children, Immigration Reform, and Same-Sex Marriage," *Politics, Groups, and Identities* (November 2018), pp.44–70.

169. Jason Zengerle, "Lines in the Sand," *New York Times Magazine,* July 21, 2019, pp.35–36.

170. Dara Lind and Dylan Scott, "Flores Agreement: Trump's Executive Order to End Family Separation May Run Afoul of a 1997 Court Ruling," *Vox,* June 21, 2018.

171. Ibid.

172. In their April 2018 memo to Nielson, McAleenan, Homan, and Cissna memo noted that the Trump administration had already run a pilot zero-tolerance program along parts of the border in Texas and New Mexico for four months in 2017 and that the number of migrant families seeking to cross illegally had decreased by 64 percent, only to rise again when the program was paused. See Zengerle, "Lines in the Sand," p.36.

173. Ibid., pp.36–37.

174. Philip Bump, "Two Thirds of Americans Oppose Trump's Family-Separation Policy," *The Washington Post,* June 18, 2018; Dylan Matthews, "Polls: Trump's Family Separation Policy Is Very Unpopular," *Vox,* June 18, 2018; and Shibley Tilhamee and Stella Rouse, "New Poll: Despite Partisan Divide on Immigration, Americans Oppose Family Separation," *Lawfare,* April 10, 2019.

175. Aric Jenkins, "Jeff Sessions: Parents and Children Illegally Crossing the Border Will Be Separated," *Time*, May 7, 2018; Aric Jenkins and Blair Guild, "Jeff Sessions Argues It's Necessary to Separate Children from Parents When Detained at Border," *CBS News*, June 10, 2018; and Philip Bump, "Here Are the Administration Officials Who Have Said that Family Separation is Meant as a Deterrrent," *The Washington Post*, June 19, 2018.

176. "Kirstjen Nielson Addresses Families Separation at the Border: Full Transcript," *The New York Times*, June 18, 2018.

177. Ron Nixon, "Migrant Detention Centers Are 'Like a Summer Camp,'" *The New York Times*, July 31, 2018.

178. Melanie Schmitz, "Conservatives Try to Defend Trump's Family Separation Policy," *Think Progress*, June 22, 2018.

179. Quoted in Marc Morial, "Civil Rights Icon Celebrates Her 80th Birthday," *Hudson Valley Press*, May 23, 2018.

Chapter 4

1. Sandra Sadek, "'Enough is Enough': Students Lead Protest against Katy Park Racism," *Katy Times*, June 5, 2020.

2. Neidi Dominguez Zamorano, Jonathan Perez, Jorge Guitierrez, and Nancy Meza, "DREAM Activists: Rejecting the Passivity of the Nonprofit, Industrial Complex," *Truthout*, September 21, 2010. https://truthout.org/articles/dream-activists-rejecting-the-passivity-of-the-nonprofit-industrial-complex/.

3. Dominguez Zamorano, Perez, Guitierrez, and Meza, "DREAM Activists: Rejecting the Passivity of the Nonprofit, Industrial Complex," *Truthout*, September 21, 2010. https://truthout.org/articles/dream-activists-rejecting-the-passivity-of-the-nonprofit-industrial-complex/.

4. Personal interviews by Daniel Tichenor with DREAMer activists and immigrant rights movement leaders, Democracy's Shadow Project, March 14–December 4, 2016. These interviewees will be anonymous to protect them from potential harms. See also Milkis and Tichenor, *Rivalry and Reform*, pp.293–297; and Daniel Tichenor, "The Demise of Immigration Reform," in Jeffrey Jenkins and Eric Pitashnik, eds., *Congress and Policymaking in the 21st Century* (New York: Cambridge University Press, 2014), pp.242–271.

5. Ibid.

6. Julia Preson, "Illegal Immigrant Students Protest at McCain Office," *The New York Times*, May 17, 2010; and Walter Nicholls, *The DREAMers: How the Undocumented Youth Movement Transformed the Immigrant Rights Debate* (Stanford, CA: Stanford University Press, 2013), pp.80–98.

7. Dominguez Zamorano, Perez, Guitierrez, and Meza, "DREAM Activists: Rejecting the Passivity of the Nonprofit, Industrial Complex."

8. Nicholls, *The DREAMers*, Chapters 2 and 3; Personal interviews: Daniel J. Tichenor with advocacy group leaders #s1–3, 5, and Dreamer organizers #s 2, 4–6, "Democracy's Shadow" Project.

9. Dominguez Zamorano, Perez, Guitierrez, and Meza, "DREAM Activists: Rejecting the Passivity of the Nonprofit, Industrial Complex."

10. J.K. Rowling, *Harry Potter and the Sorcerer's Stone* (New York: Scholastic, 1998).

11. J.K. Rowling, *Harry Potter and the Order of the Phoenix* (New York: Levine Books, 1993).

12. Suzanne Collins, *The Hunger Games* (New York: Scholastic, 2010); Collins, *Catching Fire* (New York: Scholastic, 2003); and Collins, *Mocking Jay* (New York: Scholastic 2014).

13. J. Bekken, "Newsboy Strikes," in Encyclopedia of Strikes in American History, 2009.

14. Ibid.

15. "Strike That is a Strike," *The Sun* [New York], July 22, 1899, p.3.

16. David Nasaw, "Read All About It: The Story of the Newsies; Two-Week Strike against Publishers Pulitzer, Hearst," *The New York Daily News*, August 14, 2017.

17. "Newsboys' Strike Swells," *The Sun* [New York], July 23, 1899, p.2.

18. Gillespie, 68.

19. Milan Simonich, "Centennial Flashback: A Century Ago, a Strike by New York Newsboys Sparked a Child Labor Rebellion," *The Post-Gazette*, July 11, 1999.

20. Nasaw, "Read All About It: The Story of the Newsies; Two-Week Strike against Publishers Pulitzer, Hearst."

21. Ibid.

22. David Nasaw, *Children of the City: At Work and at Play* (New York: Random House,1983).

23. Vincent DiGirolamo, *Crying the News: A History of America's Newsboys* (New York, NY: Oxford University Press, 2019), p.436.

24. Aaron Brenner, Benjamin Day, and Immanuel Ness, *The Encyclopedia of Strikes in American History* (Armonk, NY: M.E. Sharpe, 2015).

25. Martin Luther King, Jr. and Ella Baker, Announcement, "Youth leadership meeting, Shaw University, Raleigh, N.C., 4/15/1960-4/17/1960," March 1960, Martin Luther King, Jr. Papers. A month before the conference in Raleigh, Baker met with two adult advisors to the sit-in protesters, Glenn Smiley of the Fellowship of Reconciliation and Douglas Moore, an SCLC board member, who agreed that the conference "should be youth centered" with adults speaking "only when asked to do so" (Baker, Memorandum to King and Abernathy, 23 March 1960). See also SCLC and Raleigh Citizens Association, Program, "Mass meeting featuring Dr. Martin Luther King," 16 April 1960; and SCLC, "Northern students and observers to Southwide Youth Leadership Conference, Shaw University, Raleigh, N.C.," 22 April 1960.

26. Rev. J.M. Lawson Jr., Statement of Purpose, *The Student Voice*, June 1960, p.2; Clayborne Carson, *In Struggle: SNCC and the Black Awakening of the 1960s* (Cambridge, MA: Harvard University Press, 1981); Howard Zinn, *SNCC: The New Abolitionists* (New York: Haymarket Books, 2013); and Barbara Ransby, *Ella Baker and the Black Freedom Movement: A Radical Democratic Vision* (Chapel Hill: University of North Carolina Press, 2003).

27. Kotz, *Judgment Days*, 203

28. Ibid, 204–205.

29. Ibid, 206.

30. Johnson combined persuasion and ruthless methods, including FBI wiretaps on civil rights leaders, in resolving the MFDP dispute. See Kotz, *Lyndon Baines Johnson, Martin Luther King, Jr., and the Laws that Changed America*, p.206–218.

31. President Lyndon B. Johnson telephone conversation with Hubert Humphrey and Walter Reuther, August 25, 1964, Johnson White House Secret Tapes, Miller Center, University of Virginia; see also Milkis and Tichenor, *Rivalry and Reform*, pp.154–155. On the implications of the Democratic National Committee's implementation of the 1964 Convention's call for greater participation, see Sidney M. Milkis, *The President and the Parties: The Transformation of the American Party System Since the New Deal* (New York: Oxford University Press, 1993), pp.210–216.

32. President Johnson was preoccupied well before the 1964 campaign that a contentious, disorderly Democratic national convention would open the presidential nomination to other candidates, most notably his rival, Robert F. Kennedy also was concerned, even at this early stage of his presidency, that an unruly convention might open the door to a Robert Kennedy candidacy. See Milkis and Tichenor, *Rivalry and Reform*, pp.153–158.

33. Johnson telephone conversation with Walter Reuther, August 9, 1964, Johnson White House Secret Tapes, Miller Center, University of Virginia; see also Milkis and Tichenor, *Rivalry and Reform*, pp.153-158.
34. Milkis, *The President and the Parties*, pp.210–216.
35. "Jim Crowism Ruled Out," *Chicago Daily Defender*, January 20, 1968.
36. Kotz, *Judgement Days*, 220.
37. Ibid., pp.220–221.
38. Martin Luther King Jr., *Where Do We Go From Here: Chaos or Community?*(New York: Beacon Press, 2010), p.47; "Negro Leaders on 'Meet the Press,'" 89th Cong., 2d sess., *Congressional Record* 112 (29 August 1966): S 21095–21102; "Black Power for Whom?" *Christian Century*, July 20, 1966, pp.903–904; Kwame Ture and Chalres V. Hamilton, *Black Power* (New York, NY: Vintage Books, 1992).
39. Carson, *In Struggle*, 127.
40. Douglass McAdam, *Freedom Summer* (New York: Oxford University Press, 1990).
41. For example, Attorney General Robert Kennedy had proposed legislation that would only apply to federal elections, which moreover, did not include the provisions that made the 1965 Voting Rights Act so significant and controversial, including pre-clearance of changes in voting laws by the Department of Justice and the abolition of literacy tests. See Memo, Robert Kennedy to John F. Kennedy, October 23, 1963, Burke Marshall Papers, Box 8, Presidential 4-8-63 to 8-17-63, John F. Kennedy Presidential Library, Boston, Massachusetts.
42. William Nicholls, *The Dreamers: How the Undocumented Youth Movement Transformed the Immigrant Rights Debate* (Palo Alto, CA: Stanford University Press, 2013), pp.49–55.
43. Daniel Altschuler, "The Dreamers' Movement Comes of Age," *Dissent*, May 16, 2011, pp.2–3.
44. Ibid, pp.5–6.
45. Nicholls, *The Dreamers*, p.94.
46. Altschuler, "The Dreamers' Movement Comes of Age," pp.14–15.
47. Sidney Milkis and Daniel Tichenor, *Rivalry and Reform: Presidents, Social Movements, and the Transformation of American Politics* (Chicago: University of Chicago Press, 2019), 293–305.
48. Nicholls, *The Dreamers*, pp.126–128.
49. Altschuler, "The Dreamers' Movement Comes of Age," p.6.
50. Bertram Gutierrez, "Law Professors' Letter May Have Swayed Obama," *Winston-Salem Journal*, June 26, 2012; and Michael Kagan, "The New Era of Presidential Immigration Law," *Washburn Law Journal* 55 (2015), pp.117–128.

51. Milkis and Tichenor, *Rivalry and Reform*, 293–305.

52. Interviews with Cristina Jimenez, Managing Director, and Lorella Praeli, Advocacy and Policy Director, United We Dream, April 3, 2014.

53. Kenneth S. Lowande and Sidney M. Milkis, "We Can't Wait: Barack Obama, Partisan Polarization, and the Administrative Presidency," *The Forum* 12 (2014), pp.3–27.

54. Margaret Peacock, "Samantha Smith in the Land of the Bolsheviks: Peace and the Politics of Childhood in the Late Cold War," *Diplomatic History* 43 (2018) 3, pp.418–444; Anne Galicich, *Samantha Smith: A Journey for Peace* (Minneapolis: Dillon Press, 1987); and Matthias Neumann, "Child Diplomacy During the Late Cold War," *History* 104 (April 2019) 360, pp.275–308.

55. Mary Pauline Lowery, "This Is How One Sixth Grade Girl Helped Improve Flint's Water Crisis," *Oprah Magazine*, December 11, 2019.

56. Theresa Yuger, *Sor Juana Ines de la Cruz: Feminist Reconstruction of Biography and Text* (New York: Wipf and Stock, 2014); Juana Ines de la Cruz, *A Woman of Genius: The Intellectual Autobiography of Sor Juana Ines de la Cruz* (New York: Lime Rock Press, 1982); Octavio Paz, *Sor Juana: Or, The Traps of Faith* (Cambridge, MA: Harvard University Press, 1990).

57. Ibid.; Sor Juana Ines de la Cruz, *Poems, Protest, and a Dream* (New York: Penguin, 1997); and Richard Frontjes, *Between Worlds: Sor Juana on Culture, Gender, and the Desire for Knowledge* (New York: Political Animal Press, 2019).

58. Joan Sherman, *The Black Bard of North Carolina: George Moses Horton and His Poetry* (Chapel Hill: University of North Carolina Press, 1997); George Moses Horton, *Poems By a Slave* (New York: Historic Publishing, 2017); Lonnell Johnson, "George Moses Horton," in Emmanuel Nelson, ed., *African American Authors, 1745–1945* (Westport, CT: Greenwood Press, 2000), pp.238–241; and Richard Walser, *The Black Poet* (New York: Philosophical Library, 1966).

59. Jim Dwyer, "Triangle Fire: One Woman Who Changed the Rules," *The New York Times*, March 22, 2011; Annalise Orleck, *Common Sense and Little Fire: Women and Working-Class Politics in the United States, 1900– 1965* (Chapel Hill: University of North Carolina Press, 1995); Clara Shavelson, "Remembering the Waistmakers General Strike," *Jewish Currents*, November 1982; and Michelle Markel, *Brave Girl* (New York: Balzer and Bray, 2013).

60. Ibid.

61. Wayne Greenshaw, *Thunder of Angels: The Montgomery Bus Boycott and the People Who Broke the Back of Jim Crow* (Chicago: Chicago Review

Press, 2007); Phillip Hoose, *Claudette Colvin: Twice toward Justice* (New York: Farrar, Strauss and Giroux, 2009); Gary Younge, "She Would Not Be Moved," *The Guardian*, December 16, 2000; Sarah Kate Kramer, "Before Rosa Parks, A Teenager Defied Segregation," *National Public Radio*, March 2, 2015; and "Before Rosa Parks, Claudette Colvin Stayed in Her Bus Seat," *AAUW.org*, March 21, 2012.

62. Marie Brenner, "Malala Yousafzai: The 15-Year-Old Pakistani Girl Who Wanted More from Her Country," *Vanity Fair*, January 29, 2015; Malala Yousafzai and Christina Lamb, *I Am Malala: The Story of the Girl Who Stood Up for Education and Was Shot by the Taliban* (London: Weidenfeld & Nicolson, 2013); The Nobel Foundation, "Malala Yousafzai: Biography," *NobelPrize.org*; Danica Kirka, "Malala Yousafzai Completes Her Oxford Degree," *USA Today*, June 19, 2020.

63. Amy Ellis Nutt, "Becoming Nicole," *The Washington Post*, October 19, 2015.

64. Interview with Wayne Maines, "Becoming Nicole Recounts One Family's Acceptance of a Transgender Child," *Fresh Air*, National Public Radio, October 19, 2015.

65. Nutt, "Becoming Nicole."

66. Alec Kerr, "Being Nicole: Transgender Activist, 'Supergirl' Star Subject of One Book, One Valley Community Read," *The Conway Daily Sun*, October 3, 2019.

67. Evancho v. Pine-Richland School District.

68. Alison Gash, "Explainer: Why Transgender Students Need Safe Bathrooms," *The Advocate*, January 21, 2018.

69. Judy Harrison, "Maine Supreme Court Rules in Favor of Transgender Girl in Orono School Bathroom Case," *Bangor Daily News*, January 30, 2014.

70. See Alison Gash, "Anti-transgender Bills Are the Latest Version of Conservatives' Longtime Strategy to Rally Their Base," *The Conversation*, May 6, 2021; and Jo Yurcaba, "Youth Activists Lead the Fight against Anti-trans Bills," *NBC News*, March 25, 2021.

71. Ibid.

72. Ibid.

73. Alison Gash, "For Transgender Students, a Divided Pool of College Options," *The Conversation*, March 24, 2015.

74. Sarah Roth, "Transgender George Fox Student Denied Housing Request," *KGW News*, February 23, 2015.

75. Queer Heroes Northwest 2016. www.glapn.org.

76. Ina Jaffee, "1968 Chicago Riot Left Mark on Political Protests," *Weekend Edition*, National Public Radio, August 23, 2008.

77. Susanne Sproer, "1968: A Time for Dreams and Protests," *DW*, June 21, 2014.

78. Alissa Rubin, " May 1968: A Month of Revolution," *The New York Times*, May 5, 2018.

79. Daniel Walker, "Rights in Conflict: The Violent Confrontation of Demonstrators and Police in the Parks and Streets of Chicago during the Week of the Democratic National Convention of 1968."

80. Haynes Johnson, "1968 Democratic Convention: The Bosses Strike Back," *Smithsonian Magazine*, August 2008.

81. Walker, "Rights in Conflict."

82. Jaffee, "1968 Chicago Riot Left Mark on Political Protests."

83. Ibid.

84. Walker, "Rights in Conflict."

85. Ibid.

86. David Taylor and Sam Morris, "The Whole World is Watching: How the 1968 Chicago 'Police Riot' Shocked America and Divided the Nation," *The Guardian*, August 19, 2019.

87. Tanner Howard, "Journalism Still Carries the Mark of 1968," *Columbia Journalism Review*, September 13, 2018.

88. Ibid.

89. Ibid.

90. Taylor and Morris, "The Whole World is Watching."

91. Judith A. Center, "1972 Democratic Convention Reforms and Party Democracy," *Political Science Quarterly* 89 (1974) 2, pp.325–350; and Jaime Sanchez, "Revisiting McGovern-Fraser: Party Nationalization and the Rhetoric of Reform," *Journal of Policy History* 32 (2020) 1, pp.1–24.

92. John Andrew, *The Other Side of the Sixties: Young Americans for Freedom and the Rise of Conservative Politics* (New Brunswick, NJ: Rutgers University Press, 1997); and Wayne Thorburn, *A Generation Awakes* (New York: Jameson Books, 2010).

93. Peter Kihiss, "18,000 Rightests Rally at the Garden," *The New York Times*, March 8, 1962.

94. "Reagan's Candidacy is Endorsed by Young Americans for Freedom," *The New York Times*, August 19, 1979; Andrew, *The Other Side of the Sixties*; and Thorburn, *A Generation Awakes*.

95. Chloe Swarbrick, "My 'Ok Boomer' Comment In Parliament Symbolised Exhaustion of Multiple Generations," *The Guardian*, November 8, 2019.
96. Ibid.
97. Ibid.
98. Amelia Tait, "Greta Thunberg: How One Teenager became the Voice of the Planet," *Wired*, June 6, 2019.
99. Matt Vasilogambros, "After Parkland, States Pass 50 New Gun Control Laws," *Stateline*, August 2, 2018.
100. Ibid.
101. Greta Thunberg speech, U.N. Climate Action Summit, September 23, 2019.
102. "Our Leaders Are Like Children,' School Strike Founder Tells Climate Summit," *The Guardian*, December 4, 2018.
103. Albert Bandura and Lynne Cherry, "Enlisting the Power of Youth for Climate Change."
104. Ibid.
105. "Climate Change: The Impacts and the Need to Act," Oversight Hearing before the Committee on Natural Resources, U.S. House of Representatives, 116th Congress, February 6, 2019.
106. www.ourchildrenstrust.org.
107. "Parkland Survivors Turned into Activists and Inspired a New Wave of Gun Safety Laws," *CNN News*, February 11, 2009.
108. Brooke Jarvis, "The Teenagers at the End of the World," *The New York Times*, July 21, 2020.
109. Anne North, "Attacks on Greta Thunberg Expose the Stigma Autistic Girls Face," *Vox*, December 12, 2019.
110. John Paul Brammer, "'Skinhead Lesbian': GOP Candidate Attacks Parkland Teen Emma Gonzalez," March 13, 2018.
111. Allan Smith, "Trump Mocks Greta Thunberg after She Wins Time Person of the Year," *NBC News*, December 12, 2019.
112. Vivien Yee and Aan Blinder, "National School Walkout: Thousands Protest against Gun Violence across the U.S.," *The New York Times*, March 14, 2018.
113. Jarvis, "The Teenagers at the End of the World."
114. Max Boot, "Concord Coalition Aims at Federal Debt," *Christian Science Monitor*, May 10, 1993; and Michael Kinsley, "What's Not to Like: The Concord Coalition's Assault on the Deficit," *The Washington Post*, October 8, 1993.
115. Steven Powell, "Students from Concerned Youth of America Want Congress to Watch Its Spending," *The Daily Caller*, July 1, 2010.

116. "Passing on a Burden that Future Generations Don't Deserve," Blog Post, *The Concord Coalition*, October 19, 2010.

117. Ryan McNeely, "Didn't Go to Phillips Academy?" *Think Progress*, August 3, 2010.

118. Mary Kate Cary, "Behind the Scenes of 'The Can Kicks Back' Movement," *U.S. News and World Report*, February 14, 2013.

119. Lee Fang, "Generation Opportunity, New Koch-Funded Front, Says Youth Are Better Off Uninsured," *The Nation*, September 13, 2013.

120. Alex Leary, "Opt Out of Obamacare Is Conservative Group's Message to Young People," *Tampa Bay Times*, February 11, 2014.

121. David Smith, "Anti-Greta Teen Activist to Speak at Biggest U.S. Conservatives Conference," *The Guardian*, February 25, 2020.

122. Desmond Butler and Julliet Ellperin, "The Anti-Greta: A Conservative Think Tank Takes on the Global Phenomenon," *The Washington Post*, February 23, 2020.

123. Ian Spiegelman, "Larry Elder Once Said He'd Like to See a Stephen Miller Presidency," *Los Angeles Magazine*, August 30, 2021; and Tamara Keith, "Trump Aide Stephen Miller's Combative Style Goes Back to High School," *NPR.org*, August 11, 2017.

124. Andrea Gonzalez-Ramirez, "The White Nationalist Education of Stephen Miller," *Gen*, August 6, 2020; and Laurie Winer, "Trump Adviser Stephen Miller Has Always Been This Way," *Los Angeles Magazine*, October 30, 2018.

125. Paul Bond, "Here are the Young, Diverse Conservative Stars Progressives Need to Fear," *Newsweek*, September 4, 2020; and William Cohan, "How Stephen Miller Rode White Rage from Duke's Campus to Trump's West Wing," *Vanity Fair*, May 30, 2017.

126. R. Hans Miller, "Katy for Justice Organizes Protest of George Floyd's Death and Racial Injustice," *Katy Times*, June 3, 2020.

127. Kimberly Aleah, "Youth Organizers: Foyin Dosunmu of Katy4Justice," *Rollingstone*, October 14, 2020.

128. Ibid.

129. Miller, "Katy for Justice Organizes Protest of George Floyd's Death and Racial Injustice."

130. Ibid.

131. Aleah, "Youth Organizers: Foyin Dosunmu of Katy4Justice."

132. Ibid.

133. Cole McNanna, "Enough is Enough: Students Lead Protest at Katy Park against Racism," *Katy Times*, June 5, 2020.

134. Ibid.

135. Ibid.
136. Claire Goodman, "'I Grieve with Hope': Thousands Descend on Katy Park for Black Lives Matter Rally," *Houston Chronicle*, June 5, 2020.
137. Ibid.
138. Ibid.
139. www.dearasianyouth.carrd.co. See also Tiffany Yu, "The Change Makers," *Medium*, June 5, 2020.
140. Gabby Laurente, "Tesoro Teen Founds Global Movement Dear Asian Youth," *The Express*, January 16, 2021.
141. Emily Godsey, "Twitch Streamer Raises Money for LGBT Community," *The Times-Delphic*, January 20, 2022.
142. Carol J. C. Maxwell, *Pro-Life Activists in America: Meaning, Motivation, and Direct Action* (Cambridge University Press, 2002), p.33.
143. Ibid., p.29
144. Ibid., p.30.
145. Ibid., p.31.
146. Ibid.
147. Thomas W. Hilgers, "The National Youth Pro-Life Coalition: A Positive Force in a Violent World," *The Linacre Quarterly*, 41 (1974) 4, pp.285–287, p.285.
148. Ibid.
149. Ibid.
150. Maxwell, *Pro-Life Activists in America*, p.33.
151. Ibid, p.36.
152. Studentsforlife.org.
153. Andy Cush, "The Controversial Anti-Abortion 'Rock for Life' Tent is Back at Warped Tour this Year," *Spin*, June 27, 2017.
154. Carolyn Davis et al., "Young People Set to Impact the Debate on Women's Health Issues," PRRI, April 17, 2018. www.prri.org.
155. Andrew Morantz, "How Social Media Trolls Turned U.C. Berkeley into a Free-Speech Circus," *The New Yorker*, June 25, 2018.
156. Capps, Randy, et al. "Implications of immigration enforcement activities for the well-being of children in immigrant families." *Washington, DC: Urban Institute and Migration Policy Institute* (2015).
157. "UC Berkeley Scraps Breitbart Editor's Event amid Violence at Protest," *CBS News*, February 2, 2017.
158. Milo Yiannopoulos, "Milo: President Trump, Here's Why You Must Cut Federal Funding from UC Berkeley," *Breitbart*, February 9, 2017.
159. Thomas Healy, "Who's Afraid of Free Speech?" *The Atlantic*, June 18, 2017.

160. Ibid.
161. Neidi Dominguez Zamorano et al., "DREAM Movement: Challenges with the Social Justice Elite's Military Option," *TruthOut*, September 20, 2010.
162. Jennifer Lawless and Richard L. Fox, *Running from Office: Why Young Americans are Turned off to Politics* (Oxford University Press, 2015), p.17.

Chapter 5

1. Simone Abendschon, "Children and Politics," *American Behavioral Scientist* 61 (2017) 2, pp.163.
2. Rebecca Savransky, "DC Considers Letting 16-year-olds Vote," *The Hill*, April 17, 2018.
3. Alex Seitz-Wald, "Washington, DC May Let 16-year-olds Vote for President. Is That a Good Idea?" *NBC News*, April 17, 2018.
4. Jennifer Lee Kovaleski, "Should the Voting Age Be Lowered to 16 across the United States?" *Denver 7*, July 25, 2018.
5. Daniel Hart and James Youniss, *Renewing Democracy in Young America* (New York: Oxford University Press, 2017).
6. James M. Naughton, "Agnew Praises Youth for Seeking Change and Backs Vote at 18," *The New York Times*, June 18, 1970.
7. Thomas H. Neale, "Lowering the Voting Age Was Not a New Idea," in Sylvia Engdahl, ed., *Amendment XXVI: Lowering the Voting Age* (New York: Cengage Learning, 2010), p.38.
8. Robert Dahl, *Democracy and Its Critics* (New Haven, CT: Yale University Press, 1989), p.126.

Index

For the benefit of digital users, indexed terms that span two pages (e.g., 52–53) may, on occasion, appear on only one of those pages.

Tables and figures are indicated by *t* and *f* following the page number